RACKETVILLE
SLUMTOWN
HAULBURG

RACKETVILLE
SLUMTOWN
HAULBURG

AN EXPLORATORY STUDY
OF DELINQUENT SUBCULTURES BY
IRVING SPERGEL
Foreword by LLOYD E. OHLIN

THE UNIVERSITY OF CHICAGO PRESS
CHICAGO AND LONDON

Library of Congress Catalog Card Number: 64-17165

THE UNIVERSITY OF CHICAGO PRESS, CHICAGO & LONDON
The University of Toronto Press, Toronto 5, Canada

TO BERTHA, BARRY, AND MARK

FOREWORD

Different culturally supported forms of delinquent conduct are natural products of our social order under certain conditions. This is the central theme which *Racketville, Slumtown, Haulburg* documents with many insightful observations. Through intensive study of three different neighborhoods in a large city, the author reveals an intimate connection between the socially organized system of opportunities in a neighborhood and the dominant delinquent subculture of the alienated youth of the area.

The unique contribution of this book is the sharply increased understanding which comes from a comparison of different neighborhoods and their characteristic patterns of delinquent conduct. The author takes account of differences in the physical characteristics of the area, the ethnic composition of the population, family life and interaction between parents and children, occupation and income, and variations in the patterns of aspirations and expectations of success on the part of both adults and children. He points to significant differences not only in values but in beliefs about what it takes to get ahead. Above all, he stresses critical discrepancies in the availability of legitimate and illegitimate opportunities for achieving aspirations. Neighborhood youths reflect these differences in their own norms for status-producing activities. As one reads this book, the conviction grows that from a sufficiently detailed picture of a neighborhood system of learning and performance opportunities and its accessibility to youth one could successfully predict the content of the dominant youth subcultures that would emerge.

The empirical descriptions in this book may help clarify a persistent confusion in theories of delinquency between the origin of delinquent norms and delinquent acts. Many research workers are trying to account for the origin, location, content, and persistence of delinquent norms and values. Many others are trying to explain the causes of individual or group acts of delinquency. These represent two quite different objects of theoretical and practical concern. The variables used to explain them are likely to be quite different. The distribution of clearly defined delinquent subcultures in our society probably does not correspond with the distribution of delinquent acts, yet the explanation of the former is often criticized because it does not explain the latter.

In this book the author focuses clearly on a description of the content and location of delinquent norms. He is concerned with the connection between these norms and the social and cultural system of the neighborhood in which they emerge. As he notes repeatedly, however, different types of delinquent acts occur in all of the three neighborhoods he studied. The reasons why individuals are drawn into isolated acts of delinquency or involvement with delinquent gangs are not necessarily accounted for by the variables with which he is concerned. It is one thing to explain the origin and development of delinquent norms and another to explain why delinquent acts occur, as Albert Cohen stated so clearly in his initial formulation of this problem.[1]

It must be recognized that this book does not attempt to provide a complete survey of the content and distribution of delinquent subcultures throughout an entire city. A full analysis of the development of delinquent norms would probably require such a survey. Only then could one be certain of the relative concentration or dominance of certain styles of delinquent conduct in different areas of the city. This book, however, reports the research experience of one observer, working alone for the most part. To get close to the object of his in-

[1] Albert K. Cohen, *Delinquent Boys: The Culture of the Gang* (Glencoe, Ill.: Free Press, 1955), p. 18.

quiry he had to take certain short cuts. In the first place he drew on his own extensive experience with youth work in this city to select three socially distinct neighborhoods. But any one of these areas would be too large for one individual to survey adequately. Therefore, he undertook many interviews with youth-gang workers, settlement workers, police officials, and other knowledgeable persons in the community, and he examined the files on delinquents and youth gangs to identify the most typical delinquent groups in each of the areas. He then established contact with these groups, interviewed the members intensively, and acquired information from neighbors and officials about their behavior. His interviews were limited to certain topics, notably the connections with family members, neighborhood adults, and peers. It was not possible to explore all the institutional relationships of his youthful informants in these city neighborhoods or the variety of other youth subcultures which sometimes existed side by side with the delinquent ones. What he offers us instead are the careful observations of an insightful and experienced youth worker especially sensitive to theoretically relevant questions about delinquency. He presents a stimulating inquiry into the relation of delinquent norms to the social and cultural system of the neighborhoods from which they emerge. There are striking facts and relationships here that invite further theoretical speculation. However, it is the internal consistency in the various subcultural patterns of delinquency and in their differences which is particularly impressive from a theoretical standpoint.

The professional commitment of the author to social action emerges in the final chapter, where an effort is made to sketch a preventive program of neighborhood social redevelopment. The general line of attack is to increase the availability of legitimate learning and performance opportunities with appropriate supporting services. In this respect many of the recommendations are similar to programs of community redevelopment now being supported by grants from the President's Committee on Juvenile Delinquency and Youth Crime and from the Ford Foundation. Such combined action-research demonstrations should offer further validation and refinement of many of the empirical propositions presented in this book. They should also test the efficacy of many of the action programs in the final chapter. Whatever these more extensive undertakings may disclose will in any case be greatly advanced by the challenging dimensions which this pioneering study has opened up.

LLOYD E. OHLIN

COLUMBIA UNIVERSITY
SCHOOL OF SOCIAL WORK
February, 1964

PREFACE

This study assumes that delinquency is a man-made phenomenon and that it is amenable to dispassionate understanding and systematic change. My hope is that the analytical and descriptive manner selected to present the findings will contribute toward a clearer and more objective appraisal of a social problem of great concern to our communities. An attempt is made to describe and to seek causes for delinquent patterns in a detached and scientific way. This, however, does not deny my deep concern with the effects of delinquent behavior for the perpetrator, his victim, and for society.

The research is clearly exploratory, limited in scope, and in part a document of personal observations and speculations. Nevertheless, I hope that the findings and interpretations will be of value in providing significant additional understanding to social scientists, social workers, educators, and all persons interested in, and concerned with, the problems of delinquency. I am especially hopeful that the book will supply ideas and impetus for the further exploration of patterns of delinquent-group life and for the development of new approaches to community action.

Most important, I believe, social workers and social planners need to know that delinquent behavior is not merely symptomatic of personality disturbance, that delinquent groups are not all the same, and that lower-class or slum neighborhoods may differ greatly. Valid diagnosis and effective treatment or action by caseworkers, group workers, and community-organizers may depend more on the social meaning of particular delinquent patterns and subcultures than on anything else.

In a field of knowledge and professional practice in which there is much theorizing and speculation but few hard facts, there is need for systematically gathered data both about the delinquent and his social setting. Obviously, without such data, fruitful theory cannot be developed; understanding of the problem will not be achieved; and remedies will continue to be relatively ineffective. This study provides first-hand observations of three types of delinquents in their "natural habitats." It focuses on the specific neighborhood conditions which appear to give rise to discernibly distinct delinquent subcultures.

Sociological in perspective, the investigation has been largely conducted within the framework of anomie and opportunity theories developed by Robert Merton,[1] and by Richard Cloward and Lloyd Ohlin.[2] Cloward and Ohlin have formulated a theory of three major types of delinquent subcultures — criminal, conflict, and retreatist. In the present study I have used their basic ideas but have made certain significant modications. I do not regard the criminal subculture as unitary but as divided into two different types of subcultures — *racket* and *theft*. The racket subculture, probably highly developed in only a few large urban communities, represents the most sophisticated and criminal of all delinquent subcultures. The theft subculture, the most common variety, is oriented to selected and partially organized adult criminal patterns.

The study departs in another major respect from the Cloward-Ohlin formulation. The patterns of retreatists, or drug-users, have not been regarded as sufficiently distinct to comprise a special delinquent subculture. The delinquent behavior, norms, and values of drug-users and drug addicts were found to be more like than unlike the respective modes of the delinquents in each of the three types of lower-class neighborhoods. Therefore, the drug-use delinquent pattern is viewed

[1] Robert K. Merton, *Social Theory and Social Structure* (rev. ed.; Glencoe, Ill.: Free Press, 1957), especially chapters iv and v.

[2] Richard A. Cloward and Lloyd E. Ohlin, *Delinquency and Opportunity* (Glencoe, Ill.: Free Press, 1960).

as a variant or subcategory of each of the three forms of delinquent subcultures. It was observed to be primarily a late-teen-
age and young-adult phenomenon.

The term "delinquent subculture," as used in this study,
means a system of values, norms, and beliefs that conditions
the behavior of young people who seriously violate the desirable modes of conduct prescribed by official community
agents and by the broader culture in which they live. The
basic premise on which my research was undertaken was that
deviant patterns of behavior may occur in our society:

> "When a system of cultural values extols, virtually above all
> else, certain *common* success-goals *for the population at large*
> while the social structure rigorously restricts or completely closes
> access to approved modes of reaching these goals *for a considerable
> part of the same population* . . ."[3]

In other words, deviant behavior, particularly delinquent
behavior of lower-class youths, may be a response to limited
"access to approved modes" of achieving common success-
goals. Cultural requirements for all persons, regardless of
class, to become wealthy, important, and powerful and to
live "the good life" may create severe social and psychological
pressures, particularly in lower-class persons. When legitimate
or conventional means of achieving common success-goals are
not available, delinquency or crime may become an alternate
way of reaching them. Even criminal careers, however, may
not be equally available to youths in different lower-class neighborhoods. Possession of special skills, a minimal store of criminal knowledge and appropriate attitudes, and access to a
complex criminal organization or to "connections" may be
essential for the achievement of success by criminal means.
Thus, differences may exist not only in the availability of the
approved modes but also of the culturally unacceptable modes
of achieving success.[4]

For example, pursuing the career of a burglar, con man, or

[3] Merton, *Social Theory and Social Structure*, p. 146.
[4] Richard A. Cloward, "Illegitimate Means, Anomie, and Deviant Behavior," *American Sociological Review*, XXIV (April, 1959), 164–76. See also
Solomon Kobrin, "The Conflict of Values in Delinquency Areas," *American
Sociological Review*, XVI (October, 1951), 653–61.

racketeer may require the learning of certain sophisticated skills and attitudes as well as the development of good connections. All these opportunities for criminal training and contacts may not be available to youths in certain social circumstances. Alternate types of illegitimate means for achieving success-goals are then devised. For many youths in the most socially and economically deprived lower-class areas, gang fighting may be such an alternate way of achieving symbolic success.

In essence, what has just been said is that the delinquent or the criminal, as well as the conventional or conforming person, is governed by the same culturally induced motivations for obtaining significant social status. A great many people in American society, regardless of economic, social, or ethnic backgrounds, share the same kinds of aspirations, but the conditions for satisfying these aspirations are not equally accessible to all. Opportunities for acquiring a good education, a lucrative job, and useful contacts with the right people are often limited for young persons living in the deprived circumstances of lower-class neighborhoods. Parents with meager incomes and with limited education often do not provide appropriate or consistent encouragement for their children to make full use of even the inadequate conventional opportunities present in such an environment.

As a consequence, what has happened in some neighborhoods is that systems of criminal opportunity have been developed. This apparently has occurred in those neighborhoods that have older or more stable populations. However, in certain more recently settled lower-class areas — usually among the "newcomer" groups such as the Negroes, the Mexicans, and the Puerto Ricans — neither sufficient conventional nor sufficient criminal means for goal realization are present. In such areas, more primitive ways are sought for obtaining a measure of desired success status, and in such neighborhoods petty robbery or strong-arm activities are common. Systematic gang fighting may also develop among youths in these areas as an alternate illegitimate opportunity system.[5]

[5] See Cloward and Ohlin, *Delinquency and Opportunity*, and Irving Spergel, "An Exploratory Research in Delinquent Subcultures," *Social Service Review,*

The fundamental assumption of this study is that in lower-class urban communities certain distinct types of delinquent subcultures are created and thrive under the impetus of socially *unacceptable* opportunities available to youths for achieving *acceptable*, culturally induced success-goals. Three major types of such delinquent-youth subcultures, one marked by racket activities, another by violence and conflict, and a third by theft, are discernible. They develop according to definite patterns which depend on the interaction of conventional and criminal opportunities. As already suggested, drug addiction in these neighborhoods develops mainly as a variant and transitional pattern for older adolescents and young adults, many of whom have been participants in the major delinquent-youth subcultures.

The major differentiating characteristics of the subcultures are briefly described below. All names of persons and places used in this volume are fictitious or disguised. To distinguish the neighborhoods, they are metaphorically called Racketville, Slumtown, and Haulburg.

THE RACKET SUBCULTURE (RACKETVILLE)

Racketville represents the subculture of young delinquents in neighborhoods where the racket is the chief means of achieving success-goals, and it arises within a social context in which legitimate opportunities are limited but illegitimate opportunities are amply available. Here many youths with aspirations for success status find themselves under pressure, direct or indirect, to use the criminal learning opportunities accessible to them; their relatives are often engaged in the numbers, policy, gambling, and loan-shark rackets, as well as in other lucrative criminal activities.

Furthermore, the weakness or total absence in Racketville of many basic conventional norms and values does not encourage the use of the limited legitimate means present for achieving prestige, income, and influence. Youths are socialized

XXXV (March, 1961), 33–47. Also see Irving Spergel, "Male Young Adult Criminality, Deviant Values, and Differential Opportunities in Two Lower-Class Negro Neighborhoods in Chicago," *Social Problems*, X (Winter, 1963), 239–50.

into prevailing criminal role patterns; access to such illegitimate opportunities is facilitated by the close-knit organization of the population with its community and family groupings. Offenders of different age levels develop set ways of interaction. Conventional and criminal orientations and behaviors become tightly interlaced and interdependent.

THE CONFLICT SUBCULTURE (SLUMTOWN)

Slumtown represents the conflict subculture of delinquent youths in the most deteriorated slums; it is seen as a response to social conditions that provide young people with extremely limited access to either legitimate or illegitimate opportunities for reaching conventional success-goals. In such an area many youths with high aspirations create for themselves a special kind of opportunity — gang fighting. In Slumtown, a pattern of values and expectations, rules and regulations, and rewards and punishments develops which makes the reputation, or "rep," as a gang fighter equivalent to the attainment of a success-goal. On the whole, delinquents from this type of subculture appear to derive their major values, though weakly, from the larger conventional culture rather than from the local criminal one. At the same time, these delinquent gangs do not fit in well with the existing social structures prevalent in the area — conventional or criminal. There is limited age-level integration of offenders or of conventional persons. Both conventional and criminal adult groups are loosely organized and only weakly related to each other.

THE THEFT SUBCULTURE (HAULBURG)

The theft subculture in Haulburg grows out of a social condition in which there are partially limited conventional and criminal opportunities by which to achieve success-goals. The act and consequence of theft activity provide the institutionalized subcultural means by which delinquent youths may attain desired success status. For a number of reasons, a highly organized criminal system has not gained a dominant position in this neighborhood. It is possible that here, initially, access to legitimate opportunities was not so limited as in an area such as Racketville, where the development of an extensive alternate means or criminal system was required. Furthermore, a stronger and more fully accepted legitimate orientation may have set up a barrier against the creation of a fully integrated criminal structure. Access to partial significant legitimate and illegitimate opportunities has eliminated the need for new avenues to success status, such as gang fighting or organized conflict. In Haulburg, there appear to exist only semiorganized, partially integrated, yet sufficiently stable criminal routes to success status; and many of the neighborhood's lower-class youths with inadequate preparation for conventional careers can realize their aspirations for success through various some- what sophisticated delinquent or criminal activities. Here the obtaining of money and property through burglary, shoplifting, and forgery and the "borrowing" of such symbols of success as cars or motor scooters serve as less violent, more conven- tionally oriented ways of proving self-importance and achieving desired status in subcultural terms.

THE DRUG-USING OR DRUG-ADDICTION PATTERNS OF ADAPTATION

The drug-using and the drug-addict adaptations arise in the same social context which produce the three distinct types of delinquent subcultures. The drug-addict pattern is considered to be one type of response by older adolescents and young adults, most of whom were former delinquents, to certain age- role and class pressures, rather than a distinctive subculture. No longer acceptable to, or desiring acceptance from, the delinquent neighborhood groups of which they may have been members, these young men now find in drug-use a way to ease their transition to adult status, conventional or criminal. The use of drugs thus may help, in part, to sustain still un- realized and unrealizable aspirations to wealth, prestige, or power developed during the earlier adolescent years. At the same time, drug addicts are compelled by various pressures, including that of obtaining money to purchase drugs, to take on conventional or criminal jobs at the level of opportunities actually available to them in the neighborhood. A gradual closing of the gap between delinquent-adolescent aspirations and realistic adult expectations, based on knowledge of the limited existing opportunities accessible to them, may take place and in time reduce the pressure on drug addicts to continue drug-usage.

Although drug addicts as a group, regardless of the type of neighborhood, tend to share orientations and behaviors, particularly in ways of acquiring, using, and responding to drugs, they also tend to differ by virtue of their previous socialization in different types of delinquent subcultures and as a result of continuing exposure to varying levels of opportunity.

In addition, however, to the main type of delinquent behavior in each neighborhood, it should be made clear that a variety of other deviant behaviors occurred in it. For example, in Racketville there was also some gang fighting; Slumtown was also known for petty racket activity; and Haulburg had its limited share of racketeers and gang conflicts. In other words, the presence of a dominant system of delinquent orientation and behavior did not indicate the total absence of other delinquent patterns.

RESEARCH METHOD

A very large eastern city is the setting for the study of the three delinquent subcultures. Most of the data were gathered by me over an eight-month period during the summers of 1959 and 1960. I developed contacts with delinquent and drug-using groups or, in some cases, renewed contacts with delinquents and drug-users known to me from my previous work with them. These former contacts had been established over a period of six years when I served as a street-club or gang worker in these same neighborhoods. The data for the study were principally collected by means of two techniques: participant-observation and formal interviews. In many but not in all instances the subjects or group members observed were also formally interviewed.

A standardized interview was administered to 125 subjects defined on the basis of the street-club workers', community-center workers', or researcher's judgments as belonging either to a non-delinquent, delinquent, drug-addict or drug-using group or collectivity. Ten principal or core members were selected from each type of group in the three major neighborhoods, accounting for a total of 90 subjects. In addition, 22 narcotics addicts from the three selected neighborhoods — all who were receiving treatment at the local drug-treatment hospital or at its after-care clinic during a six-week period — were included in the samples. Also, a second group of 25 delinquent subjects from Haulburg and a group of 10 delinquents from a fourth neighborhood, classified as giving rise to a mixed theft-conflict subculture, were given formal interviews. The data, especially the interview data, however, deal primarily with the 90 subjects originally studied. It should be emphasized that the observation and formal-interview findings are not necessarily derived from the same groups but were always taken from the same types of groups in the same area, with one exception: interviews were obtained from a second delinquent group from a different but equivalent racket area in the city when the researcher found it impossible to follow up his observations with interviews of members of the delinquent group from Racketville.[6]

Three other techniques for obtaining data were employed: analysis of agency records on groups observed and interviewed; time study of conversations of a delinquent group in each of the three neighborhoods;[7] and, lastly, an analysis of United States Census and Big City Youth Board statistics on neighborhood population characteristics.

A discussion of the technique of time study of street-group conversations appears in chapter iv. For a description of some of the methodological problems, particularly those related to participant-observation of delinquent groups, see the Appendix. Also, it should be clearly understood that the research was neither rigorously designed nor executed. While much

[6] Mr. Russell Francione, who was a street-club worker with this group, administered a set of ten interviews to core members.

[7] Mr. Robert Rothenberg, street-club worker, assisted in the collection of time-study data for one group.

care was exercised in the collection and processing of the data, there were no systematic checks on validity or reliability. These conditions, in addition to the small size and non-random character of the samples, indicate that the findings must be considered exploratory and tentative.

Finally, it is important in all studies and particularly in a study of delinquency not only to indicate what major ideas were basic but also to indicate, even if briefly, what major perspectives and variables were *not* explored. Delinquent behavior is obviously a result of multiple factors acting on or along with each other in an individual or in a group in certain patterned ways of which we are not yet fully aware. This work probed only one set of sociocultural factors — anomie and opportunity. Also, the focus of the study was not on small-group, personality, or perceptual factors, although certain notions about group and personal functioning were used. Situational factors, such as time, place, and particular conditions immediately connected with the occurrence of delinquent acts, were not considered. Ethnic origin as a factor determining or contributing to delinquent adaptations, especially in the area of the racket subculture, was not investigated. Implicit in the research, however, was the assumption that ethnic groups occupied graduated lower rungs [8] in the stratified social structure of American society and that opportunities were unequally and inadequately accessible to them. And, while the study was concerned with conditions giving rise to particular types of delinquent youth subcultures, no hypotheses were developed about the origins of the adult criminal systems found in the various neighborhoods.

The book is organized into a descriptive section containing discussions of neighborhoods and their populations (chap. i), the patterns of delinquent behavior (chap. ii), and delinquent

[8] In the research it was assumed that certain recently arrived ethnic groups, for example, first-generation Italians, Puerto Ricans, and southern Negroes, have low status in the large urban centers in which they settle. Furthermore, these various ethnic groups were expected to occupy different levels even in the lower-class stratum. The first-generation Italians generally would be assumed to occupy a lower position than second- or third-generation Italians but a higher position than Puerto Ricans or Negroes.

life styles (chap. iii) and an analytic section which examines success goals and opportunities (chap. iv) and relationships with significant adults (chap. v). In addition, a description of postdelinquent young-adult patterns (chap. vi) and a brief discussion of approaches to community action in dealing with delinquent subcultures (chap. vii) are given.

ACKNOWLEDGMENTS

The author is grateful to the many youths who readily, and not-so-readily, permitted themselves to be interviewed and observed for purposes of the study. Most delinquents, like most people, respond to interest, friendliness, and respect. Consequently, in studying these groups, no greater — although perhaps different — difficulties were encountered than would have been met in studying non-delinquents. (Some of the difficulties encountered are discussed in the Appendix.)

It may be said that any study or human endeavor is ultimately a product of many hearts, minds, and hands. The author is much in debt to Lloyd E. Ohlin, who provided stimulus and support for the development of this research, which was originally in the form of a doctoral dissertation. To him, to Richard A. Cloward, and to Robert K. Merton must go credit for a number of basic ideas to be found in this work. Dean Alton A. Linford, School of Social Service Administration, University of Chicago, assisted and encouraged the author in every way possible toward completion of the manuscript. Many persons, including Rachel B. Marks, James F. Short, Mayer N. Zald, Edward D. Garber, and Thomas Carlsen, read and made useful comments on both the content and style of the manuscript. Special gratitude is owed to Mrs. Miriam Morton for invaluable editorial assistance. To Mrs. Frances Polson I offer thanks for extended secretarial help. Mrs. Ruth Babineau and Mrs. Agnes Nerode also assisted in typing the manuscript.

The list of agencies and their personnel who facilitated contacts with, or made available data on, the youngsters is a long one and includes: Arthur J. Rogers, Hugh K. Johnson, Russell Francione, and Robert Rothenberg, of the New York City Youth Board; Rafael Gamso, M.D., and Eric Brown, of Riverside Hospital; Antoinette Fried and Carlos Morales, of the James Weldon Johnson Community Center; and Theodore Lewis and Bernard Clyne, of the Lenox Hill Neighborhood Association. Without their help and that of many other agency workers, this study would not have been possible.

Keen appreciation is expressed to the Columbia School of Social Work and the Russell Sage Foundation for fellowship aid and to the National Institute of Mental Health, United States Public Health Service (MF–10,083 and M–4,351 A) for grant aid which permitted completion of the research.

To my wife Bertha, my children Barry and Mark, I owe an unrepayable debt for their patience and understanding and for the many hours of absence and seclusion they allowed me in consummation of this project.

It is the author, however, who bears full responsibility for the contents of this study, especially its shortcomings.

CONTENTS

CHAPTER I

The Neighborhoods and Their Characteristics **1**

CHAPTER II

Patterns of Delinquent Subcultural Behavior **29**

CHAPTER III

Differential Delinquent Life Styles **63**

CHAPTER IV

Success-Goals and Opportunities **93**

CHAPTER V

Relationships with Significant Adults **124**

CHAPTER VI

Adaptations in Young Adulthood **148**

CHAPTER VII

Community Action and Delinquent Subcultures **169**

APPENDIX

Problems in Obtaining Data on Delinquent Subcultures **190**

INDEX—**199**

TABLES

1	Male Breadwinner Occupations by Neighborhood	3
2	Median Family Yearly Income by Neighborhood	4
3	Indexes of Social Breakdown by Neighborhood	5
4	Median Family Weekly Income	6
5	Vital Statistics on Delinquents	9
6	Value Orientations	35
7	Role-Models	36
8	Attribute Considered Most Necessary To Get Ahead	37
9	Reports of Gang Fights by Members of Groups in Each Neighborhood	39
10	Major Gang-Fight Threats and Actual Gang Fights	41
11	Aspired Median Weekly Wage within Ten Years	95
12	Aspired Occupation within Ten Years	96
13	Expected Median Weekly Wage within Ten Years	102
14	Expected Occupation within Ten Years	103
15	Indexes of Differences between Aspirations and Expectations: Occupation and Wage	107
16	Gross Estimate of Number of Racketeers in Neighborhood	115
17	Status of Racketeers	117
18	Conversation Content Analysis: Number of References to Non-Criminal and Criminal Adults	120
19	Conversation Content Analysis: Number of References to Adults and Peers	121
20	Affection between Mother and Son	126

FIGURES

FIG. 1   Aspiration-Expectation Curves: The Delinquent
          Groups   110
FIG. 2   Aspiration-Expectation Curves: The Non-Delinquent
          and Drug-Addict Groups   111
FIG. 3   Aspiration-Expectation Curves: The Delinquent, Non-
          Delinquent, and Drug-Addict Groups in Each
          Neighborhood   113

CHAPTER I

THE NEIGHBORHOODS
AND THEIR
CHARACTERISTICS

The major contention of this study is that different types of delinquent subcultures arise in and are concomitant with specific kinds of neighborhoods and social contexts. In other words, the neighborhood contains the distinctive factors conditioning the type of delinquent subculture that develops in it. Lower-class populations, especially lower-class youth populations in large urban centers, are highly neighborhood-bound. Even in the present era of great mobility and change, the crucial daily contacts of lower-class youths tend to be limited to a restricted geographical area. Family living, school attendance, recreational facilities, and significant relationships with adults and peers are all largely centered within a particular city area. It is therefore important to know the general social and cultural character of each type of area to understand the basis for the development of its special variety of subculture.

The present chapter attempts to delineate briefly certain key features of three neighborhoods which determine the dominant delinquent orientation and system of delinquent behavior of each. Identifying data on the neighborhood populations, parents, and delinquents, as well as descriptions of each area and its significant patterns of neighborhood integration, are provided. Special emphasis is placed on those currents in the local stream of life that tend most importantly to fashion the criminal or delinquent adjustment of youth.

Although each of the three neighborhoods studied contains a predominantly lower-class population, their respective social

1

conditions and population characteristics are markedly different. There are important variations in ethnic composition, relative size of youth population, socioeconomic status, and in the severity of social problems.

POPULATION CHARACTERISTICS

Racketville,[1] for purposes of the research, comprised one census tract area and a population of 8,370 persons. Of this population 42.5 per cent were of Italian origin and mainly of a first-American-born generation; 25.3 per cent were Puerto Ricans; 3.6 per cent were Negroes. Irish, German, Polish, and a variety of other European ethnic groups were also represented. Although the Italians were still clearly the dominant group in the area, many families had taken flight to other parts of the city because of the influx of unwelcome non-white newcomers to the neighborhood during the past ten years. Persons twenty years old and under constituted 37.5 per cent of the population.

Slumtown included four census tracts and a population of 39,946 persons. Of its people, 66.2 per cent were Puerto Ricans, most of whom were born in Puerto Rico; 23.7 per cent were Negroes; and the remainder were largely of Irish and Italian extraction. The construction of low-income public housing had caused some population shift during the previous five years, resulting in an increased proportion of Negroes in the area. Persons twenty years old and under were 43.3 per cent of the population.

Haulburg encompassed five census tracts and a population of 43,909 persons. The lower-class element consisted mainly of first- and second-generation Irish, Germans, Czechs, and Italians. Also heavily represented in this element were Austrian, Hungarian, Ukrainian, and Polish families. The past decade had brought a change in the class distribution of Haulburg; an increase in middle- and upper-middle-class groups had resulted in a decrease of lower-class residents. The lower-

---

[1] It should be noted that the alternate racket area from which the interviews of the delinquent group were obtained was of a somewhat higher socio-economic status than the original area was. It was more residential, and families owned their own homes.

class group, however, remained a substantial one. Persons twenty years old and under accounted for 19.1 per cent of the population — a much smaller youth population than in the other two neighborhoods.

OCCUPATION OF MALE BREADWINNERS

The occupational character of the populations in each neighborhood also differed. The occupational status of male breadwinners was highest in Haulburg, lowest in Slumtown. Racketville had a relatively high proportion of its men employed as craftsmen (20.5 per cent) and as laborers (14.6 per cent). Adult laborers in this area were employed almost exclusively in the construction industry, and their jobs were highly unionized and better paying, as well as more respectable, than lower-paying factory or service employment. According to the U.S. Census Bureau count in 1959, 6.9 per cent of the male working force in Racketville was unemployed. In Slumtown, employed men were principally factory workers (29.4 per cent) and service workers (22.1 per cent). A high proportion of the male working force was listed as unemployed — 10 per cent. Haulburg's employed males, who were generally classified as middle class and upper working class, were professional people, managers, technicians, salesmen, and clerks (50.9 per cent) (see Table 1). Many of the lower-class residents of Haulburg,

TABLE 1
MALE BREADWINNER OCCUPATIONS BY NEIGHBORHOOD*

NEIGHBORHOOD	PERCENTAGE OF MALES EMPLOYED						
	Professional, Managerial, Clerical, and Sales	Craftsmen	Machine Operatives	Service Workers	Private Household Help	Laborers	Occupations Not Reported
Racketville	22.4	20.5	22.3	14.8	—	14.6	5.5
Slumtown	22.2	10.3	29.4	22.1	0.3	5.4	10.4
Haulburg	50.9	14.0	11.6	12.0	0.7	3.2	7.4

*Calculated from U.S. Department of Commerce, Bureau of the Census, *1960 United States Census of Population* (Washington, D.C.: U.S. Government Printing Office, 1962).

with whom this study was more concerned, were employed as store and office clerks, hospital attendants, night watchmen, and maintenance workers. Of the total male working force in this area, 4.6 per cent were reported as unemployed. A larger proportion of the total working force in Haulburg were women than in the other two neighborhoods. Many of these women were employed as professionals, secretaries, typists, practical nurses, and charwomen in the unusually large number of hospitals and educational institutions in the area. There had been surprisingly little shift in the dominant occupational pattern of the three neighborhoods between the 1950 and the 1960 Censuses.

The family income of persons in Haulburg, as reported in the 1960 Census, was highest of the three areas ($4,863–$7,538). However, if it were assumed that the middle-class group, with which the study was not centrally concerned, was overrepresented in Haulburg, and if it were also assumed that the figures reported represented, in the main, income from legitimate sources; then the family income in Racketville ($4,551 median) was probably as high or higher than in Haulburg, because of the non-reported income from illegitimate sources in this area. Median family income in Slumtown was extremely low — much lower than in the two other areas either at the upper end of the range ($3,930) or at the lower end ($3,788) (see Table 2).

TABLE 2

MEDIAN FAMILY YEARLY INCOME BY NEIGHBORHOOD*

NEIGHBORHOOD	INCOME PER YEAR	
	Low Census Tract	High Census Tract
Racketville	$4,551†	$4,551†
Slumtown	3,788	3,930
Haulburg	4,863	7,538

*Calculated from U.S. Department of Commerce, Bureau of the Census, *1960 United States Census of Population.*
†Only one census tract used.

SOCIAL BREAKDOWN

Indexes of social breakdown varied in each of the neighborhoods; such indexes as public assistance, home relief, aid to dependent children caseloads, infant mortality, venereal disease, termination from psychiatric clinics, and delinquency rates were highest in Slumtown and generally lowest in Haul-

TABLE 3

Indexes of Social Breakdown by Neighborhood*

Neighborhood	Per 1,000 Population		Per 1,000 Youths (6–20 years)	Per 1,000 Live Births	Per 100,000 Population	Per 100,000 Population	Per 1,000 Youths (6–20 years)
	Public Assistance Caseload (March, 1959)	Home Relief Caseload (March, 1959)	Aid to Dependent Children (March, 1959)	Infant Mortality (1957)	Venereal Disease Rate (April, 1957)	Termination from Psychiatric Clinics (Six-month period ending September, 1958)	Delinquency Rate (1958)
Racketville	37.0	5.2	52.6	22.4	393.6	170.9	55.3
Slumtown	56.1–63.5	8.3–10.1	83.1–96.1	37.8–49.6	917.5–1,283.4	356.8–432.9	94.6–95.0
Haulburg	9.9–16.8	1–3.7	8.2–16.5	8.8–38.0	141.9–290.9	131.2–231.9	30.1–48.7

*Big City Youth Board, Research Department, 1962. Rates by Health district(s) in each neighborhood.

burg. For example, the public assistance caseload was three to six times larger, the aid to dependent children caseload was five to twelve times larger, and official delinquency rates were two to three times higher in Slumtown than in Haulburg. Social problems abounded in Slumtown and were as serious as in any of the worst neighborhoods of the city. On the other hand, the level of social breakdown in Haulburg was typical of the city as a whole. Indexes of social breakdown in Racketville were at a level between those of Slumtown and Haulburg (see Table 3).

PARENTS OF INTERVIEW SUBJECTS

The interview findings on the ethnic and socioeconomic characteristics of parents of delinquents, drug-users, and non-delinquents appeared generally to be consistent with the statistical information obtained on neighborhood populations. In Racketville, for instance, parents of subjects interviewed, in the main, were born in Italy. Breadwinners, principally fathers, were reported working as carpenters, bricklayers, etc.; some were proprietors of small businesses, and others were loan sharks, numbers men, and bookmakers. The median weekly family income ($158.50) of delinquents in Racketville was higher than that of delinquents in the other areas (see Table 4). The educational level of parents was extremely low.

TABLE 4
MEDIAN FAMILY WEEKLY INCOME*

Neighborhood and Component Group	Median Family Weekly Income
Racketville	
Non-delinquent	$140.00
Delinquent	158.50
Drug addict	115.00
Slumtown	
Non-delinquent	62.50
Delinquent	105.00
Drug addict	92.50
Haulburg	
Non-delinquent	120.00
Delinquent	90.00
Drug addict	115.00

*The number in each sample or component group per neighborhood is ten.

Most of them, particularly fathers, had not gone beyond grammar school. Many of the parents of subjects in Racketville did not live together; because of death or separation half of the delinquents came from homes where only one parent was present. On the basis of the data obtained, however, there was little to indicate that significantly more delinquents came from broken homes than did non-delinquents — this finding held true in each of the three areas. Nevertheless, it was still possible that the quality of the home life of delinquents and non-delinquents differed considerably. The study did not attempt to probe the varied deeper, more dynamic aspects of the family life of subjects interviewed.

In Slumtown, the parents of subjects were, by and large, born in Puerto Rico. Breadwinners were mainly engaged as unskilled workers, factory employees, porters, and waiters. The weekly median family income of delinquents was surprisingly high ($105.00 per week), considerably higher than the weekly median family income of families of non-delinquents ($62.50) or of drug addicts ($92.50) in the same area (see Table 4).

It was likely in these families that either both parents were working or that there was more than one major breadwinner in the family. Nevertheless, it was apparent that the most impoverished families did not necessarily produce the largest number of delinquents. It is possible that in this neighborhood greater pressure for upward mobility existed among families with relatively good socioeconomic status. The disparity between aspiration for success and perception of the inadequate means for attaining it might more often be present in the homes of delinquents than in the homes of non-delinquents. The educational level of parents was considerably higher in Slumtown than in Racketville but slightly lower than in Haulburg. Yet, in Slumtown, parents of delinquents, drug-users, and non-delinquents alike had not gone much beyond junior high school. As in Racketville, there was evidence that about half the homes of delinquents were broken, principally by fathers and mothers living in separate dwellings.

In Haulburg, parents were usually reported as having been

born in the United States and mainly in the immediate metro-politan area. The occupational status of parents was about at the same level as that of parents in Racketville. Here, however, they tended more often to be employed in white-collar occupations, such as postal clerk or sales clerk, or in skilled jobs, such as jeweler or dressmaker. A few of the breadwinners were porters or superintendents in apartment houses or institutional buildings in the area. Surprisingly, median weekly incomes of the families of delinquents in Haulburg ($90.00) were the lowest of the reported incomes of families of delinquents for the three areas (see Table 4). In this area a slightly higher percentage of the parents had gone beyond the junior-high-school level than in the other two areas. A substantial number of mothers had graduated from high school. Finally, there was some evidence that a slightly higher proportion of the homes of delinquents in Haulburg was physically intact than in Racketville or Slumtown. Within this particular area, however, there was again no evidence of any difference between delinquents and non-delinquents in regard to frequency of broken homes.

THE DELINQUENTS

There were variations and consistencies in the characteristics of the groups of delinquent subjects interviewed from each of the three areas. Especially noteworthy, for purposes of the research, were the differences in age, education, and economic characteristics of the delinquents interviewed. On the other hand, it is important to note that despite variations in their residential stability from area to area, delinquents, by and large, could not be regarded as newcomers. Those interviewed had resided in the city and had lived at their current addresses for relatively long periods of time (see Table 5).

The delinquents interviewed from Racketville tended to be a little older (median age eighteen years) than those from the other two areas. All the delinquents in this neighborhood indicated their ethnic origin to be Italian, and all of them were born in the metropolitan area. The residential stability of these youths was the highest of any of the delinquent groups — a median of 17.5 years at the same home address. A few of the youngsters had lived under the same roof all their lives. All were Catholic but did not attend church regularly. The delinquents in this neighborhood, as in the other two areas, had poor records of church attendance in comparison with the non-delinquents and the drug addicts. Approximately half the delinquents in this area had records as probationers or parolees.

In some respects there was little variation in the educational level achieved by delinquents or drug addicts from any of the areas. Most had left school at the minimum permissible age

TABLE 5
VITAL STATISTICS ON DELINQUENTS*

CHARACTERISTIC	NEIGHBORHOOD		
	Racketville	Slumtown	Haulburg
Median age	18 years	16 years	17 years
Ethnic group	Italian	Puerto Rican	Irish, Italian, German
Median residence at same address	17.5 years	6.5 years	7.5 years
Median grade attainment ..	9.5 years	9.0 years	10.00 years
Number presently employed full or part time	7	1	3
Median weekly wage on current or most recently held job†	$75.00	$27.50	$60.00

*The number in each sample or component group per neighborhood is ten, except where otherwise indicated.
†Based on eight subjects per neighborhood.

of sixteen years. About half the delinquents from each area had followed a trade program at their junior or senior high school. In Racketville, however, a few more delinquents than in the other neighborhoods had taken academic or college-preparatory courses.

A higher proportion of delinquents in Racketville than in the other two areas were employed full or part time. The factor of age could have played an important role here, since the median age of delinquents from Slumtown, for instance, was two years younger; a number of youngsters from Slumtown were not even legally eligible for full-time employment. The evidence also suggested that a differential job-opportunity factor was operating across the board in favor of the youth and young-adult population in Racketville. Racketville had the highest proportion of employed non-delinquents and drug addicts, as well as of delinquents. The delinquents in Racketville also had the highest-paying and highest-status positions of any of the delinquent groups. Median wages averaged $75.00 per week, and the types of occupations reported included those of carpenter, bricklayer, and auto repairman. Several of the youths had obtained jobs through family connections and were working with a father, an uncle, or some other relative on the docks or in the construction industry.

In Slumtown the median age of delinquents was sixteen years. Almost all of those interviewed had been born in Puerto Rico. This was not, however, a recent immigrant group. The median period of residence in the metropolitan area was 13 years, and at the same address, 6.5 years. It was quite possible that the potential member of a delinquent group or, for that matter, any social group in the area (as perhaps in any of the two other areas) had to be sufficiently acculturated both to the larger society and to his neighborhood to be acceptable as a group member. In this area, members of delinquent groups attributed lower status to those persons who recently arrived from Puerto Rico. Derogatory remarks such as "cowboy," "fruit," "hick," and "square" were given to newly arrived residents. In the main, delinquents were Catholic, but they hardly ever attended church. As in the other areas, about half the delinquents indicated a present status of probationer or parolee.

Almost all delinquents in Slumtown had left school at the minimum age of sixteen. A few had stopped attending school before then. Two youngsters had not even completed their elementary-school training. Half the delinquents had pursued trade courses at school.

In Slumtown only one delinquent boy reported being employed currently. The median wage of the delinquent in his present or last job was $27.50 per week and represented both full-time and part-time employment. The factor of age ineligibility for full-time employment only partially affected the pattern of unemployment which appeared to be quite general in Slumtown. Youths and young adults had great difficulty in obtaining employment and were generally found in the lowest-status and lowest-paying positions, such as delivery boy and stock clerk. Frequently the reason for the initial relationship of the delinquent with a street-club worker or with the researcher was his need for a job opportunity.

In Haulburg the median age of delinquents was seventeen years. All those interviewed were born in the metropolitan area and were mainly of Irish, Italian, German, or mixed ethnic origin. The median period of residence of these delinquents at the same address was 7.5 years. Most of them were Catholics, and they attended church infrequently. Half of the delinquents from this area were currently on probation or on parole. The pattern of schooling was similar to that in the other areas; delinquents ceased their formal education at age sixteen or when slightly younger. As in the other areas, about half of the delinquents had pursued trade courses in junior high school or in high school. There was some evidence, however, that delinquents from Haulburg had attained a one-grade-level advantage (tenth grade) over delinquents from the other areas. More than half of them were presently employed in unskilled or semiskilled positions such as trucker's helper, gas-station attendant, or elevator operator. The median wage for those employed was $60.00 per week, which was slightly lower than the median earnings of the delinquents in Racketville. However, a far smaller number of youths in this area had obtained jobs through parents or relatives.

THE TENOR AND TEMPO OF NEIGHBORHOOD LIFE

The physical appearance of the buildings and of the people, the living space available, the cultural character, and the drama of everyday living varied in the three neighborhoods. If a lower-class person were to move from one of these neighborhoods to another, he would find not only a different physical environment but a set of social patterns and social problems unlike those to which he had been accustomed.

Racketville was a congested neighborhood, yet not so over-crowded as many other parts of the city. Its numerous five-story old tenement buildings were generally in good repair. Rows of two- and three-story bright red brick homes with attractive garden plots and trees in front were located on several of the streets. A major public housing program had made only partial inroads in the area. The impact of the housing program had not been as pervasive as in the area next to it. In comparison with the adjoining slum neighborhood, housing conditions in Racketville were fairly good. There was an essentially lower-class appearance and character to the neighborhood, however; for while only 2.2 per cent of the dwelling units were reported to be in a dilapidated condition, 20.7 per cent of the dwelling units accommodated 1.01 or more persons per room; and 8.7 per cent of the units were overcrowded, with more than 1.51 persons per room.

Neighborhood life in Racketville was brisk, particularly on the main streets. The tempo was considerably slower on the side streets. Cars, principally black Cadillacs and Chryslers, were often double-parked on the principal thoroughfare. As several street-club workers observed, these automobiles were never ticketed for traffic violations. (They were reputed to belong to "big" racketeers who conducted their business and socialized in the adjoining buildings.) One street-club worker observed that one of the funeral parlors in the neighborhood, outside of which new, expensive cars were usually parked, had been open for business every day during the three years that he was in the area, but there had never been a funeral there. According to the youths in his group, the funeral parlor had not received a corpse in six years. It was obvious that a thriving business other than that of burying the dead was the major preoccupation of the people on the premises. The extensive adult criminal activity in the area was not conducted blatantly. It was carefully shielded and could easily remain unnoticed by a newcomer or someone unfamiliar with the area. The residents of the area dressed neatly; their clothes were clean and of good quality. There was an air of stability and respectability about the people walking along the streets.

As we have already indicated, Racketville, despite recent population changes, still had an influential and numerous Italian population:

The program director of the local settlement house, used almost exclusively by youngsters of Italian extraction, believed that the Italian component of the community was still a substantial one. A number of blocks in the area were inhabited entirely by such families. She described most of these families as middle class — the men were skilled and semi-skilled workers who were highly unionized. She felt also that there had been a large in-migration of persons from Italy in recent years which was often not recognized.

There seemed to be a difference of opinion, however, about the existing population character of the neighborhood. Mr. Gambone, the assistant principal of the neighborhood high school, who had taught English there and had held his present administrative post for many years, had a reputation of having an intimate knowledge of the Italian families in the area — past and present. Here in summary is his description of the changes which had taken place in Racketville:

He was born and brought up in the neighborhood, but his family moved away when he was a teen-ager. He felt that the people in the neighborhood "were now not really Italian." He said deprecatingly that he didn't know what they were and that they had "no culture, no values, nothing." He believed that they were culturally, morally, but not economically deprived. There was a lot of money in the neighborhood. The rackets were rife and were a significant part of the way of life of the people in the area, with the kids and their families deeply involved. He was convinced that many of the young people would be moving up into "good positions" in the rackets as they got older. Many of the racketeers who were at the A —— convention had spent their youth in this neighborhood but later moved into the suburbs. He believed that the Italian community was "on the way out" and was convinced that the Puerto Ricans and the Negroes now moving into the area would ultimately replace them in the next generation in positions of racket leadership.

Slumtown had an area twice as large as Racketville, but it contained a population more than four times as large. It was, without doubt, one of the most congested and physically deteriorated sections of the city. Most of its buildings were four- and five-story old law tenements that had been put up seventy years ago. During the previous half-decade, however, the construction of an extensive public housing program had made a substantial difference in the appearance of the neighborhood. Nevertheless, housing conditions were still unquestionably the worst of the three neighborhoods: 9.9 per cent of the dwelling units were listed as dilapidated, and 26.5 per cent of the dwelling units accommodated 1.01 persons or more per room; 13

per cent of the single units were overcrowded, with more than 1.51 persons per room.

What impressed one particularly when walking Slumtown's streets was the large number of people gathered at entrance-ways and in front of buildings. The researcher observed the following scene one summer afternoon — only one small sample of the intense human drama constantly played out in these streets, regardless of the season or the time of day or night:

There were poorly clad children everywhere. A great many young and older male adults stood around in clusters, talking with each other and observing the passers-by. There were sometimes as many as a dozen such groupings on a single side of a short city block. Police cars seemed to cruise constantly in the area. A police-man walked over to a group of several youngsters about thirteen years of age and examined a piece of metal with which they were playing. He seemed to know these boys and gave them a friendly nod. Many of the adults became aware of the presence of the police officer and watched him closely. It was difficult to tell defi-nitely who among these people were Puerto Ricans and who were American Negroes, although the Puerto Rican element seemed to predominate.

On the next street there was a kosher butcher shop and next to it a newsstand with foreign-language newspapers —Italian, Jewish, Polish, and Spanish. On another street there were a number of prostitutes standing in front of a building, plying their trade, calling loudly to the men who walked past, "Hey, Babe! Come on!" or sim-ply making long, low whistling sounds at them.

At one point two large, portly women came charging down the street. The one carrying a broom caught up with the woman ahead of her and began to swat her with it. Soon the two were rolling and wrestling on the sidewalk and tearing at each other's faces, hair, and clothes. They were shouting in Spanish. Many in the quickly gathered crowd were laughing and commenting excitedly. Mickey, a member of the gang that the researcher was observing, said, with a shrug, that there was probably some man mixed up in this.

The residents of Slumtown lived at the vortex of a helpless and hopeless struggle for security and decency. Corruption and vice were rampant:

Father O. said that many of the youngsters who came to him did not believe that there were any honest people around, and he said that it had taken him a long time to convince these boys that he was not there for personal gain. They felt that everyone had his own racket. On several occasions some of them pulled him out of the church to point to the houses across the street at which police cars were parked. The policemen would dash out of the cars, run into the buildings, and soon come out, still counting the graft money.

Although it had not yet been determined precisely whether the criminal or the conventional orientations were dominant in Slumtown, there was strong evidence of the growing influence of the criminal way of life in this area:

Father O. also spoke of a funeral that took place the previous week. It was one of the biggest funerals ever seen in the neighborhood. There were dozens of Cadillacs — all the pimps, petty racketeers, small-time politicians, and even a very high city official attended it. They came to pay their last respects to one of the few big Puerto Rican racketeers. The turnout was bigger than at any other funeral of a notorious racketeer in this particular neighborhood.

Haulburg was much larger and less densely populated than either Racketville or Slumtown. This neighborhood was a study in contrasts. Tall, new, luxury apartment buildings towered over rows of old tenements. World-famous educational, cultural, and medical institutions stood side by side with a variety of local institutional structures, such as elementary schools, churches, and movie houses. There were a number of up-to-date shops along the avenue, but the stores on the side streets were old and dilapidated. There were nationality centers such as a Sokol House, attractive settlement houses, and a large shelter recently built by the American Society for the Prevention of Cruelty to Animals. There were also numerous bars.

The following is a representative scene of neighborhood activity on one summer evening in Haulburg:

It was about nine o'clock. Groups of adolescents were gathered on the side streets. They were on front stoops or in doorways playing cards or "shooting the breeze." Groups of mothers sat about talking while watching their youngsters closely. Many of the children still on the street at this hour were very young. Men in hospital uniforms, resident doctors, and nurses off duty hurried by. Attractively dressed young and middle-aged couples seemed everywhere, especially along the avenue. They stopped to window shop, entered restaurants, or moved on to fashionable apartment houses nearby. The sight of French poodles led by their masters or mistresses was common. In the midst of this strange conglomeration the researcher recognized a group of addicts, now in their middle twenties, with whom he had worked years earlier. They were a small, unobtrusive group, still "hanging around" on the same street corner. Foot patrolmen and squad cars were conspicuously absent.

Housing conditions for the lower-class population in this area were better than in Slumtown and at least as adequate as in Racketville. Only 3.4 per cent of the dwelling units in Haulburg were reported as dilapidated. The proportion of dwelling units accommodating 1.01 persons or more was 6.8 per cent; and only 2 per cent of the units were overcrowded, with more than 1.51 persons per room.

On the surface Haulburg appeared to be sedate, respectable, and cosmopolitan. A distinctly middle-class atmosphere pervaded its street life. Jackie, a young adult and former delinquent, characterized the neighborhood as follows:

The people here were really middle class. They were not just interested in food and shelter and things like that but in giving their children a decent upbringing. Parents had their kids take piano and ballet lessons. Jackie had studied the piano for eight years. He spoke of Buddy, his close friend, who had studied the violin and was now sorry he had stopped.

Karl, another young adult, summed up the characteristics of criminal activities in Haulburg which distinguished it from other neighborhoods:

This, he said, was a conservative area. There was a little bit of everything, but it was all hush-hush! Some of the criminal doings were pretty well organized but not to the extent that they were elsewhere. He said there was more stealing here because there was more to steal. The kids stole cars because they wanted more than they already had. People here already had refrigerators and TV's and things like — they had more than bare necessities, such as food and shelter and clothing. The youth group didn't have to gang-fight.

The older guys were independent and pulled their burglaries, safe-cracking, or stickup jobs "quietly." Some of these older guys lived very well, but they were not well known in the area.

A new deviant culture pattern in this neighborhood was the development of homosexual or exploitive sex arrangements involving some of the well-to-do residents and lower-class delinquent youths as role partners:

Karl and the researcher talked about the fact that men were sometimes seen kissing on the street. Karl said that there were more "fags" now than ever before. He named a bar nearby which used to be one of the roughest in the neighborhood, with fights every night and occasional shootings. Now this place was a hangout for homosexuals. None of the normal men in the area went there any more. Some of the younger boys took up with rich "fags" who kept them. The boys would of course deny it, but everyone knew what was going on. A few of them made a "good living" at it. There were also some older, "screwy," rich "dames" who were "making it" with some of the guys.

NEIGHBORHOOD INTEGRATION

Lower-class neighborhoods appeared to vary in the degree to which their significant groups and their value systems meshed or interacted. In a highly integrated area, divergent groups, such as the criminal and the conventional, would be highly interlinked. In a poorly integrated neighborhood, such groups would have considerably less contact and fewer transactions with each other. The relationships of the representatives of the significant groups or associations would be close and accommodative in a highly integrated area. In a less-well-integrated one, the relationships of persons with different orientations or of different age levels would tend to be distant and even antagonistic.

The degree of neighborhood integration indicates the accessibility to means and significant relationships in the area; the more integrated the neighborhood, the more accessible are the means and systems of interpersonal relationships. It is therefore likely that the integrated neighborhood makes greater use of existing opportunities for developing alternate, officially unacceptable routes to success status than the unintegrated neighborhood. More specifically, lower-class areas may be considered in terms of a continuum of the degree to which the relationship between adult members of the conventional and of the criminal worlds is antagonistic or accommodative. For instance, the condition of accommodation or integration could signify that the racketeer, the local businessman, and the policeman had closely and reciprocally joined for common profit.

Racketville showed that the relations of organized criminal and conventional business, the legal and illegal ways of life, were mutually supportive. The racketeer used the front of the legitimate entrepreneur to conceal or facilitate his illegal operations. The supposedly conventional businessman acquired substantial additional income through such co-operation. The policeman, by deliberately failing to enforce the law and by serving the interest of the racketeer in a variety of other ways, received a handsome payoff. The integration of criminal and conventional orientations and systems of relationship in Racketville did not necessarily constitute an association of equals. The racketeer exercised the dominant power and had great influence in the conventional structure of the neighborhood:

Frankie, a young adult who still considered himself a member of a delinquent group, when speaking about the influence of the racketeers, said that they were known to everybody in the neighborhood. If you wanted to open up a legitimate business and needed additional capital, you could sometimes borrow money from the racketeers. If you were losing out in business, they might be helpful. If somebody got "busted," or arrested, a racketeer would put up bail money and, in an emergency, the racketeer could be called upon for a payoff, since he had the right contacts in the police department. Of course this was strictly business, and you had to repay the loans or favors.

The influence of the racketeer penerated deeply into the basic family structure of the people in Racketville. It was not only that an uncle or a cousin who was a successful racketeer was accorded high status and respect, and it was not only that the family thereby derived access to jobs, money, and prestige. The racketeer played not just an instrumental role but also a significant socioemotional or maintenance role in the family system. He sustained family control and unity and was a substitute for parental authority:

Frankie put it this way: At times when a kid stepped out of line, that is, when he refused to obey his father or mother or was hanging around with the "wrong bunch," his parents would call in the racketeer. He would come and talk to the fellow and make him toe the line, or else he would get beaten up. Frankie added, "You couldn't go too far — the most you could do was give the kid a beating or two — then if he didn't listen, that was that. . . . You didn't want to kill the kid." Frankie volunteered the information that about nine out of ten families in the neighborhood had a relative in the rackets.

The racketeer was the standard-bearer of the neighborhood. He was an acknowledged source of norms and values. Even a legitimately oriented agency such as the neighborhood settlement house derived some sanction and support from the adult racket system. The director of teen-age activities at the settlement house frequented by many of the delinquents in the area depended on the racketeer as an ultimate source of control and influence over recalcitrant youths. This untrained social worker had been raised in the area and subscribed to many, but obviously not all, of the conventional values and expectations of the professional social worker:

He felt that their (the delinquent youngsters') values were all "messed up." He said that they didn't respect people and that they thought in terms of force. As they got a little older, the most important thing in life to them was to make a dollar. The only person they look up to was the racketeer. The kids in the area thought almost completely in terms of rackets and racketeers. They did not feel great affection for the racketeers; they feared them more often than not. But, just the same, these youngsters wanted to be under their protection. This settlement-house worker also said that the kids could act very tough at the settlement, sometimes; but if he wanted to, he could have them all "wiped out." I asked what he meant by "wiped out," and he said that he knew some of the racketeers and could call up one of them whom he knew quite well. This fellow could come over with four of his buddies and "take care" of the troublesome kids. The kids knew that the racketeers didn't fool around.

Slumtown was poorly integrated. The lower-echelon racketeer, such as the numbers-runner, drug-seller, petty thief, or robber, was omnipresent but did not appear to perform a significant neighborhood integrative function. The petty criminal played a circumscribed role on the block. He was one of many small independent entrepreneurs — succeeding one day, failing the next. There was constant competition for customers, who were not always satisfied with the illegitimate service or product provided. Reports of violence between criminal operators and customers and among petty racketeers and thieves were common. The criminal who exercised limited power even in controlling his own illicit business activities had little or none over others sectors of neighborhood life. His relationship with the police was not stable. For example, he was never sure when payoffs to a particular policeman or group of policemen would have to be increased. He knew that at almost any time he could be attacked or held up by a competitor or a "hoodlum" in the area.

Although there were many criminals in Slumtown, the status of the illegitimate operator was not always high. The racketeer or criminal did not exercise a major influence among conventional groups, nor were adult-criminal controls upon the behavior of delinquent youths apparent. The typical fighting group of young delinquents was as much estranged from the adult criminal system as from the adult conventional system. In general, the relationships between delinquent groups and racketeers were cool, distant, and at times openly hostile:

Zoro, a gang leader of the Regals, said he thought that they (the racketeers) were the ones who "ratted" on them so they would be picked up. He felt the racketeers sometimes wanted them out of the way. The researcher asked if any of the racketeers ever came up to him as leader to get things quieted down. Zoro said that occasionally a racketeer would do that but that it would make no difference.

A Youth Board supervisor spoke to the author about the relationship which the Noble Lords had with a young racketeer, about twenty-eight years of age, who had himself formerly been a leader of this gang:

He was a racketeer, a small-time racketeer making a couple of hundred dollars a week, but the youngsters in the Noble Lords did not look up to him. As bopping and gang-fighting kids, they even looked down on him and generally wanted to have nothing to do with him.

It was apparent that there was little accommodation here between delinquent and adult criminal orientations. The older successful criminal was not necessarily idealized by the delinquent group. The racketeer did not seem to exercise a pervasive influence in Slumtown.

Haulburg was only partially integrated. It contained a more limited, more modest racket structure than did Racketville. Its racket system was perhaps less extensive but better integrated than that of Slumtown. There was little evidence of widespread or systematic payoffs to the police. Numbers men and bookmakers operated through a few of the local grocery stores, delicatessens, and bars; but the operations were small. The police "cracked down" periodically.

A youth-officer patrolman who had been in the area for fifteen years and had the reputation of being truthful reported that he didn't know much about the other neighborhoods, but he believed there was less racketeering here than elsewhere. . . . There were some horse-betting parlors, but they had been in existence for many years. Some of the old-time bookmakers had converted their apartments into "horse parlors." Each had maybe four or five special "wires" to the track. He said that this, of course, could not have been done without the collaboration of some of the police force and of some telephone company employees.

The major system of criminal-conventional co-operation occurred with regard to "fencing," or the disposal of stolen goods. A number of the appliance, TV, radio, and auto-parts stores were known outlets for stolen material. Adolescent and young-adult thieves were frequent suppliers of stolen goods to these stores. The arrangement between the fence and the thief was, however, not always stable and mutually profitable. Fences, when it was to their advantage, were known to cheat and "rat" on the young burglars and shoplifters:

Patrolman H. recalled that several youngsters from one of the gangs had recently been falsely accused by one of the fences of selling him stolen goods. In another instance, an adolescent was outraged when he found out that the ring he had stolen from a "rich apartment," which had netted him only $25 from the fence, was worth $4,000.

Occasionally youths and young adults were given leads by fences as to where to "pull a score." Arrangements for disposal and sale of such goods were sometimes made beforehand. Often the delinquent had little need to dispose of goods to fences and crooked hock-shop dealers. In Haulburg, a criminal orientation, at least within certain limits, was acceptable to a large segment of the lower-class population:

Lester, one of the delinquents, said that he had little difficulty in selling to many of his neighbors the meat and stuff he stole from the big chain stores. He also said that sometimes even he was surprised at the number of people in the area who were willing and even anxious to buy stolen goods. The researcher asked him about the hi-fi set which had been stolen recently and who would buy it. Willie, who had stolen it, said that the set would probably bring him about $10 or $15. When new it was worth $100 to $125. A hock shop would give him $10 for it; almost any person in the neighborhood would give him $15. Asked what were the chances that a person who accepted stolen goods would be arrested, Willie said this was never a problem and that no one rejected stolen merchandise. He guessed that if the police ever asked questions, the fence would merely say he didn't know it was stolen.

It was apparent that although no highly organized criminal system was present in the area, a pattern of limited arrangements between criminal and conventional elements was fairly widespread.

Age-Level Integration

Lower-class areas may also be arranged along a continuum of the degree to which the relationships and orientations of offenders of different age levels are accommodative or antagonistic. When the relationships or orientations of children, youths, young adults, and older adults mesh closely, a condition of age-role integration may be said to exist. A system of age-level integration requires that younger youths defer to the authority of older youths and that older youths, in turn, protect and guide their juniors. It also means that the pattern of values and behavior of the older youths serves as a model for younger ones.

In Racketville the seniority and influence of the next older generation appeared to be inviolate. This was demonstrated, for instance, on the handball courts:

The Vulture Tots pushed the younger boys off simply by getting on the court and beginning to play handball. The younger boys immediately stopped their game and went elsewhere. When the Vulture Juniors, who were a little older than the Tots, came to the court, they in turn displaced the Tots. Later, Sammy, a Senior, who was smaller in size than any of the Juniors, came over, threw the ball against the wall, and told the Juniors to get off. They immediately stopped playing. Several other Seniors soon joined Sammy. After several games the Seniors left, except for Sammy — Sammy called to three of the Juniors who had stood on the side lines and suggested a game of doubles. Sammy's side won by a lopsided score. It was clear that in no way did the score reflect the skill of the respective players. The younger but lower-status Juniors were more skilled at the game than Sammy. Sammy's side should really have lost.

Older members of the Vultures eagerly performed their roles as big brothers and guides:

Little Augie, Monk, and Freddie were excited by the presence of the younger fellows. They acted as big brothers and bosses. They told them to straighten their collars, to be wary of "fags," or homosexuals, to talk straight. Monk said that the fellows had better look nice so that if they ever got into a fight and the cops picked them up, they, the cops, would be baffled and would probably conclude, "These fellows are too well dressed and too nice; they couldn't be involved," and they would be released.

Functions of authority and control were directly and vigorously exercised by members of older age groups in the youth and young-adult community:

The Youth Board supervisor spoke to me about Sam, age twenty-four years, one of the oldest of the Vultures and now an apprentice racketeer, whom he had used in the past to help settle gang fights. Recently he had used Sam's help to retrieve some items stolen from his office by members of one of the younger groups. He recounted that Sam had called the fellows into the office, lined them up, and threatened them with violence unless the stolen office records and personal property were returned. Most of the stuff had been brought back, but the agency's relationship with the young group had suffered in the process. This Youth Board supervisor suspected that this may not have been the best way to effect a change in the structure of this tightly knit delinquent system.

Members of the different delinquent groups knew one another intimately, but they also knew the members of non-delinquent groups in the area. Occasionally bickering and fighting broke out between individuals from the various groups. Individual disagreements rarely resulted in disruption of inter-group relationship. The cohesion of the youth community was never seriously threatened. Integration among offenders and non-offenders of the same and of different age levels prevailed to a marked and effective degree.

In Slumtown the relationships between offenders of different age levels were tenuous. The members of a gang-fighting group tended neither to contact nor to know directly who the older influential fighters of the gang were or had been. There seemed to be little connection between one generation and the next. The relationships of offenders of contiguous age levels were minimal in interaction, influence, and control. Older youths and young adults ordinarily were not interested in the affairs of the younger groups or in their members. On the rare occasions when a young adult attempted to influence the actions of the members of an active adolescent fighting group, the effort tended to be ineffectual:

Bobby, a former member of the Regals with a reputation as a courageous and daring gang fighter, told the researcher that he knew some of the kids in the present group fairly well. He had taken Willie or Mikey aside several times — they were now the main guys — and he tried to talk sense to them. They listened and nodded their heads, but it did no good; they went right ahead with their gang fighting.

In at least one instance, the relationship between a younger active segment and an older inactive segment of a fighting group deteriorated to the point of open conflict:

Lefty said that he had just gotten out of jail and that he had a wife and a kid and did not want to let Willie, the gang leader of the younger segment, draw some of the older fellows back into fighting and make the street too "hot" to live on. Lefty tried to straighten Willie out; he also talked to the younger kids. However, one thing led to another, and the older fellows almost decided to "call it on" with the kids because they wouldn't listen. Lefty said that Willie was crazy; Willie had even threatened to shoot him.

According to the Youth Board worker, the situation between the two segments of the group became so strained that the youth squad of the police department was alerted for fear of a serious outbreak. Flurries of fist fighting did actually occur.

There was also little accommodation in Slumtown among groups of the same age level. This was to be expected, since the very basis for the development of a conflict subculture depended on a continual state of strained relations among delinquent groups. A considerable number of the groups were in varying stages of "peace" and "war" with each other. One group would be in conflict with five or six groups at a time. The fighting was on a patterned basis and in accordance with traditional animosities; yet contacts and relationships between opposing groups were extremely vague and tenuous. The causes or reasons for group dissension and conflict were not always clearly known, even to members; indeed, sometimes the very identity and location of the antagonist group were only vaguely established.

In the neighborhood of Haulburg the extent of integration of offenders of various age levels was not as great as in Racketville; neither was it as minimal as in Slumtown. Children, youths, young adults, and older adults from the lower-class groups knew each other quite well. The pattern of relationships among different age levels was relatively stable but not so closely knit as in the racket subculture. Different-age-level relationships were loose and flexible. Younger and older boys were in contact and interacted with each other. The older ones were evidently role-models for the younger boys:

The street-club worker spoke about a young group on the block with which he was now starting to work. Until recently these boys had not been in much trouble; however, they were now beginning to "ape" the ways of the bigger boys. They were involved increasingly in drinking sprees, disorderly conduct, malicious mischief, and petty theft.

The relationships of the younger and older boys were not close, although they were consistently friendly. Direct controls were not imposed and punitive action was not taken by the senior youths:

On the way back to the front stoop from a ball game, some older boys passed a group of youngsters about twelve years old, who began to tease them. The older fellows did not respond with anger, but accepted the teasing with good nature, and responded in a casual but friendly manner. Members of both groups appeared to know each other fairly well.

Compared to the hierarchy of rigid controls present in the racket subculture, where the older boys dominated the younger youths, the system of age-level accommodation in Haulburg was flexible and open. It reflected a large element of mutual choice as to time and place, and purpose in the relationship to be developed and tasks to be achieved. Rational and calculated advantage appeared to be a basis for much of the interaction and the transactions among the individuals and groups of different age levels:

While Hughie, age eighteen, was speaking to the author, a young fellow of about fourteen or fifteen years old rode up on a bicycle. He was a chubby, angel-faced, pleasant-looking boy. He asked for Ralph, but Ralph was not around. He pulled Hughie off to the side and whispered to him, then took two dollar bills from his pocket, folded them, and gave them to him. Hughie and the boy walked over to the liquor store. Hughie walked in by himself, getting out his draft cards as he did so. He returned with a wrapped bottle of liquor — probably wine. When the boy left, Hughie opened his hand, showing the sixty cents that he had "earned"; he was very pleased with himself and soon went into a nearby grocery store to buy some beer.

In Haulburg, relationships were often established on an individuals or small-clique basis, and ties thus established were transitory. They often served a temporary social or antisocial interest or convenience. The fights which occasionally erupted between individual members of different groups rarely resulted in group conflict. They were resolved quickly and were forgotten almost as soon as they were over.

SUMMARY

The neighborhoods in which the three delinquent subcultures developed were clearly different. Racketville, with its racket subculture, probably provided the most advantageous lower-class economic circumstances. Slumtown, the conflict subculture, was characterized by the severest kind of social and economic deprivation. Haulburg, the theft subculture, provided a socially superior context for living. The indexes of social health were generally higher in Haulburg than in the other areas.

Traditional notions about the connection between poverty and delinquency were not entirely supported by the data, for not all delinquents from these neighborhoods came from impoverished families. Indeed, in Slumtown the median family income of delinquents was considerably higher than the median family income of non-delinquents. Furthermore, evidence in support of the notion that delinquents come more often from broken homes than non-delinquents was not substantial. It was, however, quite possible that the quality of the family life of delinquents and non-delinquents varied significantly.

The characteristics which did not distinguish delinquents from the three types of neighborhoods were age of leaving school, type of school program, pattern of church attendance, and probation or parole status. Other characteristics of delinquents, such as ethnic background, length of residence, and grade achievement, were different in each area. There was evidence, however, of basic residential and neighborhood stability for delinquents, regardless of neighborhood. The occupational and economic status of delinquent youths differed. The delinquent of Italian extraction, in the racket subculture, enjoyed the highest economic status; economic conditions for the Puerto Rican delinquent, from the conflict subculture, were most inferior.

The integration of criminal and conventional elements and the integration of offenders of different age levels varied in each area. Racketville was highly integrated, for criminal and conventional orientations were interlinked there, and a well-organized hierarchy of influence and responsibility existed among the offenders of different age levels. In Slumtown, integration was weak, for the various age groupings and systems of orientation did not mesh effectively. Slumtown represented, so to speak, almost a series of islands of conventional and criminal orientation and different-age-level peer associations. Haulburg was only partially integrated and lacked a pervasive and powerful racket system. In this area, an orientation to thievery seemed to predominate and was supported by a system of somewhat diffuse relationships among conventional and criminal elements and among offenders of different age levels.

On the basis of the data obtained, it became sufficiently apparent that lower-class neighborhoods were different in a variety of significant dimensions and that delinquency did not appear to arise under a single set of social, cultural, or economic circumstances. It was reasonable to expect that patterns of delinquent behavior and orientation would also differ in each of the the areas studied.

CHAPTER II

PATTERNS
OF DELINQUENT
SUBCULTURAL BEHAVIOR

The purpose of the present chapter is to describe the patterns of delinquent behavior and orientation which are characteristic of various types of delinquent social systems and subcultures. The discussion is focused on the constellations of delinquent behavior that differentiate delinquent subcultures, rather than on behavior patterns that may be common to delinquents regardless of type of lower-class neighborhood. A wide variety of provocative and aggressive behavior, such as brawling or unorganized and spontaneous fighting, is common among youths in lower-class areas. Such behavior apparently is more prevalent among lower-class than among middle-class youths. It is more typical of the delinquent than the non-delinquent adaptation. An activity such as fist fighting need not, however, necessarily reflect a delinquent orientation. It represents, at least partially, normal adolescent behavior. Its high incidence among lower-class delinquent youths may be in considerable measure a function of the greater need and striving for status and prestige and the relative lack of means, other than personal, by which to achieve them. Aspirations for success status are higher among delinquents than among non-delinquents (see chap. v). The conventional means to success-goals, however, such as academic preparation or vocational training, have not been acquired by delinquents. The gang or peer group provides the means — more significantly for the delinquent than for the non-delinquent — by which some kind of success status may be obtained. Delinquent-group interaction and activity develop pressures and provide opportunities for testing physical strength and courage — the simplest and most readily available attributes of a status of prestige. It is much less necessary for the non-delinquent to be "somebody" in his group through fighting, since a significant status can be more easily secured by him through conventional means.

Nevertheless, dominant patterns of delinquent activity, including aggressive behavior, seem to vary from one type of neighborhood to another. Certain acts of delinquency which are common in one area may occur infrequently in another. Outwardly similar kinds of delinquent behavior may be organized for different purposes in the various neighborhoods.

Not only delinquent behavior but delinquent norms and values may be distributed differently in the three neighborhoods. However, delinquent orientation and delinquent behavior may not be necessarily commensurate or correlative at a given time and place. Delinquent or criminal attitudes may be considered just as basic, in the long run, to the determination of the criminal-adult life style as is delinquent behavior. Conversely, the relative lack of current involvement by youths in delinquent behavior does not preclude the possibility of criminal-adult adjustments later.

An understanding of the delinquent adjustment requires attention to both the antisocial behavior and to the antisocial orientation. The delinquent adjustment must be viewed within a broad sociocultural framework over a sufficiently long-term perspective. For instance, a youth who does not perform delinquent acts but who has a delinquent orientation may become an adult who performs criminal acts.

THE RACKET SUBCULTURE

The rackets in Racketville and in the other neighborhoods signify highly organized criminal activities such as policy or numbers, off-track betting, loan-shark operations, narcotics-selling, and organized prostitution. These criminal operations, particularly in Racketville, involved large numbers of persons in a bureaucratic structure. There were various echelons of re-

sponsibility, power, and opportunity. Significant upper-echelon opportunities were not open to the youth of Racketville.
It was anticipated, however, that some delinquents, by virtue
of access to criminal means, would engage in significant apprentice racketeer roles, if on a limited basis. Undoubtedly,
many delinquents in this type of area would be able to assume,
in due time, significant racketeer roles without necessarily
starting at the bottom.

Policy racket. — The interview evidence did not make it
clear that more delinquents from Racketville than from the
other areas were engaged in such operations as taking numbers or making pickups of numbers receipts. Of the ten delinquents in each area sample, only four from Racketville,
two from Slumtown, and one from Haulburg said that they
had ever been involved in the policy racket.[1] There was a
strong indication, however, that of the few who reported participation in such activities, the median involvement was highest for the delinquents from Racketville — 135 days in their
entire delinquent careers. In Slumtown and Haulburg, the
median participation was merely 1 or 2 days. The risks of
serving time for this kind of law violation were minimal.

There was observational evidence from Racketville that delinquents were involved in policy operations mainly through
family connections. Since relatives were often in the upper
reaches of the racket structure, it was natural for delinquents
to be exposed and drawn into illegitimate activity in some
fashion:

Davey said to the street club worker that he had Uncle Joey's
Cadillac outside and asked if he would like to be driven home.
Davey went on to say that he was on an errand to pick up some

---

[1] It should be pointed out that no formal checks on the truthfulness of
responses of informants and subjects were made. The researcher assumed
that the delinquent would tend to be honest and accurate in his responses
when interviewed in a relaxed, non-threatening, open community situation,
by a "streetwise" skilled interviewer. Non-systematic and, at times, informal
checking of responses was made through conversations with street-club
workers and other delinquents who knew the respondents and through a
review of agency records and materials, where such were available and relevant. The validity of the responses of only two of the interviewed subjects
was strongly questioned — by street-club workers. The original responses
were, nevertheless, used.

money from the ————— Luncheonette. . . . This was the first time that he openly acknowledged to the worker that he spent part of each day in making calls at various bars, luncheonettes, and restaurants in order to pick up the day's receipts from policy. On the way home, the worker remarked that the Cadillac was beautiful and that Davey handled it extremely well. Davey replied that someday he would own a car as fine as this and go around in style.

The delinquent was given opportunities to prepare for organized criminal roles by performing seemingly minor errands. Such assignments served to put him in a position to do a small favor for the racketeer, thus showing him that he was willing and trustworthy. The communication of criminal norms and values and the opportunity to establish useful contacts with racketeers was made possible by completion of these little jobs.

Butch explained that he had to pay a fine for someone at traffic court next morning. It was for a vehicle violation. The person had given him a twenty-dollar bill. Since he wasn't going to school tomorrow anyway, Butch didn't mind doing this person a favor. He said that the guy who gave him the money had a big fat bankroll and just pulled the twenty dollars from the top. This man wasn't related to the boy but he was supposed to be a "big" man in the numbers. Butchie said this man owned, in addition, two dump trucks and an ice cream and meat-delivery business. He said this might be a break for him. . . . Someday he might get a job making a couple of hundred dollars a week hardly doing anything, which is what he wanted. He would be employed by this "big shot." He would be able to take it easy, get up late in the morning, have girls, go to night clubs . . . no one to tell him what to do.

Field observation indicated that such criminal opportunities either were not available or were not sought as much by delinquents in other kinds of areas.

Shylock or loan-shark racket.—The practice of money-lending at usurious or illegal rates of interest, often 20 per cent or higher—the Shylock or loan-shark racket—appeared to be more common to delinquents from Racketville than from the other areas. While six delinquents from Racketville had participated in money-lending, only one delinquent in each of the two other neighborhoods had done so.

Field data suggested that this type of illegal business might be conducted on the job outside as well as in the neighborhood. Involvement in loan-shark activities apparently started early. Two youths from Racketville who were still attending school were apprehended by school authorities for systematic loan-shark activities. There was little doubt that the loan-shark operator was considered "a respectable businessman" and was highly admired by delinquent youths in the area:

Jackie, Freddie, and Louie once discussed with the researcher the advantages of being a loan shark. They felt that this was a very good kind of racket to be in. It was safe. The main thing to worry about was the income-tax people, since, of course, you couldn't report all the money you would be making. Most of the fellows who borrowed money at high rates of interest paid back. The only drawback was that you had to have a little money to start with. Jackie said that he was definitely interested in becoming a loan shark when he got a little older.

Delinquents from Racketville were highly business-oriented. Indeed, they seemed to develop a keen business sense which was not characteristic of delinquents from the other areas.

Narcotics-selling or "pushing." — The interview data did not reveal that more delinquents from Racketville were involved in the sale of narcotics than were delinquents from other areas. Indeed, while two delinquents from Slumtown and one delinquent from Haulburg admitted that they sold narcotics, no delinquents from Racketville admitted such activity. "Pushing" was perhaps not a common offense among delinquents. The interview data seemed to contradict expectations.

However, the observational data supported expectations, at least at the adult level. The findings here indicated that, just prior to the researcher's arrival in the neighborhood, two major raids by treasury agents resulted in the arrest of a drug-selling ring consisting of at least fifteen adults who were distributing heroin, mainly. Also, there was evidence that although the sale of drugs on a wholesale level was approved by these adults, there was great concern about petty trafficking, particularly in the immediate area. In previous years, when drug-selling had been permitted in the neighborhood, the racketeers themselves were "hurt" when their own sons and nephews, in certain instances, succumbed to the use of drugs. Drug-selling was now prohibited in the area. Racketeers had even gone to the extreme of setting the police on the trail of small-time drug peddlers who would not obey their injunctions.

Thus the observational and interview data were not entirely contradictory. They merely indicated different patterns of involvement, depending on which segment of the drug market was studied. Upper-echelon or large-scale drug-selling was considered permissible and appropriate, but not petty trafficking, especially in the Italian neighborhood. Furthermore, it was unlikely that delinquents would be trusted with responsibility at the upper level of the drug racket.

VALUE-NORM INDEX

A value-norm index was constructed on the basis of nineteen items. Three directly indicated values — whether racketeers were good or bad, whether it was all right to cheat, and whether people should be honest. Sixteen items sought to establish the likelihood of participation in such acts as "'kill someone"; "beat up a guy"; "gang-fight"; "steal a car"; "steal a bicycle"; "steal groceries, candy, etc."; "burglary of an apartment"; "hold up a store"; "be a pimp"; "get involved in numbers"; "push narcotics"; "use narcotics"; "rape"; "con a few bucks"; "Shylock or loan shark"; "extort money." Four responses were possible — "very likely," "likely," "hardly," or "not at all."

The responses of the subjects were added to obtain a group response for each item. Then, since it was assumed that all questions tapped a single legitimacy or illegitimacy variable, the responses to the nineteen items were added for each of the groups. The resultant four intensity scores ("very likely," "likely," "hardly," or "not at all") were collapsed into two: The total illegitimate ("very likely," "likely") and the total legitimate ("hardly," "not at all") responses for each group. A criminal value score was obtained by computing the percentage of the total responses of each group which indicated an illegitimate orientation.

The findings showed marked differences in criminal orientation between delinquents from Racketville and delinquents from Slumtown or Haulburg. The delinquents from Racketville were most highly criminal in orientation; 71 per cent of their responses were illegitimately oriented (see Table 6).

TABLE 6
VALUE ORIENTATIONS*

NEIGHBORHOOD AND COMPONENT GROUP	NUMBER OF RESPONSES		PERCENTAGE OF ILLEGITIMATE RESPONSES
	Legitimate	Illegitimate	
Racketville			
Non-delinquent†	138	50	27
Delinquent	56	134	71
Drug addict	107	83	44
Slumtown			
Non-delinquent	153	37	19
Delinquent	103	87	46
Drug addict	122	68	36
Haulburg			
Non-delinquent‡	152	33	18
Delinquent	100	90	47
Drug addict	125	65	34

*The number of respondents in each component group was ten, and total responses expected per group were 190.
†Two subjects refused to answer the item on evaluation of racketeers.
‡Five subjects did not know any racketeers.

Nevertheless, an inspection of the data on antisocial activity did not reveal a greater delinquency rate for delinquents from Racketville than for those in the other areas. In other words, there did not appear to be a strict correlation between criminal value orientation and general involvement in delinquent behavior. It is possible, however, that the criminal value orientation of the delinquent from the racket subculture merely made him a likely candidate for future organized criminal activity. Although it was important for the young delinquent to develop a reputation for being tough, it was at the same time necessary that he minimize his risks of arrest. Racketeers placed a premium on smooth and unobtrusive operation of their employees. The undisciplined, trouble-making young "punk" was not acceptable. The primary condition for admission to the racket organization was not necessarily previous involvement in delinquent acts but training in attitudes and beliefs which would facilitate the smooth operation of the criminal organization. Prior development of specific skills and experiences seemed less necessary than the learning of an underlying illegitimate orientation or point of view conducive to the development of organized crime.

Role-models. — The kind of adult a young person aspires to be is manifested by the values and the way of life which he esteems highly. The role-model such a young person selects provides an indication of his current orientation to life and is suggestive of the type of adult he himself may well turn out to be.

Responses to the question, "What is the occupation of the adult in your neighborhood whom you would most want to be like ten years from now?" indicated that more delinquents from Racketville identified with the role of the racketeer than did delinquents from Slumtown or Haulburg. The sharpest contrast existed between Racketville, where eight of ten delinquents interviewed, and Haulburg, where only one of ten delinquents interviewed, considered the racketeer as a role-model. Indeed, more subjects generally from each of the three component groups of Racketville (non-delinquents, delinquents, drug addicts) identified with racketeers than those from either of the other two areas. Furthermore, it should be noted that of the nine youngsters in a total sample of ninety

TABLE 7
ROLE-MODELS*

Neighborhood and Component Group	Racketeer	Non-Racketeer
Racketville		
Non-delinquent†	1	4
Delinquent	8	1
Drug addict	5	5
Slumtown		
Non-delinquent	0	10
Delinquent	3	7
Drug addict‡	4	5
Haulburg		
Non-delinquent	0	10
Delinquent§	1	7
Drug addict	0	10

*The number in each sample or component group per neighborhood is ten.
†Five subjects responded "Nobody."
‡One subject responded "Nobody."
§Two subjects responded "Nobody."

subjects who could not find any adult to identify with in any of the three types of neighborhoods, five were non-delinquents from the racket subculture (see Table 7). This finding suggested that the non-delinquents in this area were to some extent *deviant* in relation to their own neighborhood and local culture. They would have had to be in order to develop a social or conventional orientation.

Getting ahead — education versus connections. — The subjects were asked to rank what they considered the most important quality in "getting ahead." There were four categories from which to select: "ability," "good luck," "connections," and "education." The term "connections" had a criminal connotation, particularly in Racketville.

The data revealed that delinquents from the racket subculture were highly oriented toward the use of connections as the most important factor, and education and ability as the least important factors in attaining goals. Delinquents from the other areas, particularly from Slumtown, were less oriented toward the use of connections and much more oriented to the importance of education in getting ahead (see Table 8).

TABLE 8
ATTRIBUTE CONSIDERED MOST NECESSARY TO GET AHEAD*

Neighborhood and Component Group	Ability	Good Luck	Connections	Education
Racketville				
Non-delinquent	7	0	2	1
Delinquent	0	1	9	0
Drug addict	1	0	5	4
Slumtown				
Non-delinquent	2	0	1	7
Delinquent	2	3	0	5
Drug addict	2	0	3	5
Haulburg				
Non-delinquent	3	0	0	7
Delinquent	1	0	3	6
Drug addict	3	0	5	2

*The number in each sample or component group per neighborhood is ten.

It was possible, particularly in the racket subculture, that the concepts of education and connections were antithetical. A strong value association with connections precluded an emphasis on an educational orientation. In a larger sense, the pursuit of education was the pursuit of that which was highly legitimate. The pervasive use of connections was in essence a commitment to the deviant, or that which was culturally regarded as unacceptable. Such an orientation was preeminently illegitimate. Confirmation of the validity of this deduction was obtained through an examination of the second, third, and fourth choices of attributes which were considered important in getting ahead; seven out of ten delinquents from the racket subculture chose education as the least important factor in achieving success.

THE CONFLICT SUBCULTURE

Gang fighting or "bopping." Gang fighting in its most repetitive and virulent form characterized the behavior of delinquents in Slumtown, and it could be described as group-based, systematic, and ritualized. Just the same, it was a somewhat nebulous and fluid phenomenon, difficult to observe or to identify consistently from one situation to the next. It could be unplanned, consisting of youngsters running down the street firing shots indiscriminately at one or two, ten, or twenty members of an opposing gang gathered on a front stoop, on a street corner, or in a candy store. Gang fighting sometimes was a series of planned attacks in which youngsters who were organized into squads armed themselves with sticks, knives, rifles, revolvers, zip guns, chains, can openers, bricks, ash-can covers, lead pipes, brass knuckles, or home-made bombs and converged on a large group who were similarly armed and waiting or, perhaps, not waiting and unaware of the planned attack. It could be, on rare occasions, a prearranged affair between one hundred or more youngsters from each group, meeting, head on in a park, at a dance, in a playground, or on a beach. Weapons such as revolvers, automatics, shotguns, and rifles were the preferred means of combat.

The group "brawl" was distinguished from the gang fight by being a less destructive and generally more spontaneous form of aggression in which the crucial element of gang reputation, or "rep," was not at stake. This type of fighting, found with about the same frequency among delinquents in each of the areas, occurred most often on Friday or Saturday nights after

TABLE 9

Reports of Gang Fights by Members of Groups in Each Neighborhood*

RACKETVILLE			SLUMTOWN			HAULBURG		
Non-Delinquent	Delinquent†	Drug Addict	Non-Delinquent	Delinquent†	Drug Addict	Non-Delinquent	Delinquent	Drug Addict
0	3	2	0	15	0	0	5	1
2	25	3	0	20	0	0	6	2
3	25	3	0	50	3	0	7	3
3	30	7	0	50	3	0	13	10
3	50	15	0	50	10	0	20	10
5	50	20	1	100	30	1	20	12
5	50	40	2	100	50	1	20	20
6	50	70	25	205	100	3	30	20
7	55	100	50	1,000	500	4	50	150
15	100	300	50	1,000	1,000	4	100	150

*The number in each sample or component group per neighborhood is ten. Each figure represents the number of gang fights in which a subject said he had been involved. Every gang foray, skirmish, aggressive or defensive action was included in the estimate of the subject. Figures are arranged in order of magnitude.

†Difference between Racketville and Slumtown delinquents, using a Mann-Whitney U Test, is not statistically significant — z = 1.13.

several members of a group had got drunk and had become embroiled in an argument with peers or with adults. Usually such fights were broken up quickly and did not affect group prestige. Subjects in each area were clear about the differences between a gang fight and a brawl.

The interview data revealed that delinquents from Slumtown appeared to have been involved in more gang fighting than delinquents from either of the other two areas. Although each delinquent, regardless of neighborhood, admitted to or claimed a history of gang-fighting activity, the frequency of such involvement was greater in Slumtown than in Racketville or in Haulburg, but it was not statistically significant (see Table 9). The difference in the incidence of gang fighting in Slumtown and Racketville was objectively established, however, through an analysis of agency records.[2] The frequency of major gang fights or threats of gang fights sufficiently serious to alert the police was examined in regard to four typical delinquent groups: two from Racketville — the Vultures, the observation group, and the Stompers, the formal interview group — and two from Slumtown — the Regals, the observation group and part of the formal interview group, and the Noble Lords, the other part of the formal interview group. The results indicated that there was little difference between delinquent groups from the same type of area, but that differences between delinquent groups from Racketville and Slumtown were marked and statistically significant. The frequency of gang fights reported for the Slumtown groups was approximately four times as great as the number reported for the Racketville groups (see Table 10).

Although gang fighting was a less frequent phenomenon in Racketville, when it did occur it could be just as destructive as in Slumtown.

Ralphie said the fellows used to go uptown to play around with some of the girls. One day some of the guys uptown telephoned for ten Vultures to come and meet ten of their fellows and they'd have

---

[2] The Youth Board in the city where the research was done makes use of a twenty-four-hour-a-day, seven-day-a-week telephone and secretarial service to record all incidents of gang fights or threats of gang fights reported by the street-club workers.

it out. The Vultures were so upset that eight of them jumped into a car right away. When they got uptown, a dance was in progress with a hundred or more of the fellows from the other neighborhood present. The Vultures had garrison belts and a couple of machetes. One of them had a blank pistol. Ralphie remembered that there was a big fellow who was not really involved and wanted to settle things between the groups. One of the Vultures got sore at him, took off his garrison belt, and slashed the big fellow across the face with the buckle, cutting deeply. Ralphie said the boy deserved it. When he went down, some of the Vultures cut him on the back with machetes . . . "not too badly" . . . "just sliced him a little." Then the fight started, but the other fellows got "real scared" when one of the Vultures took out the blank pistol and made believe he was going to shoot. This gave the Vultures a chance to get back to the car and drive off.

However, the street-club worker explained:

"These boys don't orient themselves to 'bopping.' Every few months they may decide to go out and get a 'spick,' but there isn't a constant tension or pressure to participate in a gang fight as in other neighborhoods. Fighting isn't the usual subject of conversation among the Italian kids."

TABLE 10
MAJOR GANG-FIGHTS THREATS AND ACTUAL GANG FIGHTS*

Neighborhood and Group	Major Threats of Gang Fights	Major Gang Fights	Total
Racketville			
Vultures	2	4	6
Stompers	3	5	8
Slumtown			
Regals	10	17	27
Noble Lords	8	19	27

*Calculated from answering service messages and street-club worker estimates, Big City Youth Board, for a twelve-month period, with age of group members and size of groups held approximately constant. A major gang-fight threat was any threat important enough to be telephoned in to the answering service.
Differences between Racketville and Slumtown groups are statistically significant, using a t test, $p(s) < .05$.

A staff worker in the settlement house frequented by the Vultures stated that the delinquent groups in the area did not talk about gang fighting. They were mainly interested in girls, a good time, and money. A gang fight, when it occurred, was "just one of those things." The nature of the gang fighting which took place from time to time appeared to be largely defensive and grew out of fear of attack, based on reality or fancied.

Some of the Vultures spoke excitedly about "a whole mess of" Puerto Ricans coming to the park about forty minutes before and about how all the fellows (the Vultures) and one of the cops from the neighborhood chased them. Some of the older boys grabbed some of the Puerto Ricans and beat them up, and three of them (the Puerto Ricans) were then picked up by the police.

Among the delinquent groups in Slumtown, the Vultures had a reputation mainly as a defensive club. Papo from the Regals commented:

"I don't like the Vultures. I always wanted to bop against the Vultures for certain reasons that everytime they catch one of us alone they want to beat us or stab us or something, but they really ain't nothing because they never hardly ever come down on us. They always wait until we come down on them. So the Vultures, I think — they got a big reputation of staying in their block, but for me they don't have no reputation at all because they never come down."

Perhaps more typical of the aggressive activity of the delinquent group in Racketville was brawling or fist fighting among several youngsters of the same or different groups over strictly momentary grievances, where group honor or "rep" was not at stake.

Big Freddie recalled that when he was fourteen years old and was with some of the older guys in the Vultures, they got into trouble with a bunch of guys who were sitting in front of them at the movies. They had a real free-for-all, Big Freddie said boastfully. He was pretty big for his age and fought three of the other guys at once. Then the cops came, broke up the fight, and he was almost picked up, but somebody said he wasn't involved, and the cops let him go. He thought this was just clean fun and loved it.

Gang fighting or "diddy bopping" in Slumtown was of a different character and frequency. For the delinquents in this area, gang fighting was a full-time preoccupation, typifying a way of life in which the achievement and maintenance of status or "rep" were paramount goals. The fighting group generated, more completely and directly than other types of delinquent groups, the means to achieve prestige and recognition:

Chico said he joined the Regals about five years ago. He joined them because he wanted to be "bad" (notorious). He wanted a reputation. He said that most guys belonged to a "bopping" club because they wanted to impress guys, girls — but also adults. The researcher asked him what he meant by that. He said that if you were not a member of a "bopping" gang, you were nobody. If you walked "four-by-four" with the other guys in the club down the street and looked everybody straight in the eye, then they noticed you. They said you were a Regal, and they respected you.

Every opportunity was sought, particularly by the up-and-coming young delinquent clique or group, to develop a reputation and to achieve the all-important status of a "down," or tough, gang-fighting group. A member of a younger segment of a fighting group described the process of achieving a "rep":

"I remember a summer when Dillinger, me, and little Lulu, we formed a club. Dillinger became the president; Cheyenne, that's me, became the vice-president. Little Lulu bcame the war counselor — only us three — we had a club. All the old Regals were in jail. Dillinger, the first time he took us down, we got a rep. We burned King Kong and Count Shadow of the Noble Lords. They were all a bunch of punks, so Papo came in, and Husky Louie and a whole lot of guys wanted to join the Regals and the Tims — that's us. We went down every day. We shanked the Noble Lords. We kicked their ass. Every day we used to go down. We went down once, twice, three times, four times . . . eleven times. The eleventh time we got busted. Dillinger got busted — he was the one who got the rep for us. He went to Youth House . . ."

The crucial component in the acquiring of a gang-fighting "rep" or reputation, was "heart," signifying toughness, daring, bravery, adventurous foolhardiness. To be called a "guy who had heart" symbolized the achievement of the sought-after ultimate goal. It was the pinnacle, the Distinguished Service

Cross for performance, by the standards of the conflict subculture:

Billy the Kid spoke of the importance of having "heart." He spoke of one of the Gonzales brothers, a former president of the Regals, who would go down with another fellow and tell him where and when to "burn" (fire a weapon). This would be a kind of training. If the other fellow became frightened or wasn't sure, this fellow would take the gun from him and "burn" for him. He wasn't afraid of anything.

The possession or lack of "heart" distinguished the worthy from the unworthy in the gang-fighting group:

Bobby said, "Just about three guys, Billy the Kid, Tito, and myself had heart . . ." All put together there were about twelve or thirteen in the club, but a lot of them "weren't worth a damn." He said they were "chicken" and would run.

Since gang fighting was the means by which to attain significant status, it was important to create a crisis, particularly if relations between groups had been quiet for too long. By calling a member of another gang a "punk," or by insulting his girl friend, or by bringing up an unsettled grievance which might be two days or two years old, a member of a group could cause a crisis. The specific factor precipitating the onset of hostilities was usually insignificant. The major consideration was that reputation, the sense of group, and, thereby, individual importance was denied or impugned. Group prestige had to be maintained or re-established. It was also important to guard against conditions which might destroy opportunities to have gang fights:

Bobby said, "It was best if the Noble Lords didn't go to the Regal's territory or the Regals to the Noble Lord's territory, otherwise we would get to know each other and become too friendly, and then it would be hard to bop."

"Bopping" was the most exciting, satisfying, and worthwhile part of life for a great many delinquents in Slumtown. It was so considered even by former delinquent group members. In a moment of stone-cold sobriety the gang member, past or present, might say "This is crazy, bopping is no good,

it only gets you busted." Yet the typical view among delinquents from Slumtown was that gang fighting was a source of
satisfaction, a means of overcoming the constrictions of slum
life, and was useful in learning the ways of the world:

"When you're a jitter-bug (gang fighter) that's the best part of
your life. . . . You have fun. It's true you go down. I think when
you're jitter-bugging you learn more about life than when you
don't, or when you go to community centers, or when you do
nothing. In jitter-bugging you learn what's happening like. . . .
You ain't doing nothing — you don't learn nothing. When you're
jitter-bugging you learn a whole lot. You learn about jury . . .
court. In a way, you could learn about court when you take up a
lawyer . . . but take someone else, they don't even know what a
courtroom is. You see, when you're jitter-bugging you know . . ."

Gang fighting occurred least frequently in Haulburg. The
difference in gang-fighting patterns among the various neighborhoods was recognized by the delinquents themselves:

Recalling his own participation in fighting, a delinquent from
Haulburg reported that certainly he was not in as many gang fights
as guys from other neighborhoods. The fellows here did not get into
many gang fights. Once in a while there was talk of a gang "bust,"
but this kind of talk "comes and goes." He remembered the time
when the fellows were interested in becoming a division of a city-
wide fighting gang. This talk lasted a few weeks, and the guys were
never sure who was in or out of the gang.

The low incidence of gang fights in Haulburg did not mean
that delinquents who had a theft orientation were inherently
less aggressive than delinquents from other types of areas.
Aggression was merely manifested in other ways. Impulsive
brawling, usually involving a small number of participants,
was the characteristic way of settling differences:

"Here we have one-man or two-men fights like me against you and
him against him, more than up in the other neighborhood. Up there
they have six or seven guys or more on one other guy or many
other guys . . ."

Fighting in this area rarely resulted in serious injury.
Weapons were seldom used. Occasionally a stick, a brick, or

a bottle was impulsively used in a fight. Once in a while, when relations between two groups deteriorated and a gang fight seemed to threaten, feeble efforts at arms preparations were made. Indeed there was indication that the delinquent code called for and accorded higher respect to the youngster or youngsters who employed physical prowess only:

Tony said he used to be president of the Devils, and they were going to fight a group on —————— Street. These guys had a reputation for being the toughest bunch in their part of the neighborhood. The Devils had a gun and a few knives, but the fellows from the other street came into their block and only had their fists and beat them up anyway. After that they dropped their club name and gave up their weapons.

In Haulburg, brawling was common on Friday and Saturday evenings after long drinking sessions. Pretexts were used to justify fighting other peers and even adults who wandered into the block. Such fighting was consistent with general lower-class norms about fighting as a permissible and approved form of behavior. Delinquents from this area recalled with pleasure the noteworthy "donnybrooks" in which they were involved or those in which others participated. Several stories glorifying the prowess of fighters were part of the folklore of the neighborhood. Some of the fights even involved their own parents:

Stan boasted that when his father was younger, right after World War II, he used to go down to the bar and get into a lot of fights. He spoke proudly of the times his father used to "string out" the other guys. "Once he took care of three guys at one time. He knocked the guy across the bar, and the other down on a table, and third into the cellar — all by himself." Stan also said that on a Friday night, like tonight, the bar would be hopping. Chairs would be broken; mirrors smashed; bottles thrown against the counters. Not quite eighteen years old, the boy spoke with anticipatory glee of the time when he would go along with the older fellows to the bar.

In general, the data showed a difference in fighting patterns in the three types of area. Gang fighting in its most organized and offensive form was prevalent in Slumtown. It occurred less frequently and more defensively in Racketville, especially when delinquents and grownups viewed themselves as threatened from outside. In Haulburg, gang fighting was not a significant phenomenon.

VALUES

Delinquents from Slumtown were considerably less oriented to criminal or illegitimate norms and values than were delinquents from Racketville. According to the data obtained from the interviews (see Table 6), delinquents from Slumtown, as those from Haulburg, were principally oriented to the standards of the legitimate or conventional culture. Delinquents from Slumtown were far less oriented to careers in the rackets than were delinquents from Racketville (see Table 7). (This does not obviate the fact that there were many criminals, including racketeers, in the neighborhood. They were in the low echelons of the criminal hierarchy, however, and possessed relatively little power or influence.) Delinquents in the conflict subculture were mainly oriented to conventional working-class and lower-middle-class occupations, such as grocery or candy-store proprietor, plumber, or photographer. Formal education, despite the uniformly negative experiences which the delinquents from this area had encountered in school, still appeared to them as the major means by which success status could be achieved.

Luck, relatively more in Slumtown than in the other areas, was valued as a means for getting ahead (see Table 8). However, the factor of luck appeared generally not to be held as significant among young people in the three neighborhoods. From the data obtained it appeared that believing in luck was not as important an aspect of lower-class culture as some writers had indicated.[3]

THE THEFT SUBCULTURE

Stealing was a pervasive activity among delinquents in the theft subculture. Although as a rule not carefully planned or

[3] See, for example, Robert K. Merton, *Social Theory and Social Structure*, (rev. ed.; Glencoe, Ill.: Free Press, 1957) pp. 147–49; Walter B. Miller, "Lower Class Culture as a Generating Milieu of Gang Delinquency," *Journal of Social Issues*, XIV (Fall, 1958), 11–12.

executed, acts of theft appeared, nevertheless, to provide the opportunity to learn skills and attitudes which might be useful for the few who chose to pursue careers of adult crime later in life.

Car theft. — "Joy riding," or car theft by delinquents, i.e., breaking into a parked automobile and going for a ride, was common in Haulburg. While the appropriation of the car itself occurred rarely, its parts or accessories were often illegally taken and disposed of by the delinquent clique or small group. The interview data showed that whereas only three out of ten delinquents from Slumtown and six out of ten delinquents from Racketville were minimally involved in car theft, nine out of ten delinquents from Haulburg reported quite frequent participation in this kind of illegitimate activity. In Haulburg, the median involvement for delinquents in car theft was thirty instances; in Racketville, two instances; and in Slumtown, three instances. For many in this particular area, therefore, car theft appeared to be a highly repetitive and patterned preoccupation.

In Haulburg car theft appeared to have a function similar to gang fighting in Slumtown or being a "tough guy" in Racketville. In each neighborhood, delinquent behavior was a way of demonstrating conformity with the model of "big shot" or "important guy." In the theft subculture the posession of material goods, including flashy cars, fine clothes, and money, was the criterion of successful status. Yet it was not so much the money as what the money could buy that was significant. Car-stealing provided, most directly, an opportunity to fulfill a desired mode of existence. A young adult of the theft subculture discussed car-stealing as follows:

> Karl said of course the younger kids were all involved in stealing cars, but he wasn't sure they sold the cars. The researcher asked why the kids stole the cars. He said it was to be a "big shot." The kids would drive around — say they got the car from their uncles or brothers-in-law — and invite the girls or other fellows to go along with them. They'd ride around for a while and then abandon the car — maybe a couple of blocks from where they'd picked it up.

The kids on the street didn't make any money — not at first, anyway. Karl said that he noticed that the kids who did a great deal of "joy riding" hung around the used-car lots which were also good outlets for stolen car parts.

Although "joy riding" was for "kicks," or excitement, according to the youths themselves, and did not necessarily result in misappropriation of the car or its parts; the theft of cars was on occasion an act of conscious criminal intent. The director of a local settlement house in the area who held this point of view reported that:

Not infrequently, when the boys stole the cars and, occasionally, a truck, they went out to other neighborhoods where either the whole vehicle was sold or parts were stripped and then sold to any of a number of secondhand car dealers with whom the boys had regular business dealings. These boys were mainly interested in the money they could make rather than in the fun that riding in the car provided.

Knowledge derived from breaking into cars and driving or from disposing of the parts of the vehicles could be useful to delinquents in later years in more sophisticated illegal operations of purchase, sale, maintenance, and repair of automobiles.

Apartment burglary. — Unlawful entry into apartments and the taking of valuables such as clothes, money, radios, TV's, and hi-fi sets was a common activity among Haulburg delinquents. Whereas in Slumtown and Racketville, respectively, two out of ten delinquents reported participation in acts of apartment burglary, in Haulburg, eight out of ten delinquents did so. Illegal entry into apartments appeared not to be limited to the luxury apartment buildings, where, although the "takings" were good, the risks were higher. It seemed to occur as often in the lower-rental apartment houses, where the advantages of knowing the layout and taking more portable goods existed.

The delinquents in Haulburg were engaged in apartment burglary generally on a planned basis. They knew who the fences in the neighborhood were and sometimes arrangements were made in advance of the staging of certain apartment burglaries. Some of the boys, even at a fairly young age, brought well-developed skills to these assigned tasks:

Karl said that he knew a group of youngsters who were involved in a whole lot of burglaries in the neighborhood. The kids broke into apartments systematically and took stuff that they knew they could sell. . . . In fact, some of them were very good at it. They had special keys for the doors. A few could even pick locks. Karl said that he himself had learned to pick locks from one of the older guys in the neighborhood.

Stickups of stores. — Robbery of stores at knife- or gunpoint by delinquents was not a common phenomenon in any of the areas. This type of activity was not reported by delinquents from either Racketville or Slumtown. However, five of ten delinquents interviewed from Haulburg reported at least one holdup. When delinquents from Haulburg participated in stickups, there was evidence that usually two boys were involved together and that some planning had taken place beforehand.

In general, the pattern of thievery was more systematic and organized in Haulburg than in the other areas. Social agency personnel and the local youth patrolman were in agreement that stealing was a serious problem in the locality. The youth patrolman had established a rating system for groups of youngsters engaged in theft. One group of twelve- and thirteen-year-olds had a particularly high score.

Patrolman K. showed me a list of names of boys from ———— Street who constituted a serious problem during the last three years. These boys, seven or eight of them, were repeatedly picked up for breaking into the coin boxes of public washing and drying machines in the building basements. They also broke into parking meters. They were constantly appearing in court but the judges were reluctant to send them to the training school at so early an age. Patrolman K. said that he had been able to persuade the local settlement house to assign a street-club worker, half-time, to this group.

Petty thievery, in particular, seemed to be common among children and younger adolescents in all three types of areas. However, it was the researcher's impression that as the delinquents got older, thieving generally diminished in Slumtown and Racketville. Other types of delinquent orientation, such as gang fighting and involvement in racket activities, would then develop with greater momentum.

This did not preclude occasional instances of thievery during middle and late adolescence in the racket and conflict subcultures. The following is an extract of a report by a street-club worker assigned to a group in Racketville. He had just started working with this group:

After a while the boys got tired of merely sitting on the swings in the playgound and "shooting the breeze," so Jerry suggested that they try to put into operation the plan they had decided upon for that night. As the worker wondered about this and saw the boys gradually drifting off in pairs, Carl remarked that they were on their way to what he jokingly referred to as some "supplies." He pointed to the stacked building materials to be used for construction of a new roadway. Although Jerry was masterminding the operation, he did not take a direct part in it. Joey and Philip, who previously had been drinking, were leading the rest of the boys in their attempt to steal whatever they could find. About ten minutes later, the boys began to return with their loot. Although the worker was sure each boy was capable of carrying off bricks, cement blocks, or cement building implements, they had taken only three saws. Jerry directed that the saws be buried and that they return for them later in the evening, when the watchman was no longer suspicious. While plans were being made to go back for a second haul, the worker tried to intervene and suggested that Jerry and Philip, as well as Joey, go with him for sodas or coffee.

In the store Jerry explained that the guys went on "raids" like these just for "kicks." He said that sometimes the guys sold or used the tools they took. But the main purpose was to have a little fun. Philip then went on to tell about their raiding the A&P and other grocery chain stores to get cake, which they ate with milk stolen from the milkman. Jerry repeated that they did this just for "kicks" and said that they really did not need the money or the stuff they took.

In Slumtown it was rare that the entire group or a substantial part of it was engaged in organized burglary, even for "kicks." When stealing occurred, it tended to be a peri-

pheral activity of one of two youngsters. However, in Slumtown, too, such actions could be quite serious in plan and
consequences:

Superman, seventeen years old, told the researchers that recently
he was in trouble. In fact, he was on probation for it now. He said
that he was picked up for gang fighting, but this was not the whole
story. The cops found $400 in his pocket and forced him to confess
that he participated in a liquor-store burglary. Superman said that an
older guy he knows worked in the liquor store and had loosened
part of the wall at the rear of the store. Superman came back at
night when the store was closed and squeezed through this opening
and took a lot of money. He gave part of the money to his family.
He did not give any of it to his partner. He "pulled a bomb"
(swindle).

The burglary or theft pattern represented a more systematic and purposeful orientation in Haulburg than in the
other areas. Although at first it was part of a game, within
a short time it might serve as a start in learning important
skills that would be useful to the older adolescent and young-
adult thief:

Pete said that when he was a kid the guys used to go around from
car to car and see if they could break into glove compartments. They
did this mainly to see who was the best "stealer." Pete recalled that
he was "busted" when he was fifteen years old for stealing hubcaps.
Actually, he didn't get much money out of it. Much of it was a matter of who could steal the most hubcaps. Richie said that you
couldn't help learning while you were doing these things . . . and
when you got older you didn't rob for "kicks" but for money. That's
what most of the guys who were in trouble did now.

While the "fun" component in stealing was common in
each of the lower-class areas, the organization of a deliberate
income-producing theft pattern was most developed in
Haulburg.

VALUES

Delinquents from Haulburg, like those from Slumtown, were
considerably less oriented to criminal or illegitimate norms
and values than were delinquents from Racketville (see Table

6). At the same time, the observational data suggested, on the whole, that the conventional standard of respectability was more firmly established in delinquents from Haulburg than in delinquents from the other two areas. Hardly any delinquents from Haulburg were oriented to careers in the rackets. Only a small number of them had ever had any contact with adult racketeers or seen them as role-models (see Table 7). Delinquents from this area attributed high status to professional people. Occupations such as those of engineer, military officer, and social worker were highly desired. Local business proprietors, such as garage owners or even landlords, were also attractive role-models. In Haulburg, as in Slumtown, formal education was considered the key to the achievement of adult success status. Connections were considered important but not nearly so important as they were regarded in Racketville (see Table 8). At the same time, partial access to criminal opportunities was available, and they were considered somewhat more important than they were in Slumtown.

DRUG-USE AND DRUG-ADDICT ADAPTATIONS

A limited number of delinquents in each of the areas experimented with using narcotics. Exploratory drug-use occurred as early as twelve or thirteen years of age but was generally restricted in these early years to the smoking of marijuana cigarettes. The use of narcotics was more likely to start around the age of fifteen. The pattern of teen-age drug-use and adult reaction to it varied in the three subcultures.

Drug-use seemed to be an infrequent and unacceptable phenomenon in Racketville. There was a great deal of pressure both from adults and from peers against the use of narcotics:

This pressure and a disdainful attitude on the part of the group membership was often due, in part, to the fact that Sandy had been an occasional drug-user (marijuana) until about a year ago. At that time, Davey had told Sandy to stay away from the group's hangouts if he could not stop using drugs. Davey had said that he, the others, and the adults in the neighborhood wanted no part of a "weakling." According to the group members, this had been enough to make Sandy give up using narcotics.

In the conflict subculture there seemed much less pressure by adult or teen-age groups against the use of narcotics. Delinquent group members were more tolerant of drug-users. Indeed, smoking marijuana was considered a helpful stimulant for gang fighting or "bopping":

The fellows in the Regals said that they used marijuana but nobody in the club used heroin. If you used marijuana, this was fine, it stimulated you. Marijuana was not "drugs," and as far as they were concerned "drugs" was using heroin and "shooting up" (injecing heroin intravenously). Marijuana was great if you wanted to "bop," if you wanted to have a good time with the girl friend, or if you wanted to go anywhere or do anything. Heroin was no good if you wanted to "bop" because it made you sleepy. It made you go to dreamland. But Brave Eagle felt that heroin wasn't bad. It was nice to dream. However, all the boys agreed that there was nothing wrong with "pot" (marijuana).

A twenty-two-year-old narcotics addict from the conflict subculture described the sequence and the meaning of drug-use as he saw it:

Mannie explained that he became a "diddy bopper" because you had to be the "baddest" (the most notorious) in the neighborhood. You had to be tough and show that you weren't afraid of anybody. Especially you had to show the girls . . . and so you began at a certain age to fight . . . to wear jackets. Then you had to be an even badder "diddy bopper," and before you knew it you used "pot." That showed the other fellows in the club that you were "badder" than they were. Of course some of them didn't use "pot." From "pot" you said you'd try a little "sniffing" (inhaling heroin in powdered form) to show that you were even "badder" and then you went from "sniffing" to "skin-popping" (subcutaneous, non-intraveneous injection of heroin), and then to "mainlining" (injection of heroin into a major vein, usually in the arm). Then you were the "baddest" in the whole club, and you didn't care what anybody thought, and you went off by yourself.

Pressures against the use of narcotics appeared to be stronger in Haulburg than in Slumtown, but they were not as strong as in Racketville. In Haulburg effective parental pressure against the use of drugs by a delinquent son was more

often used on an individual basis, rather than on a neighborhood basis, as in Racketville:

Jeff said that Jimmy Sorello began to use heroin but stopped
because his father "beat the daylights" out of him. At the same
time there were other boys in the group who had begun to use
heavily and whose parents either did not know or did not take sufficient interest.

There was no clear or consistent explanation by delinquents
as to why some of them turned to drug-use. The motivation
for experimentation with drugs was generally believed to be
due to interaction with others who were experimenting or who
were using drugs heavily. The following is a verbatim excerpt
from a conversation with several delinquents in Haulburg;
it was typical of responses of delinquents from Haulburg and
Racketville:

RESEARCHER: Do you guys have any idea as to what makes a guy
turn to using drugs?

KARL: I don't know. I guess it's just introduction . . . a guy
hangs out with three or four guys, and they turn to drugs, and he
gets a shot . . . and he likes it. Even if he don't like it, it just hap-
pens to be the fad. Two or three weeks later he might get another
shot. Pretty soon he's going to like it.

Another member of the same subculture expressed his reason why others in his group were turning to narcotics — he
felt that the fact of personal problems was not a sufficient
answer:

"A lot of guys smoke pot or something like that but never
went any further. . . . I think guys who have anything to do with
that are stupid. They say because they have a lot of trouble and
things like that. Well, those other kids who used to get into trouble
got just as much problems . . . either they work them out . . . or
they drink . . . drugs I think is stupid."

HABITUAL USE OF DRUGS

A firm commitment to the use of drugs did not appear before about the age of eighteen. Habitual users or drug addicts,
usually former members of delinquent groups, were associated

with each other in loosely knit groups. A great part of each day was spent in contact and in transactions with other drug-users for purposes of getting money and making connections with "pushers," finding a place to "shoot up," "doze," and enjoy the "high," i.e., the effects of the drug, principally heroin. Typically, in each type of area, members of the addict grouping had gone through the delinquent phase within their particular subculture. As some of the delinquents turned to drug-use they tended to be involved more often in the kinds of antisocial activity which provided them with the funds for obtaining drugs. The criminal patterns of such young adults were to some extent conditioned by the nature of the means structures available in their area. In Racketville, the addict tended to obtain funds through employment by numbers men or loan sharks or higher-echelon drug distributors. In Slumtown, the addict turned perhaps more often to robbery, petty racketeering, and thievery. In Haulburg, the habitual drug-user appeared to intensify his involvement in theft activity, especially shoplifting.

Whether the drug addict had been at one time a gang leader or a peripheral member, a high- or low-status individual in a delinquent group, in his present status as addict he obtained little positive recognition. His use of drugs made him undesirable in his self-evaluation, in the opinion of other drug addicts, or in attitude of the community. On the other hand, use of drugs was a source of great physical pleasure to the addict. In some cases drug-use appeared to facilitate the individual's functioning on a job. After the consumption of drugs, addicts seemed to be less tense, less anxious, and indeed rather pleasant in their communication and interaction with people. For some, drug-use served as an interpersonal and intrapersonal adjustive function. At the same time, this did not deny that for a great many others drug addiction resulted in severe physical deterioration and in extreme social degradation.

Addict orientations in the three types of areas appeared to be similar in many respects. The use of heroin was almost universal among addicts. In almost all cases, they administered heroin intravenously. Frequency of use and strength of dosage seemed to be similar. There was some evidence, however, that the quality of heroin used and the kind of collateral drug employed varied in the three types of area. For example, a higher quality of heroin was reputed to have been available, at least at an earlier period, to addicts in the racket subculture. Marijuana usage prior to, and collaterally with, the use of heroin was common in the conflict subculture. The addicts in the theft subculture appeared to consume the greatest variety of narcotic drugs in addition to heroin: cocaine, benzedrine, morphine, demerol, and dolophine.

VALUES

The value orientation of drug addicts reflected an ambivalence with regard to legitimate and conventional standards. The drug-using pattern appeared to provide a means, through fantasy, by which prestige, power, and success status could be achieved. Drug addicts in each area were no longer firmly committed to adolescent-delinquent patterns of behavior, nor, on the other hand, were they fully committed to adult orientations. They seemed to make halting and uncertain use of the conventional or criminal systems available in the area.

Drug addicts in each of the areas had fewer hopes than did other delinquents that they could "make it" as racketeers, as successful criminals, or, indeed, as successful conventional adults. On the whole, they were less committed than other delinquents to criminal orientations (see Table 6). This might have been due to a greater sense of personal failure or to a weaker conviction that illegitimate means were sufficiently available to them for achieving success goals. More often than not, addicts considered connections extremely important in getting ahead in the world. Nevertheless, education and, to some extent, ability were viewed as important factors in the achievement of success (see Table 8). Addicts appeared not to be sure whether they were members of a criminal or of a conventional society.

Observational data were obtained mainly for one group of drug-users and addicts — the Warrior Seniors of the racket subculture. The Warriors comprised a group of about ten male adolescents ranging in age from sixteen to twenty years, with a median age of eighteen. It was the consensus of this group and the street-club worker that eight of the members had been addicted to heroin at one time or another. The ninth boy had experimented with heroin but had quickly given it up. The tenth boy was a heavy drinker.

The group was, perhaps, uniquely cohesive. Its members convened almost every evening and during the greater part of Saturdays and Sundays. They gathered to play cards, to go on trips, to attend parties, and together they even went on dates with girls. Of the ten members, five were steadily employed at full-time jobs; two worked sporadically; two were chronically unemployed; and one, the alcoholic, was still in school. The group had participated in a variety of delinquent acts including numbers operations and loan-shark activities, as well as gang fighting. During the previous two years, coextensive with their narcotics-use, the incidence and severity of their aggressive delinquent activity appeared to have greatly diminished.

The Warriors had been initiated into drug-use by members of the previous Warrior group. One current Warrior put it this way:

"The older guys kept saying they would like to see how some of us guys would look when we were high. Well it wasn't as if they wanted to see us start . . . they just wanted to see what *our* reactions would be."

Big Freddie felt that the older guys didn't deliberately set the younger guys into using drugs. He thought it was simply a matter of their being in the neighborhood. Since they were around so much of the time, the younger fellows were bound to pick up the narcotics habit from the older guys.

The pattern of narcotics-use among members of the Warriors was erratic, consisting of alternating periods of heavy addiction, minimal use, and abstinence. It was my impression that this pattern was common to many addict groupings regardless of type of neighborhood.

One day when I was in the schoolyard, the following took place:

Charlie came over and said that I could ask whatever I wanted. (He knew I was around to ask questions about drugs.) I said okay. I asked Charlie how long he had been using drugs. He said for four years. (Charlie was now eighteen years old.) Asked how he had got started, he said, "Curiosity." Asked how much stuff he used, he said that it depended: sometimes he used it two or three times a day, and sometimes it was good stuff, and sometimes it was not. The good stuff they used to get right off the boat, and it was almost pure. The stuff they got now, from the Spanish on ———— Avenue, was lousy. He said the last time he used drugs was about a month and a half ago. Now he was getting high on beer.

I expressed doubt as to whether he really had been hooked. Charlie said he had been hooked once and probably other times, although he had never been to the Narcotics Treatment Hospital.

The street-club worker with the Warriors confirmed the group's alternating and erratic pattern of drug-use. Speaking about a member of this group, he said:

"Little Freddie is a heavy user. He has been using drugs for about three years. He has been hooked three or four times now but has always managed to kick it on his own. Last summer he stopped and stayed off narcotics for four weeks . . . but this week he got hooked again."

The group alternated narcotics-use with heavy consumption of alcoholic drinks. Simultaneous heavy narcotics-use and drinking appeared to be unusual, yet there was little doubt that for the addict who was constantly trying to break the habit, drinking was at least a partial equivalent:

Charlie, who had used drugs, said that when he came home from work he was already "stoned" (on alcohol) and when someone offered him more to drink he got worse. This bothered him. He did not want to drink so much. He said that he and the other guys had been on "powder" (heroin) for so long that when they switched to liquid it was the craziest thing in the world. Charlie said that he was getting sick from a hangover. It had taken him two hours to sober up. From breakfast to lunch he would swear off beer and then the whole thing would start again. . . . He said he did not know how long this would keep up. He spoke of having gone for a walk with his dog the other night and of how "the dog walked him," for he was completely "stoned" and fell flat on his face twice. The second time he fell, the dog began to lick his face and woke him up. Otherwise, he would have slept it off right on the sidewalk.

In each of the three areas there was a great deal of evidence of the physical, social, and psychological deterioration of the addict. The following were observations of several addicts in Haulburg:

Fred, Karl, and the researcher went for a soda. Karl said he had not had anything to eat for several days. He was strictly on "junk" (drugs). He was losing a great deal of weight. He had lost thirty pounds in the past month. He said it was very hard to hustle enough money for drugs. He mentioned that his partner, Louis, had not gotten up early enough that morning and had not made enough to buy drugs. Louis was at home now, in bed, hoping to sweat out the night. The pains would be so severe he would not be able to sleep. Fred wished the summer were over, for it was hard to "boost" (shoplift) anything. In the winter time it was easier because you wore an overcoat and could always put things under it. Lately they had been lifting meat and groceries from the chain stores, but the store managers were getting suspicious. Karl thought that with his record, breaking into apartments was too risky. He did not mind doing a petty larceny "bit" (sentence), but a felony was something else. Fred said he had been in the hospital three times in the last four months — twice for pneumonia and once because of an ulcerated leg. He said that his wife had left him. Karl added that he had been going steady with the same girl for almost five years but was afraid to marry because of his drug addiction.

The drug-addict adjustment was an alternative adaptation available to delinquents who reached an age when they could no longer maintain the status of a juvenile delinquent, i.e., they either were no longer acceptable as members of delinquent groups, or they were no longer interested in membership in such groups. On the other hand, they did not yet consider themselves ready or able to undertake conventional adult responsibilities.

Many of the young delinquents did not succumb to the addict adjustment upon leaving delinquent groups. There was some evidence in each of the types of areas that members of the gangs which had been accorded high delinquency status were less likely to develop an addict orientation than were members of gangs which had been accorded relatively low delinquency status. However, there were some significant exceptions. In conclusion, it was clear that drug behaviors and orientations in each neighborhood were complex and variable phenomena. Certainly, more systematic investigation is called for.

SUMMARY

Characteristic subcultures and concomitant behavioral systems appeared to have developed in the three areas under discussion. Delinquent behavior was highly aggressive, regardless of neighborhood. However, aggressive orientation and activities were differently organized in each area. For example, the racket subculture "toughness" was directly associated with preparation for careers in the rackets. In the conflict subculture, aggressive behavior was highly organized for purposes of group conflict. In theft subculture, aggressive orientations tended to be more indirect and were expressed through acts of theft.

In Racketville, there was little question that the value orientation of delinquents was highly criminal or illegitimate; a large proportion of delinquents aspired to be racketeers. A guide to success in this area was expressed as: "It isn't *what* you know but *whom* you know that counts." While the data did not establish a heavy involvement of delinquents from this area in racket activity, it did demonstrate the anticipatory readiness of delinquents to participate in organized criminal behavior when such opportunities became available to them. In Slumtown, systematic and continual fighting was prescribed as the means of obtaining prestige and reputation. Other types of delinquent behavior or orientation, such as involvement in theft or racket activity, were relatively minimal. This conflict subculture was not fundamentally organized within a criminal context. True, the gang-fighting response was essentially deviant, but it was not preparatory to a criminal way of life. Delinquents who subscribed to this type of orientation were largely, if weakly, governed by conventional norms and values. They aspired to legitimate careers. They saw formal education as the surest road to achievement.

In Haulburg, orientation to various types of thievery afforded the possibility of illegally appropriating the means to desired success status. Perhaps the chief characteristic of the theft subculture was its evasiveness. The commitment to conventional norms and values was verbalized, but its actual implementation was not achieved. The culture of the middle-class society, with its standards of respectability, orderliness, and self-control, was fully recognized but only partially acceptable, and a system of illicit orientation was developed which permitted an indirect and partial attack on the established value systems. While acts of theft were permitted, acts of extreme violence were not acceptable.

The drug adaptation was viewed as available to older adolescents and young adults who, because of their personal inadequacies and their perceptions of the inadequate availability of conventional or criminal means, were unable to make the transition to adult status efficiently and directly. The drug adaptation in part afforded individuals a collective support for escape from failure. It permitted and encouraged the support of the group in the use of drugs, giving rise to fantasies of success and personal well-being. Nevertheless the drug adaptation was not entirely characterized by the retreat and isolation of its adherents from the surrounding society and culture, for the need of the drug addict to obtain a continuing supply of drugs forced him into contact with a variety of adults. Thus, he remained at least partially integrated with both conventional and criminal systems.

Finally, it is important to stress that the present chapter has emphasized the *differences* in delinquent orientation and behavior of each area. Delinquent subcultures are not totally mutually exclusive. They may exist side by side and interpenetrate each other. What this chapter has pointed out is the dominant character of delinquent subcultural patterns and how they are distinctively associated with certain neighborhood conditions.

CHAPTER III

DIFFERENTIAL
DELINQUENT
LIFE STYLES

This chapter presents further evidence for the existence of differential patterns of gang life in the three areas under consideration. Data on delinquent behavior are elaborated, and relevant material on historical, cultural, and social patterns of the gangs is discussed. Although the similarities in life styles of delinquent groups are noted, emphasis is placed in this chapter mainly on the distinctions among types of groups in regard to such factors as motivation for gang formation, factors of individual and group identification, membership structure, initiation rituals, relationships to peers, and neighborhood experiences.

The focus remains on the social forces which condition both the *genesis* and the *development* of delinquent subcultures in each of the neighborhoods. In this section the analysis is based principally on the observational data gathered by the researcher.

GENESIS AND DEVELOPMENT

On the whole, the delinquent groups encountered in the study were not fly-by-night associations. Relationships among group members were often sustained over a considerable period of time, sometimes for many years. The groups, particularly in the neighborhoods of the racket and conflict subcultures, had traditions and histories predating their present memberships. The circumstances surrounding the genesis of groups provided clues to the essential functions and characteristics of different styles of gang life.

The reason for the formation of the delinquent group in Racketville was stated by group members as defense against other groups which contained mainly Puerto Rican and some Negro youths:

> George said that he was with the "crew" [1] from the beginning — eleven years ago. The group got started as a social or stickball club during World War II. After the war it turned into a fighting club. He said that the Puerto Ricans bothered them, and they had to defend themselves. They had to keep the Puerto Ricans out. George said the Vultures fought against the Negroes, the Irish, and sometimes the Italians as well. However, except against the Puerto Ricans, the fellows fought fair, with their fists.

Although the delinquent groups in Racketville engaged in occasional gang fighting with groups from other neighborhoods, conflict with groups from the same area occurred rarely:

> Sammy said that the important "crews" now in the Italian part of the neighborhood were all pretty much one big club, and their territory stretched from ———— Street to ———— Street.

The conflict with gangs in the adjacent area seemed in large part to arise from, and to be tacitly supported by, the beliefs and attitudes of the dominant local adult population with regard to unaccepted ethnic groups. The indigenous neighborhood population believed and, indeed, protested that they were compelled to leave the area and make way for the undesirable newcomers — Puerto Ricans and Negros:

> The director of teen-age activities at the settlement house spoke of the neighborhood as he knew it twenty-five or thirty years ago. It was solidly Italian then. There were no public housing projects. But, since World War II, the Italian community had been greatly "threatened" . . . the people were being "pushed out" by the public housing projects, and the adults were "sore as hell." He felt that much of the gang fighting was a reflection of the insecurity of the adults, who felt very hostile toward the Puerto Ricans and Ne-

---

[1] The delinquents in Racketville generally referred to their group as a "crew." The delinquents in Slumtown referred to their group as a "bopping," "diddy bopping," or "jitter-bugging" club. The delinquents in Haulburg tended to use a more diffuse term such as "crowd" or "guys from ———— Street."

groes because they were moving in and were perceived as "pushing them out." He considered the gangs, at least those in the Italian neighborhood, as mainly protective associations. The gang members felt they needed to be protected from attacks by Puerto Ricans and Negroes.

In some respects the genesis of the delinquent group, i.e., the fighting gang, in the conflict subculture appeared on the surface to be similar:

Indio said it (the club) started in 1947. The Regals were a stick-ball team. Since they were a Puerto Rican group, they resented other groups, mainly Negro, who were coming over from ————, the western part of the neighborhood, to date their girls and generally get mixed up in various things. The fellows organized to protect their rights to the girls.

Another version of the beginnings of the same Puerto Rican "bopping" club was the following:

Raul said the group started way back around World War II. Originally the fellows were a stickball club and "got into being" a fighting club because they were attacked by the Italians. Then, around 1949, Raul recalled, there was one big Puerto Rican club in the neighborhood which suddenly broke up. One faction became the Regals; another, the Noble Lords. The two groups began to fight each other and have fought, mainly with other Puerto Rican groups, ever since to keep or build up their reputations.

In both the Italian and Puerto Rican neighborhoods the formation of delinquent groups, at least in their fighting character, was directed toward the solution of problems of status and of group or neighborhood integrity. In the Italian sector, however, the struggle was primarily defensive, to assure the continued status of the group and the integrity of the present population. In the Puerto Rican sector the acts of aggression were committed by youths to acquire status and then to develop a sense of group security and integrity. The defensive character of the Puerto Rican group appeared to be less important than its offensive orientation.

The genesis and development of the delinquent group in Haulburg differed from that in either Racketville or Slumtown.

In this area, the delinquent group, past or present, had little or no tradition of defensive or offensive gang fighting. The street-club worker in the area recalled:

"The group originated seven years ago, in 1953, when five youngsters, aged thirteen and fourteen, banded together in a club called the Town Marauders. The boys lived in the same block or in adjoining blocks. They had known each other from early childhood. They attended the same schools, Catholic or public. Over half the families were acquainted with one another.

"The group was supposed to have organized for fighting purposes, Actually, the youngsters had previously played together for a long time in the streets. Although the group was organized expressly for fighting, no systematic gang fighting took place. Acts of truancy, running away from home, petty theft, and vandalism predominated in the early years of the group's existence. Membership in the group was constantly changing; yet a core of old members appeared to remain. About three years after its origin, it engaged in its first and last minor skirmish with a gang from another neighborhood.

"In recent years, the group has developed a pattern of participation in criminal activities. Three years ago the boys set out at least once a week in small bands of four to six to 'score' — steal cars or hubcaps; burglarize basements, apartments, and stores; mug adults; and stage occasional holdups."

The commitment to organized gang fighting was strongest for members of the delinquent group from Slumtown and weakest for members of the delinquent group from Haulburg. Still, in each area, the recollected original motivation for formal "ganging" was some kind of intergroup hostility. The delinquent-group structure seemed to crystallize at some early point around a threat of an external enemy, real or imagined. The nature of the original threat and the form of the intergroup conflict which developed varied. Only in Slumtown did gang fighting occur systematically, and primarily it was to achieve success status.

IDENTIFYING THE GANG MEMBER

Who was regarded as a gang member and how the fact of gang membership or non-membership was established were not simple matters to determine in any of the three areas. One youngster might, for a relatively short time, "hang around" a group and be recognized almost immediately as a member of that group. Another individual would be present a great deal of the time with the group and be regarded clearly as a non-member or a member of another group.

In Racketville the following situation illustrated a not atypical instance of confusion about gang membership:

Sam said that there were several other boys who were not members of their group, that is, the Vulture Juniors. These other fellows were supposed to be in a club called the Black Claws; however, Harry and Lester, themselves Vulture Seniors, seemed uncertain about this. They were unsure whether the fellows were in the Vulture Juniors or in the Black Claws. At one point Sam said that maybe actually two Vulture Junior groups were forming. However, the matter of clear-cut membership did not seem to trouble the boys.

A similar state of affairs with regard to membership identification seemed to prevail in Slumtown:

Big Willie considered that Frenchie was not in the group; yet Frenchie said that he was a full member. Later that day, after Big Willie and the others had been arrested, Frenchie said that Cowboy, Cheyenne, and Papo were the ones who were left in the group now, besides himself. He also said that Husky Louie was not a member, although he was expected to participate in a "rumble" (gang fight) if it occurred. Razor, who had just returned from "upstate" and who had formerly been the president of the group, was no longer considered, nor did he perceive himself to be, a member, although he was continually "hanging around."

In Haulburg, the structure of the delinquent group was less stable, and the need to identify group members appeared to be even less important than in the other areas. Who was or who was not a member of the group rarely appeared to be a subject for discussion. The fact of a youngster's repeated presence on the street corner in some kind of compatible interaction with the rest of the youths was sufficient reason to identify him as a group member. The street-club worker observed:

"If a boy participated in a specific activity or in a series of activities, he was considered a group member in good standing. 'He hangs around with us' or 'he doesn't hang around with us' was the way the group identified the fellow as one of them or as not one of them. Newcomers were usually tolerated and accepted into the group. In only one instance was a boy beaten and told in no uncertain terms to stay away."

Identification as a member of a gang in each of the three areas was not a stable, permanent, once-and-for-all social fact. It seemed to be a product of continually shifting attitudes and perceptions in particular social situations. Gang membership seemed to depend as much on whether the individual himself wanted to be, and perceived himself to be, a member, as on anything else.

PERSONAL AND GANG NAMES

Individual nicknames and gang names seemed to suggest the standards and values which significantly patterned the life style of the groups and their members. Youngsters were given or took names which identified them in terms of the characteristics which were deemed important in their particular subculture. The individual gang member appeared to strive for the fulfilment of the prophecy inherent in his personal pseudonym. The gang seemed to find in the club or "crew" name a special significance, and group activity appeared to be directed to the achievement of the status symbolized in the group name.

In Racketville, however, the nickname of a member of a delinquent group tended often to be derived from a certain physical or personality characteristic of the individual, e.g., "Louie the Lip," for the boy with a thick underlip who was also extremely vituperative; "Georgie Flat-Top," for a boy who always wore a crew cut and had a rather flat head; "Sally Screw," for a boy who had many personal problems and whose behavior was deviant within the group; etc.

In Slumtown, sobriquets such as those listed above abounded: "Fat Rolls," "Husky Louie," "Big Head," "Crazy Charlie," and so forth. In addition, it was common for members of the gang to have names which signified extraordinary prowess, bravery, importance, or notoriety, such as "Zoro," "Cheyenne," "Superman," "Batman," "Al Capone," "Dillinger," "Hitler," "Brave Eagle," "Count Shadow," "Sampson," "King Kong," and "Hawkeye." Such names appeared to provide a cloak of special status and prestige to their bearers. The gang member's name was an important symbol of the values and standards characteristic of the conflict subculture:

Billy the Kid said that the information I had gotten from Lefty concerning him was not right and the reason he got his name was because a few years ago he had gotten a .44 old western-style revolver from relatives in Texas near the Mexican border. He said he used to keep it in his jacket and could pull it out very fast. He had two hundred bullets for it. Also, he used to wear a black vest and one of those small-brim cowboy hats.

The street-club worker said that "Billy's" real name was Jose Morales and that he used to run down the block of the Noble Lords firing his gun into the air, shouting "Billy the Kid is here." The boys in both groups used to get a kick out of this.[2]

In the theft subculture, nicknames descriptive of physical appearance or of personality or reflective of notorious status were not commonly found. It was customary to hear delinquents refer to each other by their given first names. Occasionally a name such as Francis was shortened to Frank, or Charles became Chuck. The red-haired boy was ubiquitously called "Red." Not unusual was reference to a specific youngster by both his given and family name, particularly when there was some uncertainty as to which Johnny or Joey was being discussed. This was in stark contrast to the kinds of names that prevailed in the areas of the racket and conflict subcultures.

In the neighborhood with the racket subculture, the family name of the youngster, although well known to his intimate associates, was never or rarely used in the course of ordinary conversation — certainly not when untrustworthy or unknown adults were around. It was difficult for youth workers and staff members of leisure-time agencies to obtain accurate information about the names and addresses of delinquents. In the conflict subculture, family names were not employed in group conversation; however, the reasons were different. There often seemed to be genuine ignorance among group members about such identifying information. Besides, the given or family name

---

[2] Billy was involved, with two other members of the Regals, in a fatal shooting of a member of the Noble Lords just before the researcher terminated contact with the group.

of a delinquent from a conflict gang was not significant. It was the youth's assumed name which gave him his special subcultural identity.

As with individual names, gang names, too, appeared to have characteristic subcultural significance. These differences were not absolute but seemed to represent central tendencies, particularly in the racket and conflict subcultures. In Racketville, delinquent groups appeared more often to take names which indicated ferocity and toughness, such as "Talons," "Red Hawks," "Tigers," "Eagles," "Stompers," and the like. In Slumtown, the gang names more often mirrored high prestige or lofty status, such as "Bishops," "Chaplains," "Crowns," "Lords," "Knights," and "Sultans," and so forth. In Haulburg, gang names were uncommon, and delinquent groups were more likely to be identified by the street or location of the original, most recent, or most frequent hangout.

It was possible to speculate that the use of personal nicknames and gang names or, indeed, their absence served to develop and support characteristic delinquent subcultural patterns. In the racket subculture, toughness was a desirable characteristic for the delinquent seeking to qualify or prepare himself for a career in the organized rackets. The youngster had to make a name for himself or for his group, not the kind that might draw too much undesired attention, but one that would assure him a reputation of having the necessary attributes for moving into a criminal organization. The racket organization wanted tough but "smooth" young men as recruits.

In the conflict subculture, it was obvious that a name would signify notoriety and would help in the achievement of the "rep" or success status so strongly desired by those who subscribed to the standards of this subculture. The relative absence of special names for delinquents in groups committed to a theft orientation perhaps reflected the key elements of stealth, inconspicuousness, casualness which were useful for success by the standards of this delinquent subculture.

MEMBERSHIP IN ONE GANG OR MANY

Delinquents, like other persons, join groups to satisfy personal and social needs and interests, expressed and unexpressed.

Membership in a delinquent group had varying meanings or values to each individual. Yet there appeared to be a characteristic subcultural theme underlying the motivation for joining a delinquent group in each of the different neighborhoods. The basis for group membership was not only significant to the individual but also functional to the maintenance of each subculture and its distinctive patterns of gang life.

The youths in the delinquent group in Racketville were likely to have joined for purposes of friendship or social group interaction. They were interested personally in each other and tended to develop stable, loyal, long-term affiliations which endured even after formal ties with the adolescent gang were broken:

> Little Augie said that he had been the first of the present generation of Warrior Seniors to join the "crew." He was ten years old when he first joined, as a Tot. This had been eight years ago. Big Frankie said that he had been in the "crew" four or five years. It had been a social club at first. The fellows had jackets and played a lot of ball. It was only when the "spicks" came around that they began to fight. Actually, they were even now mainly a social club and did little fighting. They were together because they were friends.

Interaction patterns of gang members were well integrated not only within an individual group but among delinquent groups as well. There was a strong sense of collective identity among the delinquent groups:

> "The Warriors I was with since I was about thirteen. You see how, if you tell me how long you were in the Warriors, like, say — I'm going on twenty-one — I say eight years. Because even when I was on the Vultures, I always thought of myself as a Warrior, you know, because we always were . . . together . . . always friends."

In Slumtown, delinquents who joined gangs seemed not to be interested principally in developing stable friendships or long-term personal relationships. Gang membership tended to be kaleidoscopic and successive. The basis for joining a group was to share in the "rep" or prestige which the group offered. A program director of a settlement house suggested that various low-status delinquent groups might serve as loosely knit component parts of a farm system functioning to prepare youngsters for service in a major-league high-status fighting club. This was at least partially brought out by a rundown of the previous club affiliations of gang-fighting members:

The researcher and some of the youths got onto the topic of what the previous gang memberships of the fellows were. Mikie said he used to be with the Young Sultans. In fact, he used to be their president, but he gave them up because he thought they were a bunch of "faggots." [3] He used to live in Brooklyn and had been a member of the Imperial Cardinals. He had also been a member of the Bishop Kings. Dillinger said he had been a member of the Barons, the Python Princes, the Bishop Kings, and the Renegades. Little Indio said he used to be a member of the Arrows, the Young Sultans, and the Python Princes. Big Willie said he had been a member of the Python Princes, the Arrows, the Dukes, the Sports Kings, and the Royal Emperors.

The delinquent groups in Slumtown functioned at various age and aggression levels for the attainment of differential degrees of status and "rep." The conflict subculture apparently developed its own unique pattern of gang succession.

In Haulburg, delinquents appeared to join groups for at least two reasons: limited, friendly social interaction and short-run criminal gain. The group itself tended to be a collection of individuals, changing almost from week to week. Delinquents in the neighborhood seemed to know each other and developed accommodating but shifting patterns of relationships as they moved from street corner to street corner. Because of the constant circulation of delinquents, the groups appeared to merge and to constitute a large neighborhood collectivity. Loyalties to particular groups were not strong, although long-term friendships among two and occasionally three individuals did tend to develop:

Jimmy said that the guys in the neighborhood were mainly out for themselves. Usually they were looking for some one to go on a date with or to get drunk with. Sometimes two or three guys "pulled a score" together. But the next night a guy might be a half-mile away with another bunch of fellows just "messing around." Everyone knew everyone else, and they were all pretty friendly.

[3] Weak or ineffective males.

Delinquents appeared to know many other delinquents within each area. The scope and intensity of interaction, however, did vary from area to area. In the neighborhood of the racket subculture, interaction by delinquents was mainly with a single stable group of peers. The delinquent knew members of other delinquent groups, but less well. In the conflict subculture, interaction of an individual with a specific peer group tended to be confined to a period of several months. A shift of membership might then occur. The individual delinquent either joined another group, or the membership structure of the group in which he was located changed as others left and new members came in. The most fluid, least intensive, and most extensive patterning of relationships on a group basis occurred in the theft subculture.

GANG SERVICE: THE DRAFTEE AND THE VOLUNTEER

To what extent was membership in a delinquent group voluntary or coercive? Did the gang member join because he was forced or because he wanted to? Delinquents deliberately chose membership in gangs to achieve, in one form or other, success-goals. In each area delinquents were not in the final analysis prevented by others from retaining or reassuming the status of a non-delinquent. Individuals joined gangs to achieve friendship, the status of the tough guy, and maintenance of neighborhood integrity (in Racketville), reputation and prestige (in Slumtown), and short-run friendship and criminal gain (in Haulburg).

In Racketville, the researcher obtained the following response when he asked a former delinquent whether boys were ever forced to join a group:

Big Frankie said the Vultures at one point were about to beat up some of the Warriors to force them to join, but it wasn't as simple as that, since not all the Warriors who wanted to could join. They had to be voted in and then get initiated. Although six of the Warriors got in, nine of them didn't. Actually, the six who got in really wanted to. Big Frankie concluded that so far as he knew, no one had ever been forced to stay in the gang who did not want to.

In Slumtown there was also little evidence that youngsters

were forced to join and to remain in gangs. Youngsters became a part of the group of their own free will.

The researcher asked Rollo (seventeen years old), who had joined the Regals a few days earlier, why he became a member. He said he lived in the neighborhood and just decided he wanted to join. Asked what made him join, he said nothing special; he knew the guys, but they weren't his friends. He just went over and introduced himself. He said that about five months before he was knifed by somebody who he thought was a Noble Lord but he wasn't sure. He decided a few days ago that he wanted to be in the Regals.

A youngster from Slumtown insisted he was compelled to join for purposes of protection. However, direct compulsion was not implied. The need for status and not for self-defense was probably the crucial element:

"The first club I joined because of the neighborhood where I lived. In that part of the block they was all Italian guys, and we were getting slapped, you know, around. . . . I felt, I guess, that if being with a few other guys they would, you know, *respect* a little more, that's why I did."

The data on delinquent groups from the conflict subculture indicated that although on occasion active recruitment of new members occurred, new applicants frequently were discouraged from joining. A street-club worker reported:

"If anything, the Noble Lords are keeping new members out. The other week a couple of key fellows in the Lords told some new youths they couldn't join unless they would be available every night. One or two nights a week on the block is not considered enough to 'really get in with the fellows' and to do what they are really supposed to do."

In general, the evidence in both Racketville and Slumtown indicated that the process of joining the gang group was much more often voluntary than coercive. Self-protection, although it was present at times, did not seem to be a primary factor in joining or remaining in a gang.

In Haulburg the lack of group cohesion and the easy permeability of almost all delinquent associations made membership in a gang, with its many exits and entrances, a relatively simple affair. It appeared easy to either join or stay out of a group.

INITIATION RITUALS

On occasion, special ceremonies were used for the formal induction of a member into the group. Initiation rites were not systematically administered by senior members or regularly undergone by new members; they were honored more often in the breach than in practice. Nevertheless, the rites, or at least recollections of them by youngsters, became a significant part of the gangs' traditions, particularly in Racketville and Slumtown.

The following ceremony was observed in Racketville by the researcher. Its purpose was to instruct the new recruits in the importance of taking punishment without "breaking" or "ratting" to the police. The ceremony occurred in the afternoon, before the evening on which the Vulture Tots were to be graduated to the status of Vulture Juniors:

I saw a large number of fellows in the park. Louie, a Senior, was administering a certain rite referred to as "pink belly." He selected one of the Tots. The fellow lifted his shirt from his trousers, exposing his belly. Two other Seniors, Jackie and Ally, held the fellow on either side. Louis administered the slaps — at first slow and easy, then faster and harder. The skin turned light red, then dark red, then purple. The fellow writhed in pain. Louie kept urging the boy, "Don't cry, control yourself." Louis stopped several times to give the boy a breather and encouraged him to maintain control.

Later that evening a newly initiated, red-faced, out-of-breath member of the Vulture Juniors reported on the initiation he and the others had just received:

The young guys were beaten up. They were beaten with garrison belts, kicked in the body, and punched in the face. Each member of the Tots was given a severe beating by the members of the Seniors, and now they were formally Juniors.

Big Freddie, a young adult and now somewhat removed from the Senior group, was a little surprised to learn that initiation ceremonies were still held:

He remembered that he had gone through the initiation. The guys were getting lashed with belts on their "fannies" by the older guys, and he happened to be the last one in line. Everybody who had already been lashed joined the line of lashers, and they all gave it to him. He got seventy-five lashes, and it didn't hurt so much until the belt hit him in the groin. Then the pain was extreme. Big Freddie said that one of the other fellows landed in the hospital. The researcher asked Freddie what was the purpose of the beating. He said it was to see if the guys could "take it." Actually, the guys who did the whipping never hit that hard. They wanted to train the younger fellows not to "break" when the police worked them over. The researcher told Big Freddie this sounded a little far-fetched. Big Freddie insisted that this was exactly the purpose in the beating — to train the guys to keep their mouths shut and to be able to take it. This also was the purpose of the "pink-belly" business.

The function of the initiation ritual in Slumtown was somewhat different. It was to test the new member's courage and bravery and his potential usefulness as a gang member:

Big Willie said that to be admitted to the club a fellow would have to come from the area and ask to be in the club. Then they would give him a test. He would have to fight one of the fellows to see how he could take care of himself. If he passed that test, then he would "go down" with the club members to a gang fight, or "bopping session," and the boys would see how good he was under fire. However, it wasn't until the third stage, when he was able to demonstrate that he could "shank" (knife) or shoot somebody, or alternately if he himself was "shanked" or shot, that he was made a full fledged Regal.

Initiation or admission ceremonies were not detected in Haulburg. Perhaps one variety of initiation which prevailed in this area and, to some extent, in Racketville was tattooing. The scarification of the body appeared not to be related to entry into a delinquent gang but constituted rather a means of self-induction into lower-class adolescent society. It was a way of establishing identification with a popular image of adult virility and toughness. Youngsters, individually and in small groups, visited well-known tattoo artists in other parts of the city to obtain the desired body marks. In general, tattooing appeared to be less prevalent among youngsters in Slumtown, on whose darker skin such markings were less likely to show.

VARIETY OF LIFE EXPERIENCE

Although the gang boy was involved in delinquent behavior, he also participated in "social" or "quasi-social" activities. Since the gang boy was frequently a truant or, if over sixteen years of age, unemployed (especially in the conflict subculture), he spent a great deal of time on street corners or in roaming the neighborhood.

Delinquents from the racket and theft subcultures were less street-oriented than those from the conflict subculture. There seemed to be more places to go and more things to do away from the hangouts. The boys traveled to New Jersey, Staten Island, upstate New York, or even to Florida. They swam in the river, went bowling, went downtown to the movies or to where the "beatniks" hung out, for "kicks." Conversation was more sophisticated — about cars, local and national news, as well as girls, parties, jobs, trips, and delinquent acts and their consequences.

Delinquents in Slumtown were constantly on the street. In the winter time, when the weather was extremely inclement, they would hustle movie money:

Papo said that they would go to the Apex Theater every day. The researcher said that then they would be seeing the same movie over again. Papo said that didn't matter, as long as they were off the streets for at least a little while.

From time to time, group members from Slumtown left the neighborhood to visit relatives, to go across town to a dance, or to visit a nearby beach to swim. But such trips were infrequent. For the most part these youths were limited in their experience to what they could find in a twenty- or thirty-block-square area. Their usual conversations were confined to what had happened at the local party or "jump" (dance) the previous Friday night, the most recent gang incident, plans for the next rumble, or speculation as to what sentence so-and-so would get when he came before the judge.

The life space and circumstances of delinquents from Racketville and Haulburg were varied; those of delinquents from Slumtown were limited and their quality poorer.

DRINKING

The types and quantity of alcohol consumed and the frequency of the consumption varied in the three areas. The element of preference conditioned by cultural and social pressures, rather than cost per se, was probably the essential ingredient accounting for these differences. The use of alcohol outside the home was almost universal among the delinquents in each of the three areas. All of those interviewed in Slumtown and Haulburg and all but one in Racketville reported consumption of alcohol. Seventy to 80 per cent of the delinquents from each of the areas drank wine and whiskey; the heaviest wine and whiskey drinkers were those in Racketville and Haulburg. As for beer, 90 per cent of the delinquents from Racketville and Haulburg but only 60 per cent of those from Slumtown admitted drinking it. By far the heaviest beer drinkers were the delinquents of the theft subculture, with a median consumption of six quarts per member at each drinking session, two or three times per week. In general, delinquents in Haulburg drank more liquor more frequently than did delinquents from any of the other areas. Those from the neighborhood of the conflict subculture consumed alcohol in the smallest quantities and drank it least often.

The heaviest and most consistent drinking occurred during the weekends, especially on Friday and Saturday nights. Delinquent activities and drinking, that is, the occurrence of delinquent acts immediately after drinking sessions, seemed to be strongly connected. In Slumtown, cheap wine and whiskey served as stimulants to acts of "bravery" and fortifiers of courage prior to gang fights. The association of drinking with delinquent acts appeared to be most prevalent in Haulburg. The street-club worker expressed alarm over the situation:

"Night after night the group could be found in cellars, on front stoops, on the roofs, and in apartments drinking quarts of beer, wine and whiskey, often mixing them. Under the influence of alcohol, the boys quickly turned to loud and boisterous behavior, became quarrelsome, insulted people on the streets, fought amongst themselves, became destructive in their own homes, went in search of prostitutes and homosexuals, and engaged in serious criminal activity."

It was not clear whether the ethnic backgrounds of the lower-class population of Haulburg accounted largely for the wide-spread use of alcohol among adults, teen-agers, and, especially, delinquents. It was true that the Irish, Germans, and Czechs made up a substantial segment of the population and that these ethnic groups had a reputation for heavy drinking.

A settlement-house worker from the neighborhood observed that when a group of young-adult Puerto Ricans first moved to the area, its members would be found in front of their houses drinking Pepsi-Cola, but in the past year the same group had, to a man, switched to beer-drinking.

In general, non-delinquents, delinquents, and drug addicts of Haulburg consumed more alcohol more frequently than did the respective groups in the other two areas. Non-delinquents tended to drink less than the delinquents but more than the narcotic addicts, except in Slumtown, where non-delinquents consumed less alcohol less frequently than did the drug addicts. It was apparent on the basis of the interview and observational data that some particular constellation of cultural factors and neighborhood pressures was important in the determination of patterns of drinking for the subjects investigated. What it was specifically remained unclear.

RELATIONSHIP TO PEERS

Relationship to other delinquent groups. — The character of intergroup relationships was different in each of the three areas. Such relationships were a function of variations on a theme of acceptance or rejection. Dominant neighborhood patterns of age-role and conventional-criminal integration appeared to influence the nature of contacts among groups.

A network of close and usually friendly relations existed among the delinquent, the non-delinquent, and, to some extent, the addict groups in Racketville. As indicated earlier, there was little friction among delinquent groups in this area. As one delinquent put it:

"The relationship [between the Warriors and the Vultures] goes back five, six, seven years, when they [the fellows] were close friends. They were brother clubs. There are still feelings of being brother clubs. They [the Warriors and Vultures] were kind of interchangeable and very, very friendly with each other, especially as they got older."

A certain amount of "ranking," or verbal aggression, took place between members of the various groups, but it rarely resulted in intergroup hostilities or the disruption of at least tolerable relationships on a group basis. Indeed, much of the verbal hostility functioned to integrate groups and reinforce neighborhood norms. For instance:

There was some mutual teasing between Tommy [Vultures] and Russ [Warriors]. Russ seemed to be getting the worst of it. Tommy said that Russ didn't do anything to maintain the reputation of the Italians and that if it weren't the Vultures, the "spicks" and the Negroes would swoop down on the whole neighborhood. Things would be even worse than they were now.

The Vultures, in particular, took it upon themselves to maintain certain "high" standards of behavior and to enforce such standards among other groups in the area, particularly the narcotics-using group, which was acknowledged as deviant. A reprimand in the form of a mild beating was not challenged by the addicts as being undeserved or as a cause for anger and retaliation.

The Warrior seniors discussed the fact that the Vultures beat up Peewee because he was a "junkie." The boys sympathized with Peewee because it was hard to stop once you had been using drugs. Little Augie recalled, with an expression of pain, the time when he had been beaten up. In the course of the discussion, no anger or resentment was expressed against those who had given him the beatings.

When members of the narcotics-addict group became less involved in narcotics-use and again participated actively in brawling and gang fighting, they were accepted by neighborhood peers and adults, and their status was raised because they now met the standards of the subculture. A street-club worker put it this way:

"During September, the group continued to grow in numbers and get further and further away from narcotics-use. There was a return to gang fighting. Also there was less drinking. A lot of social contacts with girls on the block began again. The reputation of the group members went up among their peers and, seemingly, among the adult population as well."

Actually, the membership of the two groups, the Warriors and the Vultures, overlapped. Several narcotic addicts who were Warriors were at the same time closely related to, and had high status in, the Vulture group.

The conflict subculture, whose basic theme was gang fighting, was subject to a group-disintegrative process because of it, especially in its extreme form. A constant state of tension and hostility existed, with only brief intermittent periods of relative quiet or truce. Fighting was chronic between the two major gangs, the Regals and the Noble Lords, but warfare was also carried on against, and between, other groups. Complex and shifting constellations of fighting clubs were in intermittent conflict with each other. The search for gang "rep" and prestige was unceasing.

The quest for status was especially strong among those younger members who had not yet found a sufficient measure of success by the criteria of the conflict subculture. Shifts and changes of gang membership occurred especially among peripheral and rank-and-file members of the various fighting groups. Seldom did leadership members switch gang affiliation. Nevertheless, a gang of twelve members of one day might become a gang of fifty a day later and a few days after that melt away to four or five. It was not at all uncommon for a member of the Regals to have been a member of the Noble Lords and vice versa.

The quest for prestige made for a peculiar system of multi-group membership and role functioning. An intricate pattern of dual, triple, and quadruple membership roles existed. For instance:

Papo said that he was both a member of the Regals and the

Bishop Kings. Ralphie was president of the Satan Princes but also a member in good standing of the Regals, and he was peripherally affiliated with the Dandies, a social club.

Often a gang would seem to disappear, and another with a new name would be born a week later with essentially the same membership. The delinquent group would prefer, at certain times, to operate under a social-club name. For instance, three segments of the Noble Lords were known at several community centers as the Social Kings, the Friendly Lovers, and the Sharp Cats. It seemed that this device was partly to conceal the identity of the fighting group, but its major purpose was to provide for its members one more set of group-prestige identities.

Whether after termination of adolescent fighting careers older adolescents and young adults became friendly with former members of opposing groups appeared to be a moot question:

Tony, a former president of the Regals, remarked that he still felt "funny" when he walked down to the Noble Lords' block. Albie, once the president of a major faction of the Noble Lords, but now twenty-eight years old and a prospering small-time bookie, insisted that he would have nothing to do with past or present Regals. He spoke about them only in derogatory terms. Thus, it seemed that the attitudes of a gang fighter could not be easily unlearned. On the other hand, Frankie, a former Noble Lord, who was now a drug addict, believed that the Regals, especially those who were addicts, were his friends and that bygones were bygones.

In general, the pattern of gang hostilities ceased at the close of the adolescent period, but a residuum of ill feeling which varied in intensity remained among former delinquents.

The structure of intergroup and peer relationships in Haulburg promoted the maintenance of major subcultural commitments. Cohesive gangs, of large or small size, were less typical than in the other areas. Delinquent groups tended to be more loosely knit. There was less intergroup hostility, less conflict with immediate and larger community norms and values. There was a need for mobility and the development of limited friendships and short-run accommodation in the carrying out of illicit income-producing ventures. Although gang fighting was infrequent, brawls developed between cliques of different groups, but these were essentially non-gang-related affairs. They were settled, in the main, through fist fighting. Long-term tensions or resentments did not appear to develop.

A street-club worker from Haulburg had the following to say about group relationships within the neighborhood:

"A few name groups with some commitment to gang fighting existed in the area. However, their relations with each other are not only tolerably good but often very friendly. The pseudo-fighting character of the groups comes to the fore during the infrequent, if not rare, instances of forays. More often, they are excursions with no real hostile intent into the other areas [the racket and conflict subcultures]. Since the uptown gangs are so vastly superior in organized fighting prowess, almost all planned attacks on the part of local groups remain in the talking and boasting stage."

Each area differed in the nature of its intergroup relationships. Basic subcultural orientations appeared to determine whether such relationships would be friendly or unfriendly, associative or disassociative. In the racket and theft subcultures relations among delinquent groups generally appeared to be more friendly and integrative than they were in the conflict subculture.

Relationship to non-delinquent groups and individuals.— The same pressures that determined the character of interaction among delinquents appeared also to fashion the relationships of delinquents to non-delinquent or conventional peer groups and individuals. In all three subcultures, there were many young people, members of social clubs or informal friendship arrangements, who participated in relatively little or no delinquent activity. Such groups or groupings were present on the street side by side with delinquent gangs. Some of the social clubs appeared to have equally complex organizational structures— Seniors, Juniors, Tims, and Tots—and as long a non-delinquent tradition as the deviant groups had a delinquent one. Some of the non-delinquent clubs had high status and others low status.

The social clubs in Racketville were well known and were usually accepted by the delinquent groups as part of the order

of things in the neighborhood. A member of the delinquent
Warrior group saw it this way:

Butchie said that there was a group called the Leopards which
was social. They had several divisions of various ages. They were
all over ———— Avenue, played a lot of stickball, softball, and even
got into trouble now and then. There was another group called the
Lashers. They had been a social club but were now disintegrating.
Half of them were social; and half, just "wise guys," but his club,
the Warriors, didn't have trouble with any of these groups.

Big Freddie compared the delinquent group of which he was
formerly a member with the social club in the area:

There were more tough kids in the Vultures than in the Leopards,
but some of the kids in the Leopards could stand on their own . . .
and nobody would bother them. The Leopards were mainly a club
interested in sports . . . and if you weren't interested in sports,
you were pretty much on the sidelines. Though the Vultures and
Warriors got into a lot of trouble, the Leopards hardly got into any.
However, some of the Leopards surprisingly got "busted" (arrested) when they became older for things like "peddling junk"
(selling narcotics) or pulling a robbery, but these had really been
"fringers" and couldn't be considered fully as members of the
Leopards.

In Slumtown, the pattern of the relationship between gangs
and non-delinquent street groupings differed. More of the social groups appeared to have relatively low status in the eyes of
the delinquent gangs and were subjected by them to various
forms of depredation. A Youth Board supervisor commented
that:

The Social Gents were kids who never bothered with anybody —
they were just a little group that played basketball. Frequently
members of the "bopping" clubs shook them down and threatened
to beat them up, but the Social Gents were the kind of group that
didn't want to do anything about it.

On the other hand, a few social groups and their memberships were accorded relatively high status and deferred to, at
least to some extent, by delinquents. A temporary situation of
accommodation was somehow established:

While the researcher was talking with some of the delinquents, five members of the Spanish Counts, a social club, came over. Papo called them "coolies." Asked what he meant, Papo said these fellows were social and didn't fool around much but they were "smooth." This meant they were "all-right guys."

Earlier, I noticed that Brave Eagle had asked one of the members of the Spanish Counts to lend him some money; the fellow said he wouldn't. However, he told Brave Eagle that he and some of the other Regals were invited to a house party that night but that they would have to pay like everybody else.

Nevertheless, the possibility that a member of a social club in Slumtown might be assaulted at any given time could not be discounted. Some social clubs were converted to defensive conflict groups, but most seemed able to avoid being placed in the position of setting off or retaliating when faced with a conflict-producing situation. Certain pacific attitudes and skills of diplomacy were developed to escape or to prevent conflicts:

Johnny, president of a social club, said it was hard to avoid a fight. For instance, several years ago his club played the Noble Lords a basketball game and won. The Noble Lords wanted to beat them up. Johnny said he "used his mouth" and got his club out of the situation. He told the Noble Lords that the game wasn't important and it didn't pay to fight. He told them "this and that," and they left them alone . . .

In Haulburg, relations between the delinquent and non-delinquent or between social groups were generally peaceful, if somewhat distant. There was evidence of some friendly interaction between the "good" and the "bad" lower-class kids and even between lower-class delinquent youths and youngsters from the economically better-off segment of the population. Such limited interaction occurred in the schools and, less frequently, on the playgrounds and in community centers. On the streets, the delinquents had a rather vague awareness of the presence of non-delinquents. The existence of social groups nearby was taken for granted and did not seem to matter much in the delinquent scheme of things:

As some delinquents and the researcher were sitting in a luncheonette drinking coffee and soda, he inquired who the group of youngsters sitting at a nearby table were. Teddy and Karl did not know them, but one of the girls said that they were from the neighborhood and only recently had begun to hang around together in such a large crowd. Lucy, Karl's girl friend, said that there were a lot of kids like them in the neighborhood who grew up there and you never seemed to notice them. Teddy and Karl said they did not know any of the fellows at the other table.

There were times when delinquents in this area expressed deep resentment about the superior way of life of the middle- and upper-middle-income residents of the area. Invidious comparisons resulted in the release of much hostile feeling. Systematic aggressive action was not taken, however, beyond an occasional mugging or shakedown of a non-delinquent middle-class youngster. Feelings of envy and hostility tended more often to be dissipated in wishful thinking:

They wished they had the money like the "ritzies" and could leave town in the summer or live in nice houses. They called their own homes "dumps." They wished they had air conditioners, terraces, and luxurious furnishings in their apartments. The boys said they actually had little contact with the kids from the rich houses. Sometimes they played ball with them in the playground or in the parks. Once in a while a rich girl might hang around for a short time, but nothing ever really developed.

Relationships with non-delinquents varied in each area. They were closer in Racketville, more antagonistic in Slumtown, and casual and distant in Haulburg. Groups of delinquents and non-delinquents existed side by side on the streets, each tending to maintain its distinctive integrity and value commitments. The task of maintaining such group integrity and commitments appeared to be most difficult in the area where the conflict subculture was dominant. Special accommodative mechanisms had to be devised by non-delinquents for this purpose. In the area where the racket subculture was strong, the non-delinquent group seemed to be less sharply differentiated from the delinquent group.

RELATIONS WITH THE GIRL FRIEND

The nature of boy-girl relations in each of the areas could be described or placed along a continuum of freedom and restraint. In Racketville, parents and adults exerted strong controls, and a more restrictive type of boy-girl relationship appeared to prevail. On the other hand, in Slumtown, where neighborhood controls seemed to be weakest, boy-girl relationships were much freer. In Haulburg, an intermediate character of boy-girl relationships evolved — less restrictive than that which prevailed in Racketville, but not quite so free as in Slumtown.

Delinquents in Racketville were under pressure to sustain the traditional double standard in their relations with girls. There were the "good" girls and the "bad" girls:

Big Freddie said that when he was in the gang, he would never go around with a girl who was close to the fellows in his own or in other gangs because she would probably be no good. These girls cursed and jumped into bed right away with any of the fellows. He said it was always good to go out with a girl who was not from the neighborhood — with some girl who had a good reputation. He said it was hard to get this kind of girl these days, and once you had a girl like that you had to protect her.

He was upset because he had gone to a wedding a few days ago where he had made a play for some girl, but someone said that he was engaged, and this interfered with his play for the girl. He thought it was okay to fool around with another girl even if he were engaged or married. His financée or wife would expect it and would somehow understand that it didn't mean too much.

On another occasion, Big Freddie remarked that if he ever caught his girl friend going around with another fellow, this would be the end of their planned marriage. That was for sure. If he broke up once, it would be permanent.

On still a third occasion, Big Freddie announced that he had a problem right now. When he fools around with a girl, he has to make sure she is a bad girl, because if she's a nice girl there's no point to going with her because he "can't do anything."

The tradition of the double standard was reflected in a seeming exception to the rule about "not fooling around with a good girl." The delinquent occasionally did get "mixed-up" with a "good" girl. Serious conflict and feelings of guilt for both boy and girl resulted at such times:

Steve, eighteen years old, told the worker that he had made Gracie pregnant and that although he was willing and even anxious to marry the girl, she rebuffed him and told him she would never see him again. He was extremely offended by the girl's attitude and sought to resolve his unhappiness by beating the girl up very badly, with the result that Gracie had a miscarriage and had to be hospitalized. . . . He feels he did a great wrong to the girl, yet he continues to be greatly bothered by the fact that Gracie turned down his offer of marriage.

Relations between the sexes in Slumtown appeared to be more spontaneous and less inhibited by traditional moral standards. Sexual experimentation and intimate liaisons began a little earlier in this than in the other areas. In general, such liaisons probably were not so much approved or disapproved by adults of the neighborhood as merely tolerated. Nevertheless, the kind of relationship which developed clearly was not prescribed according to dominant cultural standards:

The street-club worker noted that Kid had been fooling around with Cindy, and it was lucky, in a way, that he went to jail. Cindy was married to a fellow who was in jail for drugs, but he was coming out now. Cindy already had a child from this first fellow, who was her husband. At present she was pregnant with Kid's child. Kid was seventeen years old, and Cindy was eighteen.

The following incident was reported by a Youth Board street-club supervisor:

He had gone to Mt. Israel Hospital to see his wife, who had just given birth to a boy. He met Jackson Taylor in the corridor, carrying a big bunch of flowers, with a sheepish smile on his face. He found out later that Jackson had come to visit his girl friend, who had also just given birth to a boy. The couple were not yet married. Jackson was sixteen; and the girl, fifteen years old.

The girl friend in Slumtown, particularly the member of the Deb group, or the girls' group affiliated with the gang, played various roles, contributing highly to the maintenance of the gang-fighting system. She was the carrier of tales — the magnifier, distorter, and fabricator of derogatory remarks which served to instigate conflict among the various clubs. On occasion, an insult to a girl friend was cause for the boy friend to avenge not so much her, but his own, honor. This kind of behavior was formally patterned and assumed ritual significance:

Pro forma, Brave Eagle, a Regal who was tiring of the month-long peace, went over to Lucy, the girl friend of Flash Gordon, one of the leaders of the Noble Lords, at the community-center dance, and said loudly so that all those nearby could hear, "You're getting fat, honey. Flash must be f——g you too much." The Noble Lord–Regal conflict broke out again the following day, with extremely serious and tragic consequences this time. Before hostilities ceased, one boy from each group had been shot to death; two women bystanders were injured; and seven young people were in jail.

Another role which the girl friend played in relation to the fighting gang was that of weapon-bearer. The weapon was usually concealed under the girl's blouse or skirt:

China said that she was seventeen years old and had just gotten out of ——— Girls' Reformatory, where she had been sent for a year for possession of a weapon. Her status now, as far as she was concerned, was former Regal Deb. She had also once been a Noble Lord Deb. China said she was now planning to go back to school and maybe even go to college. However, she doubted that this really was possible.

Finally, an important role which could be played by the gang girl was that of spy:

Little Joey's girl friend ostensibly severed contact with him because she lived in the Noble Lord territory and didn't want the Noble Lords to beat her up. However, she was still Little Joey's girl friend and said she would be getting information to him when he needed it, somehow.

In Racketville and Haulburg there was little evidence of this type of role played by girl friends. Occasionally, brawls would be set off by disputes over girls, but the brawls were likely to involve only a small number of participants and to be non-gang-related, that is, not to involve various delinquent groups directly or indirectly in the defense of group honor.

In Haulburg, the relation of delinquents to their girls was characterized by greater freedom than existed in Racketville but seemingly by more restraint than was common in Slumtown. Although heterosexual play had certainly begun by age fifteen or sixteen, few serious liaisons were established at this age. Yet traditional moral standards seem to be subscribed to more in the breach than in practice. A vague distinction between the "good" girl and the "bad" girl existed. Often a series of short liaisons by older adolescents were established with several fairly "respectable" girls in succession. There were still other girls who hung around the group and were regarded as particularly free with their sexual favors. They were given low status. Infrequently a girl would be given explicitly the status of prostitute:

The group outside the community center gathered around Barbara and began making provocative remarks to her. To the street-club worker's amazement, Barbara wasn't the least bit embarrassed. As a matter of fact, the worker felt she was "getting a big thrill" out of it all. Charlie invited the worker to come along with them and even suggested that he "go all the way" with Barbara. After all, Charlie insisted, she was the best "piece" . . . he had ever had, and she wouldn't charge the worker. When Barbara heard the worker reject Charlie's suggestion, she was upset and left. Charlie said she was a "whore."

It was generally recognized but not always admitted by the group members that many of the "nice" girls participated in sex relations. Not a few of the teen-age marriages took place after such sexual experiences, usually when it was definitely known that a child had been conceived. Pregnancy was at times resorted to in order to trick a boy into marriage:

Chuckie said he had to be on guard all the times because there were an awful lot of "slobs" around who were just looking for fellows to "knock them up" so they could get married.

In summary, patterns of relationships with girl friends among members of delinquent groups varied in each of the areas. In Racketville, where adult controls and age-role integration appeared strongest, the commitment to traditional moral standards was still firmly established; in Slumtown, where adult controls and age-role integration were at their weakest, there was no firm or explicit commitment to traditional middle-class sex

standards, and boy-girl relationships appeared to be most pro-
miscuous; in Haulburg, where adult controls and age-level integration were only partially effective, the commitment to traditional sex standards was weakened, and boy-girl relationships
were conducted with fewer restraints than existed in Racketville.

LEAVING THE DELINQUENT GROUP

On the whole, it seemed simple to leave a delinquent group in
any of the three subcultures. Just as there was usually little compulsion to join or to become a member of the gang, there was
little pressure exerted directly on the youngster to prevent him
from terminating his involvement with the group.

Big Freddie, in Racketville, spoke thus of the time when he
made his decision to quit the Vultures:

He was then seventeen years old. He remembered he had been
going around beating up various fellows, and it began to bother
him, especially since he was going steady with a girl. He felt that
he might get into trouble. He talked to one of the important guys
in the club and said he was going to drop out because he was concerned about hurting his father — if he ever got "busted," it might
kill his father, who had a weak heart.

The guy he talked to suggested that he hang around and stay
with the guys for a little longer, not to fight, just to be with them.
Big Freddie protested because he knew that if he hung around
and anybody came down to mess up the fellows he would certainly
jump in. . . . He still stayed on a little longer, finally simply drifted
away, particularly at the time the group itself broke into two segments and began hanging out at two different places. However,
even now, four years later, he still considered himself a Vulture,
although he would probably never again go along in a fight with
them.

A similar process of relatively unhindered termination with
the delinquent group appeared to take place in Slumtown:

The researcher asked Billy the Kid how a fellow got out of the
Regals. Billy said that he just stopped going with the fellows, he
just didn't hang around. This often happened when he had had
enough "bopping" and when a fellow got married or got "busted."

Angelo said that when he was fifteen years old he was a Regal for two months. He quit because he didn't want to get into any trouble. He said he was not forced to get into the Regals, and nobody told him to get out. He joined of his own will and left of his own will.

In Haulburg, it was more difficult to detect just when a member dropped out of a gang. The ebb and flow of the street-corner association made the process of the delinquents' coming and leaving hardly noticeable, especially since status of group membership was never clearly delineated. It was common for the youngster to be in the process of transferring from one group to another, although not necessarily from one role to another. The termination of delinquent status was most clearly apparent at the point when a youngster was no longer a teen-ager or when his associates were no longer juvenile delinquents.

SUMMARY

A number of aspects in the life of delinquents in each of the types of gangs were observed as clearly different. Underlying neighborhood factors such as opportunities available, adult controls and standards, age-level integration, and varied types of subcultural pressures for success symbols appeared to create distinctive delinquent styles. The delinquent patterns in one area were, in essence, not suitable to meet the social and sub-cultural needs of delinquents in another. The status of delinquents in each neighborhood and the criteria for admission to the specific delinquent subculture were significantly different. It should be noted, however, that the full range of subcultural differences among delinquents in the three types of areas was not explored. No consideration was made of such factors as family structure, ethnicity, and physical and economic geography, which may contribute to distinctive styles of delinquent-group life. The limited scope of the study prevented such explorations.

CHAPTER IV

SUCCESS-GOALS
AND
OPPORTUNITIES

The major concern of this chapter is with the cultural pressures and the social conditions in the larger community and in the neighborhoods which may give rise to different types of delinquent subcultures. *Aspiration levels*, indicators of the success-goals of delinquents, are analyzed and compared for the three neighborhoods as well as contrasted with the aspiration levels of non-delinquents and drug addicts within each area. *Expectation levels*, indicators of access to available opportunities, are also compared. Data on the availability of conventional and criminal opportunities are reported here briefly but are more fully presented in the next chapter (chap. v). The interplay of personal motivations and environmental opportunity is highlighted in that discussion.

Agreeing with Merton,[1] the author has also postulated that contemporary American culture places great stress on the success-goal mainly symbolized by the possession of material wealth. Persons situated at various positions in society, particularly those in lower-class groups, are constrained to achieve success as defined according to the standards of the middle-class group. When cultural pressure to achieve high status is coextensive with the availability of adequate institutional means for achieving it, conformity and social adjustment result. When cultural pressure to achieve high occupational and, in particular, high income goals exists *without* concomitant adequate

[1] Robert K. Merton, *Social Theory and Social Structure* (rev. ed.; Glencoe, Ill.: Free Press, 1957), chapters iv and v, pp. 131–94.

means or opportunities to attain them, a breakdown (the *anomic* condition) occurs, and deviant modes of adaptation result — especially when there is an acute breakdown.

For purposes of the research, it was anticipated that deviants in lower-class areas would aspire to success-goals but would not have the conventional means available to achieve them. Nondeviants would have acceptable or realistic success-goals in relation to the available resources or means. While this condition of aspiration to success-goals was expected to be especially true for delinquents, it was anticipated to be less true for drug addicts. The drug-addict adaptation, although regarded as deviant, was at the same time considered to be an adjustive response, moving the addict closer to a conventional mode of orientation.

Several assumptions which should be carefully noted are made in the following exploratory propositions and in the discussion of the findings. Merton, Cloward and Ohlin, and the present author assume that a state of anomie *precedes*, in some fashion, the occurrence of the delinquent or drug-addict adaptation. Also, the theoretical point of view expressed here does not deny that certain psychological states in individuals may trigger the deviant response or that there are interactive causative factors responsible for deviant behavior. The focus of this research is, however, on the sociostructural and cultural conditions conducive to the development of the deviant response. That is to say, the explanation of deviant patterns offered is only partial and is not meant to explain fully, in every case, the genesis or nature of deviant patterns in individuals or groups.

SUCCESS–GOALS

It was anticipated that delinquents in each of the neighborhoods would internalize success-goals. Indeed, it was speculated that delinquents internalize higher success-goals than non-delinquents, who conform to lower-class norms and aspirations. Delinquents may be under more direct and greater pressure from ambitious and upwardly mobile parents or from parents who were particularly dissatisfied with their own status in life, and non-delinquents may have been less baldly and forcefully exposed to general cultural pressures for success. Parents, teachers, and other community socializing agents perhaps intervened more effectively and prepared non-delinquents for the range of aspirations realistically appropriate to the limited means available to them. Furthermore, it was thought that drug addicts, by virtue of the fact that they were older than delinquents and had been made more sharply aware through negative experiences with the police, courts, and correctional institutions of the difficulties of achieving success-goals on the basis of the means available to them, had begun to lower their aspirations.

Operationalized for purposes of the exploratory research, the empirical expectations were specified as follows:

1.1 delinquents would aspire to high income and occupational achievement levels.

1.2 non-delinquents would not aspire to as high income and occupational achievement levels as did delinquents.

1.3 narcotic addicts would have lower income and occupational aspirations than did delinquents and would tend to approach the aspiration levels of non-delinquents.

The formal interview data revealed that delinquents sought to achieve success status particularly when the indicator of income aspirations was used, but not necessarily when the indicator was desired occupation (see Tables 11 and 12). The

TABLE 11

ASPIRED MEDIAN WEEKLY WAGE WITHIN TEN YEARS*

Neighborhood and Component Group	Weekly Wages
Racketville	
Non-delinquent	$200
Delinquent	325
Drug addict	275
Slumtown	
Non-delinquent	138
Delinquent	225
Drug addict	135
Haulburg	
Non-delinquent	225
Delinquent	250
Drug addict	200

*The number in each sample or component group per neighborhood is ten.

TABLE 12
ASPIRED OCCUPATION WITHIN TEN YEARS*
(By Class)

Neighborhood and Component Group	Middle-Class Occupation	Lower-Class Occupation
Racketville		
Non-delinquent	10	0
Delinquent	9	1
Drug addict	9	1
Slumtown		
Non-delinquent	5	5
Delinquent	7	3
Drug addict	5	5
Haulburg		
Non-delinquent	9	1
Delinquent	7	3
Drug addict	8	2

*The number in each sample or component group per neighborhood is ten. The procedure for gathering and interpreting data was as follows:
1. The individual was asked in a formal interview what job or position he aspired to or ideally desired in ten years.
2. The occupations were placed in rank order: large business, profession, small business, white-collar worker, skilled worker, semiskilled worker, and unskilled worker.
3. The scheme was collapsed into a twofold classification with the middle-class category containing the occupations: large business, professional, small business, white-collar worker; the lower-class category included: skilled, semiskilled and unskilled worker.

findings showed that the level of aspiration in regard to income was higher for delinquents than for non-delinquents or for narcotic addicts in all three types of areas. In Racketville, delinquents aspired within ten years to a median weekly wage of $325; non-delinquents, to $200. In Slumtown, delinquents wanted a median weekly wage of $225; non-delinquents, $138. In Haulburg, delinquents wished for a median weekly wage of $250; non-delinquents, $225. The income aspirations of drug addicts were lower than those of delinquents and generally approached those of the non-delinquents.

Support for the notion of higher occupational aspirationals of delinquents was not indicated by the results of the interview data. In the racket and theft subcultures, non-delinquents had aspirations for somewhat higher occupational status than did delinquents. The kinds of middle-class occupations desired by delinquents were as follows: in Racketville, jobs in the rackets or "business"; in Slumtown and Haulburg, professional positions of lawyer, engineer, and social worker.

At the same time, use of both indicators of success-goals revealed not only differences between types of groups (delinquent, non-delinquent, and drug addict) within each area but also between respective groups in different areas. Those from Racketville tended to have the highest income and occupation aspiration levels; the ones in Slumtown had the lowest income and occupation aspiration levels, and in groups from Haulburg the aspiration levels were intermediate.

FIELD DATA

In general, the observational data were consistent with the interview findings and indicated that delinquents from the three areas internalized conventional and criminal success-goals. Again, the types of occupations symbolizing success varied on a neighborhood basis.

The occupation of a "businessman" was extremely appealing to many of the delinquents in Racketville, not merely as a front for racket activities, but as a symbol of success in its own right. "Opening a restaurant or bar or something like that" was a common response to a question about the kind of job desired. There was some interest in professional careers, but certainly not in low-status professions such as teaching or social work. In this connection, a settlement-house worker reported:

"The fellows seem to look down on social workers and teachers and on any of the low-salaried white-collar occupations. The only professionals who seem to have real status for them are doctors and lawyers. These fellows don't think it's worth while to take all the gaff from kids and other people and make only $4,000 a year. . . . They can hang around doing practically nothing and make more money. One of the older boys from the Vultures told me that he made $9,000 a year just hanging around the streets [mainly doing odd jobs for racketeers]. This is one of the reasons that few of them have any real aspirations for college. They pretty much have it made without such effort."

The best job to have was that of racketeer — this was frequently expressed:

While driving with me in my car, Little Augie made some comment about my being a good chauffeur. He jokingly offered me a job. I said jokingly that I would take the job if Little Augie offered enough. The boy said that to do so he would have to get a better job than he had now. Asked what kind of a job this would be, he said "a job as a racketeer." Asked how much money a racketeer made, Little Augie said it depended — some of them made $100 a week, some $500. These were just local fellows. Little Augie said it wouldn't pay for him to be a racketeer unless he could make several thousand a week. The risk wasn't worth it unless you could make the money. He said a fellow like Genovese or others like him made thousands and thousands of dollars a week . . .

Delinquents in Slumtown had different views about what were desirable careers. Whereas the professions of medicine, law, dentistry, or engineering seemed beyond their grasp, the position of social worker — the street-club worker and the community-center worker — was familiar and understandable to them. The social worker's job was not menial, had high status, and called for understanding and skills which the delinquent from the conflict subculture believed he, too, possessed:

Billy the Kid said he would like to be a social worker more than anything else. . . . He said he would like to be a social worker out in the streets, helping the kids. He had gone through a lot of experiences and had a lot of feeling for the kids. He could help them even more than somebody who had never been a "diddy bopper" and who did not have that kind of experience.

Delinquents in this area were also interested in careers in the rackets, but at a level lower than that desired by delinquents from Racketville. A common desire was to be part of a local criminal association which might be involved in something such as "protection." The protection racket would effectively utilize the aggressive attitudes and assault skills developed by the "bopper."

Frankie said the Seniors were planning to organize a protection association, and he wished to get involved. They were going to get money from bar-owners, prostitutes, numbers men, and others in the neighborhood. If the people didn't pay up, it would be his job and that of the others to do the beating up, the knifing, or shooting . . .

The major fear of the delinquent from Slumtown was that he would have to settle for a job as errand boy or porter in a factory where he would "break his back" and get little in return for his hard labor. He wanted to make money — easy money. He knew there was money around to be made. Among delinquents in Slumtown there was also occasionally an element of faith or trust in the "lucky break" as it was associated with aspirations for success:

Joey said that he was just out of jail and that he was waiting for his chance to to come, whether legal or illegal. He said that he was going to be patient and would wait. Someday he would be driving around in a car and have all the money he needed. People hold him that he just had to have patience for the right moment to come along.

Again, it is worth pointing out that the belief in luck was not a dominant theme in any of the three subcultures, although it was relatively more evident in the conflict subculture than in the other two (see Table 8).

Delinquents in Haulburg had high middle-class aspirations. They appeared not to be interested mainly in making a lot of money per se or in the power which derived from being a "big gun" and controlling many underlings in an organized racket structure. They were principally interested in the style of living inherent in certain success statuses, often conventional and highly respectable:

Jackie, aged twenty-one years, continued to express an interest in going to medical school and becoming a surgeon, although he had not gone to college or even completed high school. He said he had gone for a time to the Eastview School of Printing. Recently he had been fired from his job because he had a fight with his boss. He believed that if he became a printer in ten years he might make about $300 or $400 a week. Of course, if he were a doctor he might make more, although he was not absolutely sure of this. Actually, it it wasn't the money alone that interested him, he said. It was that the field of medicine meant a lot to him.

Our popular culture exalts certain glamour roles. The status of the movie star is conceived to be at the apex of the occupational pyramid. The street-club worker in Haulburg described the job aspirations of the members of the group he served in this way:

"Well, most of the boys — some of them are more realistic about it, the more intelligent ones — but most of the boys would like to get jobs where they have to do a minimum of work, the work being as glamorous as possible and offering fantastic sums of money. They would like to get into the movies. One twenty-year-old boy kidded himself for quite a while that he was going to be discovered and would go Hollywood like Robert Mitchum, who was also a truck driver once. They tell themselves only success stories of the fantastic, legendary fortunes of poor street-corner boys who were discovered by talent scouts and offered thousands of dollars and so on . . ."

All delinquents or delinquent groups were not necessarily committed to the characteristic delinquent orientation which prevailed in their neighborhood. A range of delinquent orientations existed in each area. One such exceptional or atypical orientation in Haulburg was revealed by Benny, a young adult formerly known to the researcher as a fringe member of a gang. He was presently employed in a conventional white-collar job. He had many relatives in the rackets who were not from the area.

Benny said that he would like to be a racketeer when he was a little older. The racketeers he knew made $1,500 to $2,000 a week. He'd like to make all that money. . . . He said that the important thing was to be smart, keep your mouth shut, and to have connections. He said that most of the fellows in his neighborhood did not have connections. Mainly they could become shoplifters and burglars. He looked down on them. That type of activity was "stupid." He said that he had already spent six month helping a particular bookmaker. . . . Bookmaking was really just like a business. The people in it were decent and honest. It was true they stuck together. He had no hesitation about getting involved. . . . It wasn't like being a gangster in the old sense. Now, it was like being in a clean business.

In summary, each of the three types of neighborhoods, delinquents, in comparison to non-delinquents and drug addicts, had the highest aspiration levels when the indicator of status was income. Differences between the groups using the indicator of occupation were not clearly established. In general, delinquents from Racketville had the highest income and occupational aspirations; they aspired to high positions in the rackets or, less often, to top-level conventional careers as businessmen, doctors, or lawyers. Delinquents from Slumtown had, relative to other delinquents, the lowest income aspirations. They aspired to lower-level criminal or middle-class conventional careers. Delinquents from Haulburg generally were intermediate in the range of their income and occupational aspirations. They particularly desired upper-middle-class status and a conventionally glamorous style of life.

EXPECTATION LEVELS

The expectation level of the individual as to future income or occupational status is normally conditioned by the opportunities realistically available to him in the present or in the predictable future. It was assumed that the interview subjects were able normally to differentiate between expected achievement and ideal attainment. Since delinquents in lower-class areas had limited access to conventional means structures, mainly because of their inadequate academic and conventional vocational preparation, it was anticipated that:

2.1 delinquents would have lower income and occupational expectations than did non-delinquents, particularly in Slumtown, where very limited alternative criminal means were available, and in Haulburg, where commonly only moderate criminal means were available.

2.2 delinquents from Racketville would have relatively high income and occupational expectations, since substantial criminal means were available.

2.3 narcotic addicts generally would have higher income and occupational expectations than did delinquents, except in Racketville, and would tend to approach the expectation level of non-delinquents. It was expected that narcotic addicts, as young adults, generally would have more access to means than did delinquent adolescents. The additional status opportunities available to the young adult would tend to compensate for the lack of means available to them as adolescent delinquents. In Racketville, of course, the delinquent would have access to greater means, especially criminal means, than either the drug addict or non-delinquent.

The formal interview data, in the main, supported the above notions — at least when the indicator of expected income was used (see Table 13). In the conflict and theft subcultures, de-

TABLE 13

EXPECTED MEDIAN WEEKLY WAGE WITHIN TEN YEARS*

Neighborhood and Component Group	Weekly Wages
Racketville	
Non-delinquent	$150
Delinquent	200
Drug addict	138
Slumtown	
Non-delinquent	100
Delinquent	75
Drug addict	110
Haulburg	
Non-delinquent	135
Delinquent	80
Drug addict	118

*The number in each sample or component group per neighborhood is ten.

linquents had lower income expectation levels than did non-delinquents and drug addicts. In Slumtown, delinquents had a median weekly wage expectation within ten years of $75; non-delinquents, of $100; drug addicts, of $110. In Haulburg, delinquents had a median weekly wage expectation of $80; non-delinquents, of $135; drug addicts, of $118. In the racket subculture, delinquents had higher income expectation levels than did non-delinquents and drug addicts. These delinquents had a median weekly wage expectation of $200; non-delinquents, of $150; drug addicts, of $138. In general, the income level expected by drug addicts tended to approach that anticipated by non-delinquents.

The data on occupational expectations did not support the exploratory notions. The expectations of non-delinquents in

Slumtown were as low as those of delinquents but lower than those of drug addicts. The expectations of drug addicts in Haulburg were also lower than had been predicted for they should have approached the level of the non-delinquent group (see Table 14). As in the case of aspiration levels based on the indicator of ideal occupation, the patterns were not entirely clear or consistent for the groups in each area. It was likely

TABLE 14
EXPECTED OCCUPATION WITHIN TEN YEARS*

Neighborhood and Component Group	Middle-Class Occupation	Lower-Class Occupation
Racketville		
Non-delinquent	8	2
Delinquent	9	1
Drug addict	2	8
Slumtown		
Non-delinquent	1	9
Delinquent	1	9
Drug addict	4	6
Haulburg		
Non-delinquent	8	2
Delinquent	3	7
Drug addict	2	8

*See note to Table 12. The individual was asked what job or position he expected to have in ten years.

that occupation was not as valid an indicator as income in measuring status. Success status is probably more closely associated with income than is occupational status in lower-class areas, where the visibility and knowledge of many types of middle-class occupational status are exceedingly low. In general, delinquents from the racket subculture expected to attain positions in "business," as members of racket organizations. Delinquents from the conflict subculture expected to be factory workers, porters, and delivery boys. Delinquents from the theft subculture expected to land jobs as mechanics and clerks.

Regardless of the type of group, there were general neighborhood differences in respect to expectation levels. Subjects from Racketville tended to expect the highest income and occupational levels; subjects from Slumtown had the lowest income and occupation expectation levels; the expectation levels of subjects from Haulburg were, in the main, between those of subjects from Racketville and the ones from Slumtown.

FIELD DATA

The observational data generally supported the interview findings. Expectations of future income and occupational status were differentially viewed by delinquents in the three areas.

Delinquents from Racketville had little question that they could obtain at least fairly decent-paying conventional jobs. In such cases the occupational status level might be quite low:

Jackie said that wanted very much to finish school. He wasn't sure he would be able to. He hoped to take up a trade as a mechanic and wanted to be a good mechanic — maybe going into business for himself. He expected some day to make as much as $150 a week. Actually, what he felt would happen would be that he wouldn't finish school, and ten years from now he'd be settled and married making only about $120 a week at some construction job.

In most cases, however, delinquents from this area felt they could obtain substantially better paying and more prestigeful jobs in such rackets as numbers, loan-shark activities, or juke-box operations.

The expectations of delinquents from Slumtown were very different. The following is a verbatim excerpt from a recorded interview which reflected the much bleaker outlook of the delinquent from the conflict subculture:

RESEARCHER: How many of the older boys really made it at something big or important?

FRANK: Yeah, Rudy's supposed to be a big something . . . I don't know what he is. . . . You know, come to think of it, ain't none of the old Regals became something . . . like lawyers. . . . The only Regal that I know ever became something . . . joined the army.

RESEARCHER: What did he become?

FRANK: Nothing. He just joined the army . . . digging ditches.

RESEARCHER: Do some of the guys make it in the rackets?

FRANK: Some of them . . . like, you see . . . some of them are in the rackets. Most of them are junkies. . . . Most of the Regals are busted. So they haven't made any.

RESEARCHER: Do you think they will?

FRANK: No. None of them. They haven't got a chance.

RESEARCHER: What do you mean — they don't have a chance?

FRANK: They come back to the neighborhood.

RESEARCHER: What's the neighborhood got to do with it?

FRANK: Can't find nothing to do but mess around and get into trouble. Push some dope, be a junkie . . .

Delinquents from Haulburg, in their moments of more realistic appraisal of future occupations, pitched their job expectations to a semiskilled level. On this matter the street-club worker comented as follows:

"They'll probably be the same thing, in a way, that their fathers are — cab drivers, janitors, truck drivers . . . and so on. Most of them are not very willing to talk about it because the subject is full of anxieties and frustrations for them."

In the theft subculture, a premium was placed on jobs where "you don't get your hands dirty" and "you can dress well." The money alone was not everything. A factory job was not as acceptable as some other types of work. The conventional job had to provide at least a semblance of middle-class status. The street-club worker continued:

"A job like an elevator operator or a doorman is desirable because it does not seem to involve any work — you just have to stand and go up and down. It brings a fairly good salary, about $65 to $90 a week."

Income and job expectations for delinquents varied in the three types of neighborhoods. By virtue of their educational background and training, delinquents in each area were equipped to perform only in unskilled or, at best, in semi-skilled positions. Yet delinquents from the racket subculture realistically anticipated fairly high-paying, high-prestige jobs, usually in some kind of criminal enterprise, while delinquents from the conflict subculture anticipated the lowest-paying menial positions. Those from the theft subculture looked forward to relatively low-paying unskilled and semiskilled positions. Particularly clear was the fact that delinquents from Racketville were considerably more optimistic than were delinquents from Slumtown about future job opportunities. Delinquents who were in gang-fighting groups were extremely pessimistic about future income and job prospects.

DISPARITY BETWEEN SUCCESS-GOALS AND OPPORTUNITIES — THE ANOMIC GAP

The purpose of the present section is to focus attention more directly and graphically on the disparity between culturally induced success-goals and the institutional means available to achieve them. In the exploratory research, aspiration and expectation levels were considered to be characteristics of individuals and also structural indicators, respectively, of the cultural pressures of success-goals and of the institutional means available to groups. In this section attention will be directed to the gap between the aspiration levels (success-goals) and the expectation levels (institutional means) of delinquents, non-delinquents, and narcotics addicts from the three areas.

On the basis of our conceptual model (see Preface) it was anticipated, especially in relation to the indicator of income, that:

3.1 the largest gap or the greatest disjunction between aspirations and expectations would occur for delinquents from the conflict subculture — Slumtown.

3.2 the smallest gap or the least disjunction between aspirations and expectations would occur for delinquents from the racket subculture — Racketville.

3.3 the disparity between aspirations and expectations for delinquents from the theft subculture — Haulburg — would be intermediate.

3.4 in each area the disparity between aspirations and expectations would be smaller for non-delinquents than for delinquents.

3.5 the disparity for drug addicts would be variable, generally approaching that of the non-delinquents in the respective areas, except Racketville.

3.6 in the racket subculture the disparity between aspirations and expectations would be largest for the drug addicts. (In this neighborhood, while aspiration levels would be high and realistically related to the presence of illegitimate means, access to such means would tend to be denied to its most deviant inhabitants — the drug addicts.)

INDEX OF DISPARITY: OCCUPATIONAL STATUS

An index of disparity was devised, based on the difference between levels of occupational aspiration and expectation for the various groups in each area. The data revealed (see Table 15) that the gap between aspirations and expectations was

TABLE 15
INDEXES OF DIFFERENCES BETWEEN ASPIRATIONS AND EXPECTATIONS: OCCUPATION AND WAGE*

Neighborhood and Component Group	Occupation: Aspiration-Expectation Gap†‡	Weekly Wage: Aspiration-Expectation Gap in Per cent‡
Racketville		
Non-delinquent	2	25
Delinquent	0	38
Drug addict	7	50
Slumtown		
Non-delinquent	4	27
Delinquent	6	67
Drug addict	1	19
Haulburg		
Non-delinquent	1	40
Delinquent	4	68
Drug addict	6	41

*Calculated from Tables 11, 12, 13, and 14.
†The number of subjects expecting to achieve middle-class job status was subtracted from the number of subjects for each group aspiring to middle-class status. The resultant figure indicates a measure of shift from middle-class aspirations to lower-class expectations.
‡The correlation of the two indexes is .607 $p < .05$, using a Spearman-Rank Test.

largest for delinquents from Slumtown (value of 6) and smallest for the delinquents from Racketville (value of 0). The disjunction between occupational aspirations and expectations, was intermediate for delinquents from Haulburg (value of 4). The level of disjunction for delinquents from Haulburg was quite high and tended to approach the level obtained for the delinquents from Slumtown.

Anomie theory contends that acute discrepancy or disjunction between aspirations and expectations (success-goals and socially structured capacities) is a requisite for the development of the deviant adaptation. It was obvious from the interview data that the delinquents from Racketville were not anomic by this standard. The genesis of this type of delinquent adaptation can not be explained strictly in terms of Merton's Anomie Theory or, at least, not without the aid of a proposition about some intervening variable or condition. The presence of ample and accessible illegitimate means in this neighborhood constitutes the intervening condition.[2]

The gap for non-delinquents between job aspirations and job expectations appeared to be relatively small in Racketville (value of 2) and in Haulburg (value of 1) but fairly large in Slumtown (value of 4). The interpretation made was that non-delinquents generally were able to choose goals in conformity with the means actually available. In Slumtown, however, the availability of means was probably so limited that, even though non-delinquents had set their aspiration levels fairly low, certainly lower than did delinquents, sufficient means were still lacking to meet reasonable lower-middle-class goals. It seemed probable that there was greater pressure exerted on non-delinquents in Slumtown for adaptation to a deviant mode, although not necessarily a delinquent mode, than there was on non-delinquents in other areas.

The index of disjunction based on the level of job aspirations and job expectations did not appear to bear out anticipations in respect to drug addicts. The gap between aspirations and expectations for drug addicts in both Racketville (value of 7) and Haulburg (value of 6) was relatively high. In Racketville the gap between aspirations and expectations was greater for the drug-addict group than for any other type of group. In Slumtown, however, the occupational disjunction level appeared to be unexpectedly low for drug addicts (value of 1). Moreover, there was no clear evidence that the disjunction level for drug addicts approached the disjunction level of non-delinquents in the three areas.

The significance of the data found by employing the occupational index is not fully explainable, particularly in relation to drug addicts. It is indeed possible, as indicated earlier, that an index based on job status is less valid in lower-class areas than one based on income.

[2] See Richard A. Cloward and Lloyd E. Ohlin, *Delinquency and Opportunity* (Glencoe, Ill.: Free Press, 1960).

INDEX OF DISPARITY: INCOME.

Income is very likely a more valid and precise index of aspiration and expectation levels than job status. It was employed to examine more critically the exploratory predictions. The results obtained with the income index supported the original predictions more than did those obtained with the job index. Nevertheless, both indexes appeared to be significantly related (see ‡, Table 15).

More specifically, the differences between ideal and expected income levels of delinquents from Slumtown and Haulburg appeared again to be quite marked. The computed income aspiration-expectation gap was 67 per cent in Slumtown and 68 per cent in Haulburg. The disparity between aspirations and expectations for delinquents from Racketville was considerably lower — 38 per cent. The operation of an illegitimate means system was regarded as the important intervening condition which tended to close the gap between income aspirations and expectations for delinquents from the racket subculture.

The income disjunction levels of non-delinquents and drug addicts in each of the areas appeared, in the main, to follow the expected pattern. It was noteworthy again, however, that the level of disjunction for addicts from the area of the conflict subculture was unexpectedly low — 19 per cent. Why this was so was not clear.

Anomie, the structural condition of disjunction between success-goals and institutional means as indicated by the disparity between income aspiration and expectation levels, appeared to characterize mainly delinquents from Slumtown and Haulburg and drug addicts from Racketville.

GRAPHS

It was possible to plot the differences in disjunction level among the various groups investigated.[3] For this purpose an index of disjunction based on income was considered more ap-

[3] Data supplied by a second sample of twenty-five delinquents from the theft subculture and also by a sample of ten American Negro delinquents from an area containing a mixed conflict and theft subculture were also used for illustrative purposes.

propriate, since income was regarded as a clearer and more representative indicator of success status in lower-class neighborhoods than was occupation. Also, occupational status could not be so easily or accurately plotted on a graph. Income was regarded as a simpler, continuous, and more homogeneous variable. Three points on a graph were plotted for each group: ideal (or aspired) income, expected income (both already discussed), and lowest expected income. The resulting curves highlighted the following patterns:

1. The curves for the delinquent groups were fairly similar (see Fig. 1). They were distinguished by the steepness of their

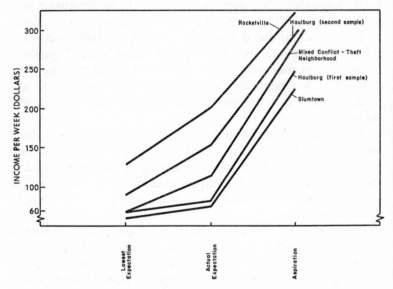

FIG. 1 Aspiration-Expectation Curves: The Delinquent Groups

slopes between the points of ideal income and expected income. Severe disjunction prevailed generally, except among the delinquents from Racketville and the second sample of delinquents — perhaps not so delinquent as the first sample — from Haulburg. The graph clearly portrayed the radical lowering of aspirations to expectations: in Slumtown from a weekly median of $225 to $75; in Haulburg (original sample) from a weekly median of $250 to $80; and in the area of the mixed conflict-theft subculture from a weekly median of $300 to $110.

2. The curves for the non-delinquent groups were generally quite different from those of the delinquent groups (see Fig. 2). The slopes were more gradual, indicating that aspirations

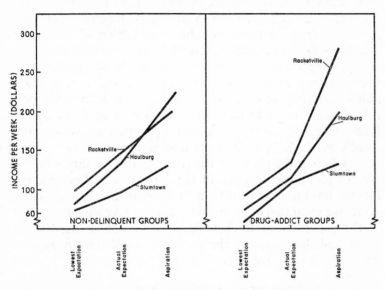

FIG. 2 Aspiration-Expectation Curves: The Non-Delinquent and Drug-Addict Groups

were higher than expectations but not greatly higher. Furthermore, aspiration levels were not as high as they were for the delinquent groups. In Racketville, the lowering of aspirations to expectations for non-delinquents was from $200 to $150; in Slumtown, from $138 to $100; in Haulburg, from $225 to $135.

3. The curves for the drug-addict groups reflected considerable variation which was, perhaps, after all, systematic (see Fig. 2). Suggested was the possibility that drug-use served essentially as a help in adjusting to reality — aspiration levels of addicts were lower than those of delinquents. The influence of reality, i.e., actual means available, on the aspiration levels

of young-adult addicts had to be given due attention. The slope of the curves between the points of ideal income and expected income probably approximated the actual availability of resources or means in each of the neighborhoods. The shape of the curve in Haulburg ($200 to $118) suggested that addicts were aware of the availability of some means, not so many as were present in Racketville ($275 to $138), but considerably more than in Slumtown ($135 to $110). Regardless of area, however, drug-use made possible a condition of fantasy in which the lack of availability or the inaccessability of means to significant status in reality was partially overcome. Drug addicts viewed at least some possible access to means as available — certainly more than non-drug-using delinquents perceived as available to them in Slumtown or in Haulburg. In Racketville, of course, criminal opportunities were more readily available to delinquents than to drug addicts.

4. Whereas the shape of the curve tended to vary with the type of group, the location of the curve at a higher or lower income level appeared to be a function of the general socio-economic condition of the neighborhood. Invariably, the curves of the groups from Racketville were located at the highest levels and the curves of the groups from Slumtown were at the lowest levels (see Figs. 1, 2, and especially 3).

MEANS STRUCTURES — OPPORTUNITIES

Up to this point, the discussion has been concerned primarily with aspiration and expectation levels and their relation to each other. Further elaboration of the social factors which determine the relationship of individual expectations to means structures will now follow.

Merton has maintained that a breakdown in the cultural structure occurs particularly when there is an "acute disjunction between the cultural norms and goals and the socially structured capacities of members of the group to act in accord with them." [4] The conception of "socially structured capacities . . . to act . . ." may be divided into at least four elements: first, it implies the *presence* of institutional means — resources

[4] Merton, *Social Theory and Social Structure*, p. 162.

or learning environments; second, the *accessibility* of the means to a segment of a population; third, the *capacity* of members of the population to use the means which are accessible; fourth, the desire or the *motivation* of the members to use the means toward desired ends. Although these are analytically distinct concepts or elements, it may be extremely difficult to deal with them separately for research purposes.

This research focused mainly on the awareness of the subjects of the presence or access to goal-reaching means available

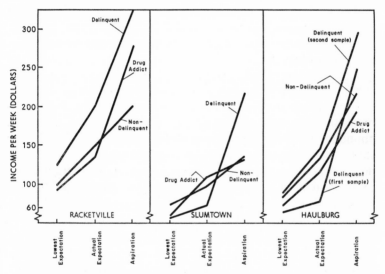

Fig. 3 Aspiration-Expectation Curves: The Delinquent, Non-Delinquent, and Drug-Addict Groups in Each Neighborhood

in the neighborhood. It was assumed for purposes of the research that the concepts of presence and of accessibility of resources were equivalent. The term "access to means" signified direct admission or approach to resources or learning environments. Finally, the differential capacities and motivations of groups of youths to utilize the means accessible to them were dealt with only secondarily and often inferentially.

Certain exploratory expectations were held:

4.1 the delinquent group in Racketville would have ample access to means, mainly illegitimate.

4.2 the delinquent group in Slumtown would have very limited access to means, legitimate or illegitimate.

4.3 the delinquent group in Haulburg would have partial access to means, legitimate or illegitimate.

4.4 in general, groups in Racketville would have the greatest access to means. The groups in Slumtown would have the least access to means. The groups in Haulburg would have an intermediate range of accessibility to means.

These ideas were examined mainly in relation to three sets of variables: neighborhood racket structure, adult or peer-group integration, and relationships to significant adults (considered in chap. v).

ILLEGITIMATE MEANS

Cloward has developed the cogent thesis that not only legitimate but illegitimate means to success may be either in abundant or short supply in a particular neighborhood.[5] He states that differential access to illegitimate means in certain neighborhoods accounts for the prevalence of different types of delinquent activity. He uses Kobrin's illustration of two polar kinds of neighborhoods. In one, conventional and criminal values and norms are highly integrated, and the neighborhood constitutes a "training ground" for the "acquisition of criminal values and skills." Criminal activity is highly organized and controlled. In the present investigation, Racketville essentially represents this pattern of orientation and behavior. In the other neighborhood, conventional and criminal value systems have not been integrated. "Systematic and organized adult activity in violation of the law" does not exist, "despite the fact that many adults in these areas commit violations." Opportunities for stable role performance are limited, and criminal behavior is not well organized.[6] Roughly, this corresponds to a description of Slumtown, the conflict subculture.

Neighborhood racketeers — It was expected not only that

[5] Richard A. Cloward, "Illegitimate Means, Anomie, and Deviant Behavior," *American Sociological Review*, XXIV (April, 1959), 165–76.

[6] *Ibid.*, pp. 171–72.

the integration of adult conventional and criminal systems of values would influence or reflect the extent of organized criminal means available to the youths of an area but that the sheer relative numbers (or presence) of racketeers, particularly successful racketeers, would also be associated with accessibility to criminal means. If this were so, then young people in Racketville would be more likely to perceive the presence of a greater number of more powerful racketeers in their neighborhood than would young people from Slumtown or Haulburg, respectively. Furthermore, it was likely that subjects from Haulburg would perceive the presence of a larger number of adult thieves than of racketeers. Fewer successful adult thieves would probably be perceived in Racketville and in Slumtown.

Data were not available to explore all of these notions. Interview subjects were asked to estimate the gross number of racketeers they thought were present in their neighborhoods. They could select any of four categories in response: "a lot," "some," "hardly any," "none." In the three neighborhoods no subject selected the "none" category. There were two refusals to answer the question by non-delinquents from Racketville. Non-delinquents from this area and, to some extent, from Haulburg showed great reluctance or ambivalence in answering questions about criminal operations or conditions.

In the main, the findings supported expectations (see Table

TABLE 16

GROSS ESTIMATE OF NUMBER OF RACKETEERS IN NEIGHBORHOOD*

Neighborhood and Component Group	A Lot	Some	Hardly Any
Racketville			
Non-delinquent†	7	1	0
Delinquent	7	3	0
Drug addict	9	1	0
Slumtown			
Non-delinquent	7	3	0
Delinquent	6	3	1
Drug addict	6	4	0
Haulburg			
Non-delinquent	3	2	5
Delinquent	4	5	1
Drug addict	1	6	3

*The number in each sample or component group per neighborhood is ten.
†Two non-delinquent subjects from Racketville refused to answer.

16). Subjects from Racketville perceived the presence of the highest number, or density, of racketeers. Subjects from Haulburg reported the lowest density of racketeers in their neighborhood. The majority of responses of the subjects from Racketville and Slumtown [7] fell into the "a lot" category. The majority of responses of the subjects from Haulburg were in the "some" category.

At a later time, interviews were administered to a second sample of twenty-five delinquents from Haulburg; this sample contained delinquents who were not so seriously deviant as those in the first one. In the second round of interviews, a series of additional questions were posed about adult thieves. In response to one of the questions, twenty of the subjects answered that there were more thieves, burglars, and fences than there were racketeers in the area. Only four responded that there were more racketeers. One individual refused to answer. Since the responses of delinquents from the two Haulburg samples of delinquents were highly similar in almost all other respects, it was assumed that to the delinquents in this area a theft structure of means was relatively more available than a racket structure of means. Unanswered, however, is the question of whether Racketville and Slumtown young people, particularly delinquents, perceived the presence of more or fewer racketeers than thieves in their respective areas.

The subjects were also asked to discuss a racketeer they knew quite well and, in the course of this part of the interview, to rank the status of this particular racketeer: Was he a "big shot," a "medium-echelon" criminal, or a "small-time operator?" The findings (see Table 17) clearly supported expectations and were highly consistent with the theoretical formulation guiding the research. The power and prestige of racketeers in the various neighborhoods varied considerably. In Racketville, the overwhelming majority of subjects perceived racketeers to fall into the "big-shot" category. Subjects from

[7] The size of the neighborhoods varied. There were indications that the largest number of criminals were to be found in the neighborhood containing the conflict subculture, since the population was larger. The proportion of adult racketeers to population, however, was probably greater in the neighborhood of the racket subculture.

Slumtown regarded the racketeers whom they knew as falling largely in the "medium" or "small-time" categories, particularly in the "small-time" category. The estimates of the subjects from Haulburg were distributed about equally in all three possible response categories. More of their responses, however, fell into the "big-shot" category than those of delinquents from Slumtown, but fewer than those of delinquents from Racketville.

Thus, not only did the relative numbers or density of criminals, mainly racketeers, appear to vary according to the perceptions of interviewed subjects, but the status of criminals

TABLE 17
STATUS OF RACKETEERS*

Neighborhood and Component Group	Big-Shot	Medium	Small-Time
Racketville			
Non-delinquent†	2	0	2
Delinquent	8	2	0
Drug addict	8	1	1
Slumtown			
Non-delinquent	0	3	7
Delinquent	1	4	5
Drug addict	2	4	4
Haulburg			
Non-delinquent‡	4	1	0
Delinquent	4	3	3
Drug addict	0	4	6

*The number in each sample or component group per neighborhood is ten. If medium and "small-time" columns are combined, the difference between delinquents from Racketville and Slumtown is significant, using a Fisher Test, $p < .055$.
†Six members of group refused to answer.
‡Five members of group did not know any racketeers.

particularly racketeers, seemed to vary by neighborhood as well. A strong implication was that subjects, especially delinquents, had potentially the greatest motivation and access to significant criminal means in Racketville, least access to such means in Slumtown, and intermediate access to them in Haulburg.

ADULTS AND PEER GROUPS AS OPPORTUNITY SOURCES.

It was speculated that the extent to which a group was positively oriented to neighborhood adults might indicate the degree of access the group had to means controlled by those adults. In other words, it was assumed that adults provided access to various kinds of skills and attitudes requisite for the acquisition of rewards, advancement, and status desired by youths. The greater the reference to adults, the greater the likely interaction with adults, and the greater the possible access to means (and thereby to goals) which adults control. On the other hand, to the degree that the group was oriented to peer associates, to that degree might adult means be closed off. The greater the orientation to peers, the greater the possibility that routes to significant status were denied to youths. An assumption here was that adults controlled more significant means by which culturally induced goals might be attained than did peers.

It was believed that the content of natural conversation of young people might indicate the extent of orientation to, or integration with, adult or peer systems and that samples of free-flowing conversation in delinquent groups could be analyzed into such gross component parts as references to criminal adults and peers. A more refined breakdown of conversation, for instance into categories which would signify the affective or instrumental character of such references, was not attempted.

It was thought that the delinquent group from Racketville would be most likely to direct its verbal references to adults; that the delinquent group from Slumtown would tend least to direct its verbal references to adults; and that the delinquent group from Haulburg would tend to direct its verbal references to adults less than did the delinquent group from Racketville but more than did the delinquent group from Slumtown.

EXTRACTING THE DATA: CONDITION AND PROCEDURES.

Several general conditions or requisites were established for the gathering of these data:

1. The researcher had to be sufficiently familiar with the group so that the type of verbal references made to adults — criminal and non-criminal — and to peers could be accurately recognized.

2. An easy, comfortable relationship between the researcher

and the group had to prevail so that group conversation would be spontaneous and unimpeded.

3. A group of three or more youngsters had to be present continuously during the time periods established. Movement in and out of the group was permissible as long as a core of at least three members remained in direct physical proximity with each other, allowing for possible communication.

4. The researcher had to remain uninvolved in initiating, sustaining, terminating, or in any manner influencing the extent and nature of the conversation.

The specific procedures for extracting and analyzing the data were as follows:

1. Ten successive fifteen-minute periods of group conversation, divided into references to non-criminal and criminal adults, were analyzed for the three types of delinquent groups. Group cohesion was not always maintained for a minimum of fifteen minutes, and therefore certain counts were discarded because of incompleteness.

2. The researcher at first hid small mechanical clickers or counters in each of his trouser pockets to record the number of specific references to non-criminal and criminal adults. Later, when some skill had been developed in the use of the technique of picking up and differentiating verbal references, the employment of memory replaced the use of mechanical devices which, if detected, might have created an inhibiting, if not seriously embarrassing, situation.

3. A click or a count was made for every word — noun or pronoun — referring to a specific adult mentioned by the youngsters. The words referred mainly to neighborhood adults, racketeers, parents, and relatives but also to teachers, employers, baseball players, movie stars, and persons in the news.

4. All curse words or references to non-specific adults were disregarded. Any reference to the researcher was also eliminated.

5. Not more than two successive counts were made during an afternoon or an evening. The counts were taken from the mechanical devices or from memory not more than an hour after the termination of the contact with the group.

6. Finally, a second series of ten successive five-minute periods of conversation, divided into "adult" and "peer" categories, were analyzed for the same group, using exactly the same procedures. The second series served, in part, as a check on the assumption that the total verbal productivity of each group was approximately the same and, in part, as a way of testing the reliability of the data.

The findings were entirely consistent with expectations: the data revealed that the delinquent group from Racketville was highly oriented to adults, both criminal and non-criminal (see

TABLE 18

CONVERSATION CONTENT ANALYSIS: NUMBER OF REFERENCES
TO NON-CRIMINAL AND CRIMINAL ADULTS*

RACKETVILLE DELINQUENT GROUP			SLUMTOWN DELINQUENT GROUP			HAULBURG DELINQUENT GROUP		
Non-Criminal Adult†	Criminal Adult‡	Total§	Non-Criminal Adult†	Criminal Adult‡	Total§	Non-Criminal Adult	Criminal Adult	Total
12	2	14	3	1	4	5	0	5
11	5	16	6	0	6	7	0	7
16	1	17	6	0	6	10	0	10
19	4	23	7	0	7	12	0	12
26	0	26	7	0	7	18	0	18
10	18	28	10	0	10	18	0	18
23	7	30	10	0	10	24	0	24
30	0	30	10	0	10	29	0	29
38	1	39	12	0	12	29	5	34
49	9	58	12	0	12	36	4	40

*The number in each sample or component group per neighborhood is ten. Data were arranged in order of magnitude of total scores for fifteen-minute periods.
†Difference is significant, using a t test — $t = 3.87$, d.f. 9, $p < .005$.
‡Difference is significant — $t = 2.86$, d.f. 9, $p < .01$.
§Difference is significant — $t = 4.48$, d.f. 9, $p < .005$.

Table 18); the delinquent group from Slumtown was much less oriented to adults but, on the other hand, much more oriented to peers (see Table 19); the delinquent group from Haulburg was less oriented to adults than was the delinquent group from Racketville but more oriented to adults than was the delinquent group from Slumtown.

Particularly noteworthy was the fact that delinquents from Racketville made the largest number of references dealing with criminal adults; delinquents from Slumtown made the smallest number of references to criminal adults; delinquents from Haulburg were intermediate between the other two groups in their number of references to criminal adults.

Finally, as was expected, the total number of references made to adults and peers by each of the delinquent groups was substantially similar, demonstrating a measure of control or equivalence of verbal productivity (see Table 19). It should be noted, however, that in the second series of counts the difference in the proportion of references to adults and peers between the delinquent groups from Racketville and those of Slumtown continued in the expected direction and were still

TABLE 19

CONVERSATION CONTENT ANALYSIS: NUMBER OF REFERENCES
TO ADULTS AND PEERS*

RACKETVILLE DELINQUENT GROUP			SLUMTOWN DELINQUENT GROUP			HAULBURG DELINQUENT GROUP		
Peer†	Adult‡	Total§	Peer†	Adult‡	Total§	Peer	Adult	Total
30	18	48	60	3	63	75	0	75
36	18	54	54	18	72	81	36	117
57	27	84	96	0	96	87	36	123
36	51	87	81	24	105	129	0	129
42	57	99	90	30	120	90	45	135
39	66	105	114	6	120	99	36	135
72	33	105	135	9	144	114	39	153
93	24	117	162	6	168	159	6	165
102	21	123	120	60	180	150	30	180
84	126	210	195	15	210	165	18	183

*The number in each sample or component group per neighborhood is ten. Data were obtained for five minute periods and then multiplied by a factor of three to make them equivalent with data presented in Table 18.
  The data are arranged in order of magnitude of total scores.
†Difference is significant, using a t test — $t = 3.28$, d.f. 9, $p < .005$.
‡Difference is significant — $t = 2.21$, d.f. 9, $p < .05$.
§There is *no* statistical difference, when level of significance is .05, $t = 1.14$, d.f. 9.

statistically significant, but the confidence level was considerably reduced (see §, Table 18 and ‡, Table 19). Additional counts of conversation would have been highly desirable.

In any case, there appeared to be consistent evidence that the delinquent group from the racket subculture was much more expressly oriented toward, and possibly integrated with, the adult community, both criminal and conventional, than was the delinquent group from the conflict subculture. The character of the references of the delinquents from the theft subculture was in an intermediate position. This evidence points to the strong possibility that delinquents from Racketville were most closely related to adults, to their value systems, and to the learning situations they controlled, than were delinquents from the other areas. Those from Slumtown appeared to be relatively isolated from contacts with adults and adult influence. Again, Haulburg delinquents seemed neither so very closely related to, nor so isolated from, adults.

SUMMARY

Evidence from the formal interviews and the field data showed that delinquents aspired to high success-goals, particularly when the indicator of desired income status was used. Amply demonstrated were the consistent and significant differentials in income expectations; these were assumed to be related to access to the means structures, legitimate and illegitimate, in each of the areas. Striking in contrast were the relatively high expectation levels developed by delinquents from Racketville and the extremely low expectation levels manifested by delinquents from Slumtown. While a structural condition of anomie and its psychological correlate — disparity between aspirations and expectations — might account for pressure toward deviant behavior in Slumtown and Haulburg, it could not, however, strictly speaking account for the existence of pressure toward deviant behavior among delinquents in Racketville. The disparity between aspirations and expectations for delinquents in this area appeared to be minimal, perhaps because of the availability of a criminal system of means. Again, the implication drawn was that in the racket subculture delinquents were *not* "deviant" but were subjected to "normative" processes of induction and socialization to a criminal neighborhood culture and organization.

On the basis of the data relevant to the two sets of indicators of means — awareness of neighborhood racket structure and group references to adults or peers — it was further demonstrated that access to means was differentially distributed according to kind of neighborhood in which the delinquent group was found. The evidence was clear that delinquents from the racket subculture had most access to illegitimate and

probably to legitimate means; those from the conflict subculture had very limited access to means, legitimate and illegitimate; and delinquents from the theft subculture appeared
to have an intermediate range of access to means. It was apparent that in the different types of subcultures access to the
means by which youths might attain desired goals systematically varied.

CHAPTER V

RELATIONSHIPS
WITH SIGNIFICANT
ADULTS

Positive and co-operative relationships with significant adults offer to youths learning opportunities by which they may acquire knowledge, attitudes, and skills useful in the performance of conventional or criminal roles. Adults are the guardians of the important routes to success status. As parents, teachers, employers, and others, they provide the access to means which young people need to acquire desired ends. But to conceive of the relationship with adults as an index to the means structure has a major limitation, for adults of the same general status may provide differential access to means. For example, a moderately positive and co-operative relationship with a wealthy father or uncle may signify accessibility to greater means than would a highly positive and co-operative relationship with an impoverished father or uncle. Nevertheless, if the quality of the relationships developed by delinquents with various kinds of adults, undifferentiated as to the level of means to which access is provided by them, does vary in a *patterned* manner on a subcultural basis, then the index will be at least partially useful. The focus of the present analysis and discussion is on the character or quality of the relationships rather than on the quantity of opportunities derivable from the relationships.

It was anticipated that the type of delinquent subculture would vary with the nature and extent of means available to youths located in different neighborhoods. If the kind of relationships established with significant adults provides an index to the means structure then the particular type of delinquent subculture will tend to depend upon the character of these relationships. The following empirical expectations were held:

5.1 delinquents from the racket subculture would have very positive and co-operative relationships with criminal adults, especially with racketeers, and less positive and co-operative relationships with conventional adults.

5.2 delinquents from the conflict subculture would have very limited positive and co-operative relationships with adults, conventional or criminal.

5.3 delinquents from the theft subculture would have somewhat positive and co-operative relationships with criminals, especially thieves, as well as with conventional adults.

The relationships of youngsters from the various types of neighborhoods to a selected group of significant adults were investigated. The subjects studied were expected to have established some relationship with a number of, or all of, the following kinds of persons: mothers, fathers, teachers, employers, community-center workers, policemen, street-club workers, neighborhood adults, racketeers, and thieves.[1] The data in this chapter deal principally with the responses of delinquents to interview questions on their relationships with these persons, except for teachers and employers, with whom many delinquents did not have present contacts. The interview findings are supplemented by observational reports.

Four measures of relationship with adults were developed. An affective dimension was tapped by asking the subject whether he liked or disliked the particular adult discussed. Four responses were possible: "like very much" (love), "like" (love), "dislike," "dislike very much." A more comprehensive interaction dimension — co-operativeness — measuring both affectivity and instrumentality was also investigated. Responses to the question of whether a subject co-operated or got along with a particular adult could be: "very well," "somewhat," "slightly," "not at all." A partially instrumental dimension (in the sense that the subject might admit the adult's helpfulness

[1] Only the second sample of twenty-five delinquents from the theft subculture was questioned specifically on the nature of their relationships with adult thieves.

but not use it) was also employed: Did the subject view the adult as helpful? In respect to various categories of helping, his response could be: "very much," "somewhat," "slightly," or "not at all." The interviewer did not seek to determine whether or not the subject utilized the help. Finally, the subject was asked how much time he spent with a given adult or how frequently he saw this adult. Specific time periods or frequencies were obtained and median measures determined. The data are closely summarized and only the more important findings are presented here.

Relationship with Mothers. Just as everyone appears to be against sin, probably even the delinquents interviewed, nearly all subjects said that they loved and were loved by their mothers. However, the degree of loving found in the different groups, particularly in the delinquent groups, varied. Delinquents from Racketville appeared to have relatively the most positive relationships with their mothers. Delinquents from Haulburg seemed to have the least positive relationships with their mothers (see Table 20). More often than delinquents from

TABLE 20
AFFECTION BETWEEN MOTHER AND SON

Neighborhood and Component Group	Like Very Much		Like	
	Son for Mother	Mother for Son	Son for Mother	Mother for Son
Racketville				
Non-delinquent	9	8	1	2
Delinquent*	9	8	1	1
Drug addict	9	9	1	1
Slumtown				
Non-delinquent	8	9	2	1
Delinquent	6	5	4	5
Drug addict	10	8	0	2
Haulburg				
Non-delinquent	7	6	3	4
Delinquent*	2	3	7	7
Drug addict*	8	8	1	2

*One youngster in each of these groups indicated he disliked or was disliked by his mother.

other neighborhoods they seemed to be lukewarm in their feelings to their mothers and less often did they perceive mothers to be very loving. Delinquents from Slumtown were neither so positive as the delinquents from Racketville nor so negative as the delinquents from Haulburg about their relationships with their mothers.

As has been noted above, the data suggested that problems of interpersonal functioning in this crucial relationship were most prevalent in Haulburg, the theft subculture. Possibly the influence of generational ethnic variables operated more effectively to maintain the positive character of mother-child relationship in the racket subculture than in the theft subculture. In first-generation Italian families the affectional ties of the children to mother may be stronger than in second, third, or succeeding generations of more Americanized families. This possibility was enhanced by the findings that in Haulburg, a mainly second- and third-generation mixed-ethnic neighborhood containing a substantial Italian group, non-delinquents were not quite so positive in their relationships with their mothers as were non-delinquents in Racketville, a largely first-generation Italian community. The findings on drug addicts in each of the areas were consistent with previous research which indicated that drug addicts tended to be exceedingly close and positive in their relationships with their mothers.[2]

With regard to the measure of co-operation with mothers — particularly by helping with work around the house and running errands — delinquents from each of the areas showed slight variations in their responses. Generally, delinquents seemed to be more co-operative than not in this aspect of their relationships with mothers. Those from Racketville and Slumtown gave similarly high estimates of the helpfulness of mothers in giving advice and guidance and in providing material welfare as well as spending money or allowances. But the delinquents from Haulburg considered mothers to be less helpful than did the delinquents from other areas.

The evidence that delinquents appeared to get along rather well with their mothers was heightened by the fact that in Slumtown, for example, delinquents viewed mothers as even more helpful than did non-delinquents. The implication was that problems of interpersonal functioning between mothers and

[2] See Donald L. Gerard *etc. al.,* *Post-Hospitalization Adjustment: A Follow-up Study of Adolescent Opiate Addicts* (New York: New York University Research Center for Human Relations, October, 1955).

sons, at least at a conscious level, were not significantly present and could not, therefore, be associated with the creation of an antisocial orientation in Racketville and in Slumtown. In view of the poorer relationships between Haulburg delinquents and their mothers, as compared to the relationships of non-delinquents in the same area and to delinquents in other areas with mothers, it was conjectured that a psychological or interpersonal variable might be particularly important in the development of a delinquent adaptation in this neighborhood.

Relationship with Fathers. The findings indicated that the relationships of subjects with their fathers were generally positive but less so than with their mothers. Delinquents from Racketville expressed the greatest degree of liking for, and being liked by, their fathers; the ones from Haulburg indicated the least positive relationships with their fathers; those from Slumtown were intermediate in the character of their relationships with their fathers and tended to express only mildly positive feelings in regard to them.

The non-delinquent subjects generally expressed the opinion that they co-operated and got along well with their fathers, assisted them with errands, and did things around the house or outside. Delinquents from Racketville, however, reported they were only slightly co-operative in their relationships with their fathers. Delinquents from Slumtown and Haulburg were even less accommodative in their relationships with fathers. While delinquents from the racket and conflict subcultures saw their fathers as somewhat helpful in giving advice and guidance, material welfare, and spending money, delinquents from the theft subculture considered their fathers to be less helpful.

The data indicated, on the whole, that non-delinquents had developed positive and productive relationships with parents while delinquents had developed somewhat less fruitful and positive relationships with parents. Just the same, there was considerable variation among the delinquent groups in their relationships with their mothers and fathers. Delinquents from the racket subculture had the most satisfactory relationships with their parents, and delinquents from the theft subculture the most strained and negative relationships. The tentative conclu-

sion drawn was that expressed problems of interpersonal functioning manifested in, and perhaps arising from, inadequate
family situations might constitute an especially significant factor in the development of the delinquent adaptation in the theft
subculture.

FIELD DATA ON RELATIONSHIPS WITH PARENTS

In each of the areas there was some evidence that interpersonal
relations of families of delinquents were poor by gross mental-
hygiene criteria. Severe conflict, divorce, desertion, and infidel-
ity were not uncommon. This did not deny the possibility that
some of the same conditions were also present in the homes of
non-delinquent youths. We are not certain how important the
broken home — especially the psychologically broken home —
is in its association with, or determination of, the delinquent
orientation. This line of inquiry, significant as it is, was not pursued in the research. Very important for purposes of the investigation, however, were the differential cultural meanings and
consequences of a broken home for delinquents in the various
neighborhoods.

In the racket subculture a broken or inadequate home appeared to be mitigated by the presence of an extended family
structure. The destinies of uncles, aunts, fathers, mothers,
nephews, and cousins were complexly interwoven through the
sharing of common personal, social, and "business" interests.
If a father was absent or ineffective, an uncle (perhaps a powerful figure in the local racket structure) might exert authority
and provide affection and support in a benevolent, if autocratic,
way:

The street-club worker said that Little Augie's uncle had sent
word inviting him to come and have some beer with him and talk
about the boy, in whom he was very interested. Little Augie's uncle
was a "big man" in the numbers racket. The worker was unable to
meet the uncle at that time but subsequently was introduced to him
at a family wedding. He expressed much gratitude to the worker for
"taking care" of Little Augie and wanted to do him a good turn.
The worker observed that Little Augie was very close to his uncle,

perhaps more so than to his own father. At the wedding everyone "kowtowed" to the uncle as if he were a Roman senator.

Patterns of authority in the racket subculture were such that a youth, even of an advanced adolescent age, frequently received beatings from his elders — mainly his father. Yet this did not inhibit the youth from strongly identifying with the authority figure. In Racketville obedience and respect were characteristic of the relationship of the delinquent youth to his father. There tended to be little criticism of the father's or the father substitute's dominating role. The authoritarian father developed a close relationship with his son and exerted a major influence upon him. For instance:

Jerry spent a good deal of time describing his father, who had died the year before, and focused especially on the fact that he was a very strong person and could beat up men much stronger and bigger than himself. It was evident that Jerry took pride that his father was so competent with his fists, and he indicated throughout the conversation that he wished to be just like his father. He mentioned, guardedly, that his only criticism was that his father had been sometimes a little quick to lose his temper when it came to him.

While in the racket subculture delinquents referred to parents frequently and positively in the course of conversation, in the conflict subculture parents ordinarily were not a topic for discussion or reference. Families of lower-class Negroes and Puerto Ricans in Slumtown were often quite large. The family unit was not cohesive, and the relationships to parents appeared distant and tenuous, although not necessarily negative. The family, whether broken or not, appeared not to have much impact on the life experience of delinquents in this area. Frankie's situation was typical:

Frankie (seventeen years old) said that his father was dead and that since coming out of the protective institution he had been living with his mother, who had remarried. He said he had about — but wasn't sure — six full brothers and sisters and about nine half-brothers and half-sisters. In addition, his father had been married twice.

In the past year his mother had moved to Jersey City, and he had gone home only two or three times a week. The rest of the time he usually stayed with an older brother.

The character of relationships of delinquents from the neighborhood of the theft subculture with parents seemed markedly different from that prevalent in the other two neighborhoods. Delinquents in Haulburg expressed considerable hostility and resentment toward parents in the course of group discussion. It appeared to the observer that here "ranking," or making fun of parents, was a sufficiently common and expected occurrence to be classified as a subcultural norm:

During the discussion Harry, Jackie, and Karl said in different ways that they did not like their parents. A common lament was that parents were still "Old World peasants." Karl said that his mother was too fat and ate too much candy. Jackie said his mother was also fat and waddled like a duck when she walked. Harry said that his father was no good, especially because he had refused to let his brother keep his driver's license. Karl said his father had left home many years ago, and they had never heard from him. He hated his father for this.

The unsolicited comments of the delinquents from the theft subculture were consistently in line with current and popular theories of delinquency causation which placed the blame on parental inadequacies. A significant comment was:

"Well . . . me . . . I always had a great resentment, you know, for my father . . . If my father wasn't living at home [he drank a lot], I think I wouldn't have gotten in any trouble. Maybe it doesn't sound like it makes sense . . . I just feel he had something to do with it, somewhere in there.

"Everybody used to have troubles at home, you know. In one way or another it was troubles with their father; their father used to drink too much; or, you know, this or that . . ."

Both interview and field data demonstrated that the relationships of delinquents with their parents or substitute parents varied from area to area. A stable and integrated pattern of relationships in the racket subculture appeared to control and make for a positive and co-operative relationship between delinquents and their parents. In the conflict subculture the lack of stable and cohesive family structure seemed not to induce hostility toward parental figures so much as a mild but affectionate tolerance of them. In the theft subculture the intermediate degree of family cohesion and stability appeared somehow to result in considerable protest and dissatisfaction with parents by delinquents.

RELATIONSHIP WITH COMMUNITY CENTERS AND COMMUNITY-CENTER WORKERS

A variety of youth-serving agencies offering recreational and group-work programs appeared to be available in the three types of neighborhoods. Subjects from Racketville attended mainly church-sponsored programs. Subjects from Slumtown were members of several kinds of agencies, including a Boys' Club, a church-sponsored agency, and a settlement house. Subjects from Haulburg participated mainly in the activities of two settlement houses. Although a very large majority of all subjects had at some time or other participated in organized youth programs, not all individuals were presently connected with such agencies. Age appeared to be a factor in determining whether or not a young person was still likely to be a member of such a program.

The somewhat younger subjects, including those from the three non-delinquent groups and the delinquents in the conflict subculture, were generally still participating in youth-serving programs. While relatively few of the delinquents from the racket subculture were presently participating in agency programs, most of the delinquents from the conflict subculture were alternately in attendance at two youth-serving organizations. The contacts of delinquents from Slumtown with agency personnel tended to be frequent but of short duration. The time spent per contact with any particular staff person was considerably less in this neighborhood than in the others investigated. The implication was that despite the high frequency of agency and staff contact, there was probably very little significant involvement in programs on the part of delinquents from Slumtown.

Delinquents from Haulburg appeared to have positive and accommodative (if at times ambivalent) relationships with staff

personnel. Delinquents from Racketville had uniformly negative and antagonistic relationships with youth-agency workers.
Delinquents from Slumtown had intermediate relationships
with agency personnel — mildly positive but distant.

FIELD DATA ON RELATIONSHIP WITH COMMUNITY-CENTER WORKERS

The field observation generally supported the data obtained
through the formal interviews. In Racketville, the relationships
of delinquents with youth-serving personnel were characterized
by lack of friendliness and respect; indeed, they frequently reflected outright contempt:

Mr. Ippolito, the supervisor of teen-age activities who had been
brought up in the neighborhood and worked in the settlement for a
great many years but now was somewhat alienated from the neighborhood culture, spoke of the complete absence of respect that the
youngsters (in this case the Vultures) had for adults. The kids
thought nothing of insulting an adult, breaking up furniture, and,
occasionally, even threatening to hit a staff member.

A priest, in charge of the Catholic Youth Organization program, reported an incident that occurred several months before:

He had had to eject the Vultures from a dance because they were
causing too much disturbance. A short time later that evening several of the Seniors came to him and threatened to burn the church
down if he did not permit them to return to the dance. He warned
them not to carry out the threat, or they would suffer the consequences. The boys returned next day to apologize to the priest
because some of the adults in the neighborhood had put pressure
on them for making the threat.

The program director at the settlement house objected to the
attitudes of the Racketville delinquents:

There was one thing in particular that troubled her — the fact
that the Vultures thought they were so superior. . . . They felt superior to social workers and "oh, so many people!" . . . They felt
they owned the agency and that social workers were merely public
servants.

The only staff person with whom the Vultures appeared to
have a genuinely positive and affective relationship was the

registrar of the settlement, an older man who had been raised in the neighborhood and therefore completely identified with its criminal value system. Of this particular person, whose relationship with the rest of the staff was tenuous and not always compatible, another staff person commented:

"He is the most unusual person in the house — the only way he can possibly keep order among the kids is to be a racketeer himself. . . . If he were not in the rackets, the fellows wouldn't respect him as much as they do. His values are just like theirs."

Delinquents in Slumtown appeared to develop an entirely different type of relationship with agency staff. Threatening and aggressive behavior toward staff personnel occurred rarely. Instead, the primary difficulty and the basic source of concern to youth workers were the tension and problems which arose in the relationships of delinquent groups to each other. To repeat, relationships to the staff tended to be distant and uninvolved, although somewhat positive. The following is an account of the ejection of the Regals from a community center (located in a public school) of which they had been members for several months:

The youngsters were gathered into one room, and Mr. K., the district supervisor who had been called in especially for the purpose, addressed the group. He spoke eloquently of the efforts of the center to make a "go" of having the Regals in the program, but this had not been possible. He pointed out that other youngsters were no longer as orderly as they used to be — these youngsters cursed now and discipline was generally poor — because of the influence of the Regals. Mr. K. said that some of the Regals were themselves orderly, but it was their presence that seemed to affect the atmosphere of the center. Attendance, he said, had dropped off, and many of the parents were keeping their children home. There were complaints that gang fights starting in the streets were brought into the center. Mr. K. spoke of the previous week, when shots were fired by the Noble Lords as they chased the Regals into the center. The district supervisor's final words were that the community, especially the P.T.A., was putting pressure on the center to keep the Regals out. The Regals were now officially to leave the center and could return only after they had changed their behavior. None of the boys made a sound during the entire fifteen-minute talk.

When the speaker finished, Billy the Kid, the president of the group, said, "You going to pay back our fifty-cent membership?" There were snickers among the group, and this seemed to relieve the tension a little. Mr. K. gave the signal to Mr. H., the center director, to start refunding the money to the boys. On the way out Billy the Kid collected the refunded money from the boys to buy wine for the group.

The character of the relationships of the delinquents in Haulburg with community-center workers was essentially an ambivalent one. At times it could be highly positive and cooperative, particularly when needs and interests of the delinquents, as they saw and expressed them, were met. Use of agency facilities and services were often interpreted by staff as essentially manipulative:

"As long as they can make use of me," said an agency staff worker, "they like me; but even during the same meeting or activity, if they don't get exactly what they want, they turn hostile."

On occasion the delinquents from Haulburg could wreak havoc in the agency:

The boys resented the presence of the church worker. Two of them, G. and A., left the club room and set out "to explore" their surroundings. It was later discovered that they had urinated on various objects of the church — doors, pews, etc. They also had broken into the caretaker's apartment and insulted his wife. The caretaker, when informed of the boys' actions, came storming into the club room, threatening to use the baseball bat that he had in his hands. A. immediately accepted the caretaker's challenge and began to swing at him. The situation was finally brought under control by a street-club worker in attendance.

In the discussion which followed, the group reproached G. and A. for urinating in the church. G. and A. justified their action by stating that the minister had gotten them "pissed off," so they decided to "piss on the church." The street-club worker made the two boys apologize, and they said they didn't realize what they were doing and promised never to do such a thing again.

In summary, field data showed that delinquents in each of the areas had characteristic ways of relating to youth-serving programs. In Racketville delinquents developed antagonistic and unproductive relationships with the conventionally oriented staff. They severely abused youth workers or wanted to have nothing to do with them. In Slumtown delinquents appeared to establish tolerable but distant relationships with staff; however, due to the hazards of their gang-fighting behavior, they were often rejected by the staff. In Haulburg relationships with the staff were positive and co-operative when staff were perceived as meeting the delinquents' needs and interests or destructive when such conditions were not met.

Relationship with Street-Club Workers. — Street-club workers were ordinarily assigned to provide special intensive group work and recreational and counseling services to delinquents or "troublesome" youths who were not effectively utilizing existing social and community resources. Non-delinquents and drug addicts were not, in the main, currently served by street-club workers.

Delinquents from the three areas generally reported positive relationships with street-club workers. Of the various types of relationships with adults examined, only relationships with mothers and street-club workers elicited consistently positive responses from almost all delinquents. Those from Racketville reported the most positive involvement with the street-club workers.[3] Delinquents from Racketville and Haulburg appeared to develop the most co-operative relationships. Street-club workers were considered helpful in giving advice and guidance, providing material welfare and opportunities for jobs, and arranging camping trips and other recreational programs. Delinquents from Racketville placed the highest valuation on these services. Those from Haulburg set relatively the lowest value on them. There was evidence that delinquents from Slumtown developed the least substantive relationships with street-club workers, at least from the point of view of the time spent with them. Delinquents from Racketville appeared to be most intensely involved, judging by the amount of time they spent with the street-club workers.

[3] It was possible, however, to raise the question about contamination of data. The street-club worker himself did the formal interviews with the group of delinquents in Racketville. The data were not wholly consistent with the observational material.

A comparison of the data on relationships established with street-club workers and community-center workers revealed major differences. Delinquents appeared to be much more positive and co-operative in their contacts with street-club workers and considered them to be more genuinely helpful people. The difference seemed particularly marked in the relationships developed by delinquents from Racketville. In general, the differences were to be expected, since community-center programs were largely recreational in purpose and were directed to a cross-section of youths, most of whom were conforming, while street-club workers specialized in a highly personalized, intensive, problem-focused service to delinquents.

Field Data on Relationship with Street-club Workers. — The observational data only partially supported the interview material, especially with regard to the relationships of the delinquents from the racket subculture. Observations indicated that in this area only under certain circumstances were the relationships of delinquents with street-club workers positive. Much depended on the character of relationship developed by the worker. His approach to the delinquents had to be extremely warm and personal. The following were typical reactions:

"You don't know how much Dick has helped us guys when we were in trouble. He went to court for us. He visited our families. He tried in every way he could possibly think of to be good to us."

"You ask him [the street-club worker] for a favor. If he can do it, he does it. . . . The kids used to enjoy being with him."

On the other hand, the street-club worker would run into difficulty in the exercise of a legitimate authority function. The worker was required, when the occasion demanded, to call the police. Such contact with a law-enforcement agency made him instantly *persona non grata*. On one such occasion this is what happened, as reported by the street-club worker:

On the following day the group refused to talk to him and started to walk away whenever he came up to them. The worker stationed himself on the stoop across from the school yard. Most of the fellows began to wander over. Little Augie and Butchie seemed to be leading the opposition, saying that they couldn't have a worker around if he was going to continually squeal on them. The worker continued to sit on the stoop. The group then went back into the school yard. After about a half-hour they sent a girl on some pretext to get the worker into the school yard, and when he came they pelted him with eggs. The worker then said, "Now that it's out of your system, let's talk about it." This appeared to infuriate them even more, but the end effect was a long conversation, which at times became fiercely argumentative, about the worker's right to call the cops. One of the delinquents went and bought more eggs. The worker then said, "Well, there's no sense to this at all — I'm going home," and left the area for that day.

A worker with the Vultures decided to give up his job after a brief period rather than face their persistent aggression and hostility:

On one occasion the Vultures became so enraged at the way he refereed a basketball game that one of the Juniors walked over and kicked him in the groin. On other occasions the worker was beaten when members of the group accused him of being a "stool pigeon." Appointments for special trips and events arranged for the group were rarely kept. There was a constant, violent "ranking" of the worker because he was regarded as a representative of an agency that kept records on the delinquents' behavior and communicated with the police department.

The relationship of delinquents with street-club workers in the conflict subculture was both similar and dissimilar to that in the neighborhood of the racket subculture. Youths tended to like their street-club workers and often utilized the help that was provided. One of them expressed himself as follows:

"I say that Youth Board is pretty good. Some guys just can't be helped. But as far as Youth Board is concerned, I think they do a pretty good job. . . . They help you a lot — in jobs, with your problems. If you have a problem you sit down with a worker and talk about it. . . . Most of the workers are very good guys . . . easy to get along with. Maybe some of the guys in the club don't care for Youth Board somehow or other. They say they are like cops, and they run to the cops and tell them everything. Well, to me it was different. I think they're strictly out to help us."

The crucial difference in the relationships established by

the delinquents in Slumtown appeared to lie in the lack of outrage and violent reaction to the street worker's contact with the police:

Billy the Kid said that Parker was a nice guy, but a lot of the fellows didn't like him because he sent some of them to jail. Parker said he was helping them, and maybe some of the guys thought so, too, but jail is jail. . . . Billy said he wouldn't trust Parker . . . he wouldn't trust any of the Youth Board workers. But this didn't mean he didn't get along with Parker.

Actually, there was evidence that gang members in Slumtown actively invited the intervention of street-club workers in the preservation of law and order:

During one afternoon several youngsters appeared at the door of the lounge and wanted to speak with the street-club worker. They were members of a group called the Corsair Lords, a forever "bopping" club. They were upset because the street-club worker had not been around when Cowboy was killed. They shouted through the doors, "Where are your God-damn social workers?"

A major complaint of delinquents in the conflict subculture was that the resources provided by the street-club workers were highly inadequate:

Once, on leaving the agency office, one of the delinquents expressed dissatisfaction with the street-club worker because he wasn't taking the group on any trips or developing enough programs for them. He said that the street-club worker was around when they got into trouble — when they were fighting — but when there was anything they needed he was not around.

Husky Louie said that Jim, the street-club worker, wasn't around enough. Monte nodded his head. Dillinger also agreed.

In the theft subculture delinquents appeared to develop a somewhat less intense relationship with street-club workers than did those delinquents from the other areas. Perhaps this was due to the relatively larger caseloads which workers in this neighborhood carried. The kind of relationships developed by the delinquents from Haulburg with street-club workers closely resembled the character of involvement generally established by them with community-center workers. The street-club worker in Haulburg often was regarded as the recreational specialist who could assist groups and their memberships to participate in new and exciting experiences. He was seen as someone who, because he could involve youths in recreational programs, was thereby able to keep them out of trouble:

Joe said that the worker did a lot for the fellows. He was really able to keep them out of trouble by taking them on camping trips. This didn't mean they didn't get into trouble at the state parks where they went — they were kicked out of almost all of them. Once they were arrested for breaking into a summer cottage. Joe felt, however, that if they had remained in the city on those weekends, they would have gotten into even more trouble. He said the fellows would always remember the wild times they had had on the trips.

Those street-club workers who, on occasion, were not sensitive to the interests and needs of the delinquents would be subjected to abuse, threats of violence, and ostracism. Considerable strain could set in:

The supervisor of the street-club unit told the researcher that he did not know what to do with one of his workers and feared that he would have to get rid of him. This worker just did not understand the kids. He had almost gotten into a fight with one of the members, who had threatened to beat him up. The worker was very frightened and was planning to retaliate next time he saw the youth who had threatened him. He told the supervisor that he was going to carry a gun in self-defense should any attack be made on him in the course of his contacts with the youngsters on the street.

In general, street-club workers and delinquents were able to establish satisfactory relationships with each other. The delinquents appeared to want street-club workers to help with personal and court problems and to provide job referals and opportunities for new social and recreational experiences. Major problems in these relationships, depending on the type of neighborhood, tended to arise in situations where the worker set legitimate authoritative limits, where he did not make adequate social opportunities available, or where he lacked sufficient understanding and skill to assist these youngsters in a manner acceptable to them.

Relationship with the Police. — Delinquents from each of the areas disliked policemen and perceived policemen as disliking them. There was some evidence, however, that delinquents from Racketville were not so intense in their dislike of the police; whereas delinquents from Slumtown reported the most negative relationship with policemen. In the main, all the delinquents reported they did not co-operate with policemen and that policemen were not helpful to them. Again, there was evidence that delinquents from Racketville were able to get along with the police somewhat better and perceived them as slightly more helpful than did delinquents from the other areas.

Field Data. — Field observation tended to substantiate the findings of the formal interviews and further helped to emphasize the characteristic subcultural differences. Delinquents in Racketville appeared to be neither fearful of the police nor concerned with possible harassment by them, and the police appeared to leave these youngsters alone in their hangouts. On occasion, when a police officer exerted his legitimate authority, delinquents from this subculture responded in a cocksure and brazen fashion, secure in the fact that their parents and relatives (racketeers) would control and blunt the effectiveness of the officer in performing his duty:

Little Augie and Louie were in the school yard, drinking beer, cursing, and making a great deal of noise. A policeman came in after them. The researcher and some of the gang members were waiting on the street corner nearby to see what would happen. Soon the boys came out of the school yard and came over. Little Augie said the cop was a nice guy and had just come in because they were making too much noise. Louie, slightly drunk, said in a loud voice and with much gesticulation, "As soon as the cop came in, I told him to take me to my uncle." Louie added that he wouldn't let the cop take him to the precinct and had threatened to get his uncle after him, but that the cop had turned out to be nice. He said he knew that they had been drinking and said if they'd be a little quieter he wouldn't bother them. Before leaving the policeman gave them cigarettes, Louie said.

Delinquents from Racketville disliked the police but managed to get along with them. The fact that the group could say of several policemen, "They're good cops; they never bother us," was not an expression of friendship or respect for them but, rather, of condescension, especially if they were "cops who took taps," or bribes. The way to assure a minimum of clashes between delinquents and the police was the payoff:

Sandy felt it necessary to bring the researcher up to date on developments leading up to the arrests of that Monday night: He phoned the street-club worker to report that Tommy C. was being held for possession of a forged draft card and that Mikey had also been brought to the precinct and questioned about the draft cards (a racket they had devised). However, Sandy's older brother, Sal, came to the police station. The result was that Sandy and Mikey were let off. Sandy said that his family had been tipped off that the FBI was going to be called in on the case. He and Mikey had decided to pull out of the situation completely. The charge against them had been manufacturing and selling phony draft cards.

The police in Slumtown were, without question, least restrained with delinquents. They constantly harassed members of gangs and, indeed, others in the area:

Frenchie urged the worker to take the fellows for a ride or at least to keep moving — the police were forcing them off the streets. He said that yesterday he was stopped twice by the police, and each time he was "hit." The researcher asked why, and Frenchie said, "for being around." (The researcher noted to himself that on the previous Saturday a group of five Regals had been forced by a policeman to leave a street corner in broad daylight. The group had been conversing quietly.) Dillinger said this was so — the police were constantly picking on them.

Cheyenne, an older ex-member of the Regals, came over. He was highly agitated and was staggering, yelling, and screaming "Come on, Irv [addressing the researcher], we'll go out to the cop." He complained bitterly that he had merely been walking along the avenue when some cop came over and told him to be quiet. When Cheyenne began to talk to the cop, the cop took the end of his billy and shoved it into Cheyenne's stomach. After describing this encounter with the law, the youth again began to scream at the top of his lungs. He insisted that the researcher come along with him to the policeman because the researcher had "the authority." The researcher suggested that Cheyenne take it easy and that he didn't think he could accomplish very much anyway. Cheyenne quieted down.

The absence of a *modus vivendi* between the police and the residents in Slumtown made the operation of various illegitimate and semilegitimate enterprises difficult and dangerous. The police, for example, continually beleaguered young adults in the area, many of them former members of the Regals who were now engaged in petty racket activities:

The researcher ran into Johnny, a twenty-three-year-old Regal who was operating a street game — a game in which about fifteen adults and young adults placed bets on the numbers *1* to *6* and three dice were thrown. While the game was in process, Johnny reported, the detectives had come around and made them stop playing, but they had refused to pay off. Johnny said the payoff asked was too high — the cops wanted from five to ten dollars each. For two or three dollars each, it would have been okay, Johnny said.

About half an hour later, a squad car and a detective's car pulled up. The game was broken up, and eight of the players were hauled off to the precinct. Johnny later informed the researcher that the fines which they had had to pay were only two or three dollars, and he pointed out that it was cheaper that way.

The delinquents from Haulburg verbalized considerable hostility toward the police, yet believed the police were useful under certain conditions:

"Let's put it this way — Sam, Karl, and me are on a burglary, and a cop will pick us up that we know. And nobody seen him pick us up. In other words, he was clear — he could let us go; he might take a payoff. He probably would take a payoff. Might even take half the burglary money, split down the middle or something. But like there was somebody there, like somebody reported a burglary and seen him go in and grab us. He would have to, you know, arrest us, even though he would probably take some money, you know, to put in a good word for us at court and everything. Maybe say he caught us outside the place, and he didn't see us in there and everything."

They also reported that occasionally the police gave them leads on good "jobs" which they could pull:

Ted said that sometimes the cops were involved; they would often tell some of the kids that they would be going off duty at a certain hour and encourage them to go ahead and do what they wanted to do in certain shops. There would be a payoff later, of course.

Regardless of neighborhood, delinquents had no love for the police and generally wanted to have as little to do with them as possible. While delinquents from Racketville and, to a lesser extent, from Haulburg had developed channels of communication and ways of getting along with the police — mainly through bribery or payoffs — delinquents from Slumtown had not as yet found effective ways of getting along with the police. No basis for tolerance of their behavior or for preferred treatment had apparently been worked out.

RELATIONSHIP WITH NEIGHBORHOOD ADULTS

Delinquent youths spent a great deal of time on the streets and in neighborhood shops. This led to contact with a variety of neighborhood adults. The local grocer, the candy-store or luncheonette proprietor, the worker on his way to the factory or his office, and many others were known to them. Contacts were also established with a variety of adults engaged in illegitimate and quasi-legitimate occupations who seemed just to "hang around" the neighborhood.

In the main, delinquents, non-delinquents, and drug addicts had relatively friendly relationships with the people of the neighborhood. The character of involvement with such adults, however, varied on a subcultural basis: delinquents from Racketville developed the most positive and co-operative of relationships with neighborhood adults; delinquents from Slumtown developed the least positive and co-operative relationships with these adults. Again, delinquents from Haulburg tended to place between the delinquents from Racketville and those from Slumtown in their feelings about, and their degree of co-operation with, neighborhood adults.

The interview and observational evidence (see, especially, chap. i) consistently showed that delinquents from Racketville were highly integrated with neighborhood adults and that delinquents from Slumtown were poorly integrated with them. In Haulburg such integration was intermediate.

RELATIONSHIP WITH RACKETEERS

Each subject was asked to identify the type of illegal enterprise in which the racketeer whom he knew best was engaged. The subject was also requested to rank the racketeer in order of importance or prestige. In Racketville all subjects — delinquents, non-delinquents, and drug addicts — tended to speak of "big-time" or Syndicate racketeers engaged in multiple criminal enterprises; Slumtown subjects appeared to be familiar with "small-time" and some in-between-status racketeers, mainly numbers-runners and local bankers; in Haulburg, subjects were acquainted mainly with numbers men and bookmakers ranging from "small-time" to "big-time operators." As indicated earlier, the difference between the status of racketeers known to subjects in Racketville and in Slumtown was especially marked (see Table 17). It was interesting also to observe that subjects from Racketville did not select narcotics-peddlers or dealers for any identification, although there was evidence of the presence of "big-time" drug-peddlers in the neighborhood. The prestige of narcotics-peddlers was extremely low, and the sale of drugs to youths of the area was strictly proscribed.

The data was not complete for all subjects, yet it was clear that delinquents from Racketville had the most positive and co-operative involvement with racketeers, that those from Slumtown had the least positive and co-operative relation with them, and that the character of the involvement with racketeers was intermediate among Haulburg delinquents.

RELATIONSHIP WITH ADULT THIEVES AND FENCES

Comparative data were not available on the relationships of subjects from all of the subcultures with adult thieves. Findings were available, however, from a second series of interviews with a group of twenty-five delinquents from Haulburg. Of the twenty-five subjects questioned, twenty-two were willing to discuss their relationships with adult thieves. Each of the twenty-two subjects was asked to select and comment on a single adult thief. Of the twenty-two adult criminals discussed, fifteen were described as burglars; three were shoplifters; three were stickup men; and one was described as a fence. In regard to the status of these adult criminals, four were categorized as "big-time" operators; fifteen were viewed as "small-time" criminals; and three were identified as of intermediate status. The Haulburg delinquents regarded their relationships with such criminal adults as positive, although not so intensely positive as the relationships described by Racketville delinquents with racketeers. They indicated merely that they got along well with adult thieves. In general, there was evidence that delinquents in Haulburg knew relatively more adult thieves and appeared to have developed somewhat more positive and accommodative relationships with them than they did with racketeers.

SUMMARY

The major proposition underlying the discussion in this chapter was that adults did influence, *directly and indirectly*, the patterns of behavior and orientation of delinquent adolescents. The data indicated that the delinquent group within a subculture was not a social system necessarily closed off from the adult world. Delinquents did appear to establish one kind of relationship or another with a variety of adults.

Adults were considered functionally to be the controllers or the providers of access to social means for desired status. It was evident from the data that delinquents in the racket subculture had the greatest access to means controlled by adults. Generally they had close and effective ties with the representatives of the organized criminal world and maintained differentially negative relationships with adults who symbolized conventional and legitimate orientations. A major exception appeared to be the relatively positive relationships which Racketville delinquents developed with street-club workers. Delinquents from Slumtown appeared to have least access to means provided through adult relationships; they were relatively isolated from both conventional and criminal systems. Delinquents in Haulburg had some access to conventional and

criminal means controlled by adults, yet they were unexpectedly negative and unproductive in their relationships with
parents; they perceived adults generally as less helpful than
did delinquents from other areas. The data examined gave rise
to speculation about the possible presence of a psychological
variable which produced disturbed interpersonal functioning
and furthered the development of a delinquent adaptation in
the theft subculture.

CHAPTER VI

ADAPTATIONS IN YOUNG ADULTHOOD

Delinquent orientations established in adolescence are not immutable in postadolescence or young adulthood. No inherent or acquired pattern of social behavior developed during any one stage of the human life cycle inexorably carries over to the next. The delinquent of today is the socialized adult, the drug addict, the petty criminal, the professional thief, the racketeer, or any one of a range of social types of tomorrow. Much, but not all, depends on the nature of the socio-cultural context in which the individual and his group find themselves.

The end of adolescence confronts the lower-class youth in our society with new rights and responsibilities, new opportunities for significant status, and new powerful legal and normative restraints on his behavior. Marriage and employment, in particular, compel the patterns of orientation and behavior previously developed during the stage of adolescent delinquency to change. Great pressure is now exerted on the young adult to conform to conventional norms. Whether the proportion of delinquents who negotiate the shift from illegitimate to legitimate orientation is greater in one type of lower-class area than another is not yet known. Logically, it would be expected that the largest proportion of delinquents developing adult criminal careers would be found in the racket subculture, where norms and means conducive to the adult criminal orientation are, respectively, strongest and most amply provided. Perhaps the smallest proportion of delinquents who continue on to criminal careers would be found in the theft subculture, where middle-class conventional norms are relatively most securely established and where at least partial means exist to facilitate the conventional adult adaptation. Nevertheless, there are indications that in each area a significantly large number of youths who have been members of delinquent groups move on to conventional adult adjustments.

It ought not to be assumed, however, that the stage of young adulthood and the provision of some additional opportunities automatically signal the end of modes of behavior and orientation learned earlier. The patterns developed by adolescents under conditions of limited conventional opportunity, while functional for performance in the delinquent subculture, may be *dysfunctional* for performance in the role of conventional young adult. For example, gang fighting or burglary does not prepare the adolescent for a conventional career. The lack of adequate formal education and the limited skills in conventional interpersonal relations of the delinquent youth subsequently handicap him as a young adult in attaining and developing significant occupation status. Only relatively low-status conventional careers are ordinarily accessible to him.

THE CONVENTIONAL ADAPTATION

Field observations indicated that at a certain point in late adolescence the delinquent suddenly became aware that he was through with his teen-age status and was becoming a man. He stated with greater frequency that he "didn't want to get into any more trouble." He was going steady or engaged to be married, and he "couldn't be fooling around much longer." He would say "This is my last year for bopping . . . after next summer I quit." He became aware that fighting and brawling led "nowhere." More and more he would think and talk about his needs "to make a dollar" the best way, the right way, or perhaps the easiest way he knew how.

The conventional adaptation took place if at least four major socioeconomic and sociopsychological conditions were present: the availability of at least partial opportunities for fulfilling conventional adult status, the increased cultural pressure to attain conventional adult status, the appearance of a new set of motivations, and the development of a system of personal controls to secure the conventional way of life. The data derived from the research did not permit easy assessment of the variations in cultural pressures, motivations, or personal control systems characteristic of the postadolescent in each of the areas. It was somewhat less difficult to evaluate the conventional means which were newly accessible. These four conditions, however, were interrelated variables and therefore difficult to separate from one another in reality.

In the racket subculture, conventional means were available to older delinquent youths. Parents, relatives, and neighbors were often in a position to assist the young adult to make a start at a reasonably good job:

Sammy said that when he quit high school he started working in his father's printing shop — first part time, then full time. At first he didn't like it, but he had no complaints now. His father helped him out. He was on salary — making a pretty good living. He hoped to expand the business or maybe take it over some day. If he got into the printer's union there wouldn't be any problem; he would be making at least $120 a week.

Sammy said he still had trouble getting used to things. The other day a wholesaler called up and got "snotty," which made Sammy sore, and he threatened to come over and kill the guy. Sammy ran out of the store, jumped into the car, and was about to go over to the other fellow's place when he suddenly stopped and realized what he was doing.

Sammy had criminal as well as conventional means available to him. He told the researcher:

"There are a great many ways of getting into trouble in the neighborhood. . . . You don't know the temptations around here. It's hard for a guy to go straight. It would be the easiest thing in the world to make $60 or $70 extra a week for just an hour of night work — say taking numbers." Sammy added that he would have been in trouble many times if it hadn't been for the fact that he loved his family, particularly his father.

The older youth in Slumtown had limited means for acquiring sufficient background and skill to get started in a decent job, even after he had made the decision to abandon his career as a delinquent:

Indio said that life was better for him now. "Bopping" was not worthwhile. It only got him into trouble. He had definitely learned his lesson at ――― Prison. He learned how to be neat and clean and how to be nice. He went to the auto shop regularly and learned how to take a car apart. He hoped some day to get a job as a mechanic, but he had been looking for a job for a month, without success. He didn't want to push a hand truck in the garment district again.

On the other hand, it was hardly worthwhile to take the risks involved in making a few dollars by illegitimate means:

Indio said that he knew a lot of people on the street and could "connect up" for a few dollars here or there, but the money he would make would not be enough. He didn't want to take the chance of going back to jail. Besides, he had developed a new reputation. People looked up to him and said he was a nice guy. Now they invited him to the bar to have a drink. Before, when he was "gang busting" and doing bad things, they avoided him.

The older delinquent from Haulburg, as in Racketville, could look forward to assistance from relatives and neighborhood adults in locating fairly good legitimate jobs:

The boys discussed Frank, who now lived out of the neighborhood. He was married (he had been forced into it) and had a child and another one on the way. Although he was only nineteen years old, the fellows considered him a success. His father, who had connections in the tugboat union, was able to get him a job. Frank was now making close to $150 a week. He had started to study for the pilot's exam. The last time he came around, he told the boys he was buying a brand new red Mercury convertible.

Not all older youths who had been members of delinquent groups in the theft subculture had such impressive connections. More often the process of adjustment to conventional young-adult status involved acceptance of a not-so-good job. The older youths came to realize that the "slow and hard honest dollar" might go farther than the "fast and easy dollar" dishonestly made. Nevertheless, temptations and pressures to engage in criminal activity continued to be present and had to be warded off:

Larry, age twenty years, said that he was now working in a factory and making $65 a week. His take-home pay was about $56. He said that he had been working for a year. He liked his work but wished he could get better wages. Still, he was saving more than he ever had before. He planned to get married next spring.

He said he used to make a lot of money in burglaries, including one in which he broke into a safe in a warehouse and got $500. He spoke of his last court case. The charge was mugging a doctor. Before that he was up for stealing a car. He was on probation for the assault charge, but the car-theft case was still pending. He believed his delinquent career was over. He had decided that it just wasn't worthwhile, particularly when he was sitting in jail and nobody came to see him.

Larry mentioned that late one night a few months ago he met Tommy, who had been a member of the same street group. Tommy wanted him to stand lookout while he climbed a building — Tommy was one of the best cat burglars around. Larry refused and found out later that Tommy had made about $300 on that "score" but was picked up for something else a few days later and was now in ———— Prison on a three- to five-year sentence.

In each of the three types of neighborhoods many former delinquents were developing a new set of motivations for attaining conventional status. The significant development of conventional norms and controls occurred during the post-adolescent or transitional phase. Substantial gains, both tangible and intangible, accrued to those young adults who were successful in making the shift to conventional roles. Increasingly, heavy penalties were meted out to those who persisted in their criminal endeavors. To what extent the multiple conditions facilitating the conventional adjustment for the post-adolescent varied in the different types of areas remained unknown. Certainly, better conventional opportunities (but also better illegitimate ones) were present in the racket and theft subcultures than in the conflict subculture.

NEAR–HIPSTERISM

One variant of the conventional adaptation was the "beatnik" or "hipster" adjustment. It was a marginal adjustment, not characterized by strong commitment to an unconventional or, for that matter, to a conventional value orientation. The young-adult ex-delinquent of this type was either unemployed or worked sporadically or part time. He had some interest in jazz and in "beat" literature. He smoked an occasional marijuana cigarette. There was a strong orientation to sensual experience or "having a good time" in a rather "cool," or unemotional, way. The adaptation to hipsterism or, rather, to near-hipsterism (since the former delinquent was merely on the fringe of the hipster subculture) occurred most frequently in the conflict and the theft subcultures:

The researcher stopped to speak with three of the boys. Bobby, age twenty, said he had recently begun to work as a steam fitter, but since his union was now on strike, he was again unemployed. He was carrying a book under his arm. It was *A History of Zen*. Bobby said that he liked the book and that he was also reading stuff by Huxley, Kerouac, and Mailer. The boys said they were on the way to a "beat" party on the West Side.

Jackie spoke of his smoking marijuana. He preferred it to heroin and used marijuana mainly at jazz parties, which he liked very much. Jackie said that he played conga drums and trumpet. He was the only member of the group to complete high school and had even attended City College for one term in the evening.

Bobby and Patty spoke of the "crazy" drunken party they had gone to the other night. "Beat" poetry — or homosexual poetry as they regarded it — was read. There were lesbians and "fags," and everybody was trying to "make out" with everybody else. Patty laughed as he described a scene at the party — a girl trying to "make out" with another girl.

These former delinquents did not seem to have a serious commitment to a "beat" or bohemian orientation. Such young adults were essentially on the fringe of "beat" society. They identified with these groups only temporarily, until more substantial access to conventional roles became available.

Finally, in a limited sense, it is possible to classify the drug-using adaptation as a variant of a conventional adjustment. To the extent that the drug-user or addict has separated himself from the delinquent subculture, avoids a commitment to the criminal adaptation, and adopts conventional practices, norsm, and values, a quasi-conventional role may be attributed to him. There need not be, after all, a necessary connection between drug-use and criminality, particularly if the acquisition of drugs is made legal.

CRIMINAL ADAPTATIONS

It is obvious that various types of criminal roles were not equally distributed in the different kinds of lower-class neighborhoods. Top-flight criminal positions were not accessible to postdelinquents, even in Racketville, because of the immaturity and lack of experience of these young-adult aspirants. Yet, access to lower-level criminal careers did appear to vary by neighborhood. The most lucrative beginning-racket-career opportunities — connected with illegal gambling, policy, off-track betting, loan-shark operations, protection, prostitution, narcotics-sale, and certain types of union organizations — were, of course, mainly available in Racketville. Good opportunities for the development of careers as professional thieves were obviously available in Haulburg. Only minimal opportunities for successful criminal careers as racketeers and thieves were present in Slumtown.

THE YOUNG RACKETEER

Delinquents in Racketville generally aspired to the career of a racketeer. It was apparent, on the basis of prospective and retrospective accounts, that at least some members of delinquent groups in this area would and did realize their criminal ambitions. That many a mature racketeer had at an early stage been a member of a delinquent group was generally accepted in the racket subculture:

In response to the researcher's question as to what the fellows (age twenty-five to thirty years) who were now in the rackets had been doing ten years ago, Big Freddie said that most of them had been in delinquent groups, that maybe a few of them had been in social clubs, a few on the fringes of clubs, but most had been in the delinquent groups.

The director of teen-age activities in the settlement house emphasized that it was the delinquent youngsters from a group in the racket subculture who had been around a long time, like the Vultures, who had the best chance for making it in the rackets:

He said that the youngster gets a reputation in the neighborhood as a tough kid, a member of a tough gang. He gets known that way, makes his connections. He doesn't move in right away, at first he feels his way around . . .

Yet some reservations were expressed. In a highly integrated neighborhood, even members of non-delinquent groups had fairly good opportunities to develop racket careers, particularly if relatives provided ready access to a criminal organization:

Ralphy, a narcotics addict and "pusher," felt that most of the future racketeers were going to come from a group like the Leopards, rather than from the Vultures or Warriors. He said that the Leopards didn't "take crap" from anybody. They had tremendous respect in the neighborhood and knew how to control themselves. They were the kind of guys who could take orders from people and could be respectful; yet they were tough.

Ralphy thought some more and concluded that he wasn't really sure. What he was certain of was that the racketeers were highly involved in the whole neighborhood. Almost everyone had a cousin, or an uncle, or distant relative in the rackets, and it wasn't hard to make a connection.

The researcher spoke with a street-club worker who had been raised in Racketville but had not returned there after military service. Repeatedly this street-club worker expressed amazement and puzzlement as to how the seemingly wild, undisciplined, tough delinquent youngster could grow up to be the often very servile and extremely well-disciplined apprentice or hireling of the mature racketeer. It was possible that aggressive and delinquent behavior was not so purposeless and that such behavior served to call the young delinquent to the attention of the older racketeer, although this particular purpose of the aberrant behavior was not usually verbalized.[1]

[1] See the discussion of the concept of "over-conformity by individuals to the norms of groups to which they aspire but do not belong. Richard A. Cloward and Lloyd E. Ohlin, *Delinquency and Opportunity* (Glencoe, Ill.: Free Press, 1960) pp. 166–71.

Big Freddie said that you never could find out who wanted to be a racketeer and who didn't. It was the kind of thing you felt. In other words, if someone went around being tough and acting like he wanted to be a "big shot," this was the kind of guy who might get into the rackets. Or, if a guy made a deliberate effort to contact and do favors for the racketeers — this was a guy who wanted in. Now a kid in a club would never say that he wanted to be in the rackets, that he was training to be a racketeer. If he did the other guys would laugh him out.

While there was some question as to whether the larger proportion of up-and-coming young racketeers in Racketville were formerly members of delinquent groups or members of social clubs, there was little question that in Slumtown nearly all of the young-adult racketeers — mainly petty racketeers — had previously been members of delinquent groups.

A street-club worker who himself had been, for several years, a gambler in a neighborhood containing a conflict subculture said that every small-time racketeer that he knew had been a "bopper" or connected with kind of "bopping" gang when he was younger. He had to have this as a basis for moving in. He had to make his connections. He had to learn "what the score was" from his early days, and the best place to learn was in a "bopping" gang.

The following is an excerpt from a recorded interview in which a young man, now twenty-three, who formerly had been president of a fighting club, reported his brief and relatively unsuccessful attempt to establish himself as a successful young racketeer. Somewhat better than average criminal opportunities were probably available to him by virtue of the fact that he resided in, and his group was located in, an area immediately contiguous to one containing a racket subculture:

RESEARCHER: You mentioned that you were involved in some of this. You made, apparently, quite a bit of money?

MANNY: Yeah.

RESEARCHER: How did you get involved? How did you begin?

MANNY: Well, I always had a lot of chances to get involved in . . . any kind of rackets . . . because I knew a lot of guys.

RESEARCHER: What made you know so many guys?

MANNY: Well, I guess just being involved in the club. I knew quite a few guys in the neighborhood. I knew guys that were in the numbers rackets and drugs and what not.

RESEARCHER: How did being involved in the club help you know all this?

MANNY: Well, I guess you just know, that's all. You're always running around, and you see everything. You see things that a lot of other people don't. For instance, if your club is fighting you always got your eyes open, always watching out for somebody, a guy behind you. You always turn around, and anybody's passing something, you find out that guy's passing a bet. . . . You see him a few times; you get to know the guy. Now the guy knows you; he knows you're a club leader. You're a good guy. You're a stand-up guy. You say, "Look, I'd like to make a few dollars. You know of anything I can do?" The guy might turn around, and if you know him well enough he'll say, "Well, look, I'm doing business. If you're interested . . ." So from there it starts.

RESEARCHER: Is that pretty much how it worked with you?

MANNY: With me? We were fighting an Italian club; we were shooting back and forth in the Italian neighborhood, and a lot of racketeers were very disturbed about it because there were cops around most of the time. So they had some Spanish guys who were working in the neighborhood, collecting numbers, call us together; and they told us that the racketeers were getting very disturbed. They were getting very angry. Naturally, as a kid, you know a racketeer to you is something great. So it's something you respect. You hear a lot of stories, and you're afraid, and all that crap. So they called us together, and we had a meeting. They told us they wanted it stopped, and naturally we respected them. And we stopped. From there I knew that this guy [the Spanish numbers man] was doing something with him [the Italian racketeer]. At first I wasn't too interested in getting in any of the rackets. I was very much with the club, you know. But then a couple of years later I was waiting in a place, and some guy was telling me there was so much money involved in drugs. He kept asking me if I knew anybody. So I started thinking. I remembered the Spanish guy and the other guy [in the Italian neighborhood]. From there I got right into it. And we hooked a pretty big business out of it. Something like $1,800 a week. And we got something like five guys working together, and we used to split somewhere from $300 a week to $400. But most of the money we used to blow it. Then I quit. A couple of weeks later I was broke so I went back in. A week later I was caught . . . that was the end of it.

Whereas ex-delinquents in Racketville tended to move into safe jobs, at fairly good base wages or commissions in the large well-organized rackets; the ex-delinquents in Slumtown held relatively low-paying jobs, often in riskier, less well-established criminal operations.

Papo said that Chicky, a former vice president of the Regals, was involved in a protection racket. Chicky had some of the former members of the club working for him. They would do certain kinds of jobs. For instance, a local bookie would come to him and say that someone else was trying to horn in on his territory or that one of his customers was complaining about being shortchanged in his winnings and making a big fuss about it. Chicky would get one or two guys, and they would go down and pay a visit to the numbers man who was horning in or, for that matter, to the complaining customer and either threaten to beat up these people or actually do it, depending on what was called for. Things would be okay after the visit.

Even when seemingly equivalent kinds of illegal or quasi-legal jobs were performed, former delinquents from the racket subculture received better financial returns than did former delinquents from the conflict subculture. For instance, youths who were former leaders of gangs, in both areas, were employed on occasion as union-organizers, performing basically similar tasks. The rewards for the former delinquents from Racketville were greater, however:

On his last job Franky was working as a union organizer. He claimed that with the money he made, which was $75 a day, he was able to buy a new car.

The former president of a gang from Slumtown made considerably less money as a union-organizer; he worked half of a week for the amount Franky earned in one day:

When Louie got out of jail, he was offered a job as a union-organizer at one of the farms run by a large city-wide grocery chain. The farm employed a great many migrant laborers from Puerto Rico. Louie brought along two of his friends from the club. His job was to make sure that the migrant laborers joined the union. He made $150 a week. He had this job for several weeks but gave it up because his wife complained he wasn't home often enough.

A former president of the Vultures in Racketville, now engaged part time in a juke-box racket and also part time in selling drugs, boasted to a street-club worker:

"Dick, I just got back from Florida. I spent $1,300 in one week. I flew to Cuba and then back to New York — $1,300, Dick"

But a former president of the Noble Lords in Slumtown was described as having a much more modest income:

He was working in some sort of plastics factory, making about enough money to live on, but not comfortably. On the side he received stolen goods — mainly clothes — and sold them to a fence he knew. The take was probably no more than $30 or $40 a week.

QUALIFYING FOR THE RACKETS

The older adolescent who wanted to move into the rackets had to possess certain characteristics for proper functioning in a racket organization. Four significant qualifications which had to be demonstrated were "brains," "heart," "connections," and "trust."

"Brains" were absolutely essential for entry into the rackets and for moving ahead:

Big Freddy said the racketeers weren't tough the way they used to be years ago. They didn't put on the air of being tough hoods. They now could get a lot of things done quietly, by being respectable, by being in business. Racketeering was a business, and you had to have brains to make out. There wasn't much killing going on. In fact, the racketeer often didn't want some tough, loud-mouth hoodlum in an important spot. He wanted someone who was quiet, who could talk clearly and carefully.

In the conflict subculture, brains were also a necessary qualification for a position in the racket organization. Whether or not the aspirant actually achieved his goal, he knew that appropriate use of intelligence was an essential requirement for success:

The researcher asked Billy the Kid, president of the Regals, if anybody in the club was thinking about getting into the rackets. Billy said that he didn't think so. He said they didn't use their brains. The important thing was to use your head to get someone else to do your work for you. Billy said he had been thinking of this for a long time.

A former president of a gang in Slumtown who was now a successful, small-time numbers man bemoaned the sad state of affairs among the current generation of gang youths:

"These kids don't know what they're bopping for. Things are worse than they used to be. The kids don't finish school and don't get their education. You have to read and write to get ahead. You got to know how to count to be a numbers man. Not all the kids could do that, today."

At one point, the researcher remarked to a key young-adult informant in Racketville that if brains were so essential, then the college-trained young man would be admirably qualified for admission to the racket organization:

Big Freddy said this was definitely not so. The kids from the neighborhood who went to college were really outsiders. These fellows began going around with other college guys and became different. The guys who went into the rackets were from street clubs (delinquent groups) in the neighborhood. None of them went to college, although most of them had some high-school education.

"Toughness" was another essential attribute qualifying the former gang member for a racket career. The street-club worker who had been brought up in the neighborhood containing the racket subculture explained:

"The youngster has to be afraid of nothing. He has to have little or no respect for the law. He has to be able to protect himself and to engage in a good street fight. He has to come to the attention of the racketeer by being the toughest, roughest kid in the neighborhood and by having a sort of defiance of the law. However, toughness alone was not enough to make a go of it in the rackets. If he was only tough, he stayed in the lowest ranks, maybe as a bodyguard."

"Heart," the superordinate characteristic of the "bopper," epitomized the quality of toughness desired and, to the extent that he possessed it, partially qualified the delinquent for entry into the rackets.

The *ideal* condition qualifying the former gang member for

a position in a criminal organization was, however, to have a father or a close relative already established in some illegitimate enterprise. But, such a connection, even in the racket subculture, was not always present. Nevertheless, it could be developed or earned:

> Big Freddy said that some of the boys did a lot of "brown nosing" just to get into the rackets. These people were called "Lobos." They did not have much respect in the neighborhood. They were not the real old timers — the tough racketeers. It was a matter of doing favors for people, sticking around until you got your break and your connection.

Occasionally, in Racketville, a non-indigenous or non-Italian youth who had been accepted into the delinquent group faced the problem of lack of connections on leaving it and therefore the inability to gain access to the racket structure:

> Polack said he wasn't working or going to school. He didn't know what he would be doing. When he said that he would like to be a bookie, Vince, a fellow gang member, laughed, and Polack shamefacedly admitted that he didn't have any connections.

In Slumtown the importance of connections was equally recognized. In this subculture connections were commonly not available through family ties but could sometimes be earned:

> Larry explained that if he were going to become a bookie, he would start hanging around a fellow who was already established. He would get to know him well, doing favors for him. He would, first of all, have to come with a good reputation — he would be somebody who didn't "talk." If the bookie liked him, he might get part of his territory. The guy who was eager to get in might even come with a proposition — telling the bookie, "Oh, I know a lot of people in the so-and-so block. I have a good contact with them. I can take their numbers. Would you let me come in with you?"

There was also a set of attributes which the aspiring former delinquent had to possess which could be included under the rubric of "trust." This was a complex trait that was important and widely cultivated in Racketville. The aspirant would have to demonstrate to the racketeers that he could be trusted to do as he was told and thus protect their interests:

George said it was a matter of being asked to do something like delivering a package, and if you did that right and didn't ask questions, then you would be asked to do other things. If you were caught and you didn't "rat," you'd surely be in.

A street-club worker described how the leader of a club, now on the verge of dissolving because its members were getting older, was qualifying himself for the rackets:

He now works for his uncle on the side and gets a sizable commission for this. He makes collections (number receipts) in his uncle's Cadillac. He feels that he "has it made" because he'll move up in the organization when he's older. This is the best thing that could happen, he feels, because he'll not have to be a flunky. He also feels he must work hard and remain loyal to the uncle for his "break."

The uncle mentioned in the above situation was one of the "big guns" in the city and had attended a notorious national convention of racketeers held several years earlier.

In Slumtown the idea of trust was not as well developed. Nevertheless it implied, at least, "keeping your mouth shut," if you wanted to get into the rackets: Billy the Kid said:

"You are not supposed to rat. . . . A lot of guys rat when they are gang busting . . . but to be a good racketeer, you have to keep your mouth shut, and not everybody can do that."

Billy the Kid was drawing an important distinction here between the fighting-gang member and the youth who fights but is also oriented to criminal values. For the gang fighter it was important that news of battle accomplishments be known to a great many people as quickly as possible. Delinquents from Slumtown were well known for their readiness to divulge the most complete details of their gang battles. The racket-oriented youngster tended to be much more close-mouthed.

For Larry, a young man from the conflict subculture who had "made it" in the rackets, if only for a short time, the concept of trust had taken on special significance:

"In other words, in the rackets there's such a thing as . . . you do your time alone, you don't take anybody else with you . . . I'd say in such a neighborhood to be a stand-up guy is something to be proud of. Something that everybody looks up to; and they say, well, this guy, you know, went away, done his time . . ."

Finally, certain types of criminal activity by the young adult tended to make him untrustworthy and ineligible for consideration in a highly organized racket system. The significance of undesirable traits was most clearly recognized in the racket subculture. The street-club worker who had been raised in Racketville commented as follows:

"For instance, a holdup man, a notorious holdup man who is well known to all the racketeers and perhaps liked, was for some reason never taken in. I guess they find out who the compulsive ones are . . . in the sense, the way this fellow is always getting arrested; or he's always going out with a gun — they'd rather not get involved with a guy who's always loud and noisy and is always getting arrested and being caught in the most embarrassing situations."

From Racketeer to Holder of a Legitimate Job

There was substantial evidence in the racket subculture that the young adult was not engaged in organized criminal activity merely for short-term gains. Ties to the racket organization were not easily severed. There was little to indicate that the successful racketeer, even in possession of lucrative legitimate as well as illegitimate business interests, could or would give up his basic orientation to the racket organization.

In the conflict subculture the ties of the young adult to the racket organization were weaker. There was less opportunity for progress in the criminal structure. Few of the former delinquents appeared to rise above the lower-status levels of the racket organization. It was much easier to sever connections — the career of the petty racketeer in this area could be temporary and transitional:

Indio said that his older brother had been knifed once when he was a gang member. He had quit gang fighting; then he sold narcotics for a short while and made enough money to pay off his debts and buy some new furniture for his family as well as clothes for himself. He set himself up well and was now working in a factory. He was no longer selling drugs.

Not infrequently the former delinquents in Slumtown would clearly perceive a brief career at some criminal activity as a stepping stone to a more desirable, conventional middle-class status:

Papo spoke of Robert — a pimp — who was doing well. He had a couple of girls working for him and was trying to make enough money "to go legitimate," to buy some property. In discussing the rackets, Papo said the idea was for the guys to get into the rackets; make money; and then buy a restaurant, a candy or liquor store, even an apartment house; and then to get out of the rackets. The risk was always there. Even in the numbers, where the risks were minimal, there was still the possibility of getting "busted."

THE YOUNG-ADULT THIEF

In the theft subculture the dominant or central criminal pattern was professional or semiprofessional thievery. This reflected a commitment at various levels of knowledge, skill, and attitudes to careers of burglary, shoplifting, forgery, pocket-picking, hi-jacking, safe-cracking, and pay-roll robbery. Successful prac-titioners had to develop considerable individual "craft" ability, often within the framework of a small, independent team or-ganization.

Former delinquents from Haulburg seemed not to have op-portunities for the development of careers in the highly organ-ized rackets available to them. This was not to say that burglary, shoplifting, or like activity at high levels of organization was not, in essence, a racket. There was evidence that limited theft-oriented racket structures which required the employment of skills and knowledge uniquely possessed by former delinquents and criminals from Haulburg did evolve later.

Also, racket and theft activities and orientations appeared to be integrated at the upper levels. For example, it was re-ported that after a major haul of jewels or furs, thieves from Haulburg often called on big-time fences in Racketville to dis-pose of the goods. Occasionally, by virtue of special skills and interests, the former delinquent from the theft subculture could fit into a racket devised and controlled by criminals from the racket subculture:

Les had been involved in a great many car thefts when he was young and served two short sentences, one of them a term in a federal penitentiary, for taking a vehicle across the state line. He loved cars and was constantly tinkering with them. The researcher met him again some years later. He was now twenty years old. He was taller, heavier, and more at ease than when the researcher had known him four years ago. He proudly took the researcher to his tow truck, parked outside. He said that it had cost him $3,800. He was in partnership with another fellow, also from the neighborhood. They were "ambulance-chasers." Whenever there was a wreck, especially on a main highway or bridge, he or his partner — whoever was driving the truck — would race to it. He had an illegal police radio in the truck which picked up all the police calls and he knew about accidents right after they had occurred. If he got to the wrecked car first, he would take it to a body shop that he knew and get a 15 per cent commission on all body work done. Of course, he also collected stiff towing charges. He pointed out that his vehicle did not have a special license or medallion for this type of work but said it didn't matter. He and his partners were usually able to pay off the cops, who collected about $30 or $40 per wreck. Payoffs were not made on the spot but at an agreed-upon meeting place a few days later. He and his partner were able to do the work because they had an arrangement with the "big boys" located uptown. Les said he enjoyed the work; it kept him close to cars.

The former delinquent from Haulburg did not, usually, move into large-scale, well-organized, highly protected criminal operations. He tended, rather, to develop more independent, highly stylized, and specialized criminal patterns. A successful thief was regarded as someone who made a lot of money and lived well but who also was a master craftsman: A conversation with two former delinquents went as follows:

RESEARCHER: You were talking about a booster (shoplifter) who makes $20,000 a year.
KARL: Yeah, he lives in a $30,000 home in Connecticut.
RESEARCHER: How old is he?
KARL: The guy is thirty-five.
RESEARCHER: Where is he from?
KARL: The neighborhood, originally.
RESEARCHER: What kind of kid was he?

KARL: He was very good at burglaries, stickups, and everything like that.

RESEARCHER: What about now? How does he operate?

KARL: He works with a partner, and they'll get a station wagon, and they'll go upstate New York, like say Albany, and start working their way back. By the time they get back they'll have their station wagon full of stuff.

RESEARCHER: What do they boost?

KARL: Like good typewriters, recorders — sometimes clothes; but they got to be good clothes, where they can get $75 a suit.

LEFTY: There's another booster. He can go into a store with a suitcase. People won't notice him. He can fill up that suitcase full of suits. Don't ask me how he does it. They just got a certain way. They wrap the suits when nobody is looking. What they do lots of times is take the hanger and hook it on to the sleeve . . . on one side and fold it right across in a certain way under the arm and take it out. . . . This particular guy isn't like most of the average boosters, like us. When we take a suit out of the store, we love to keep the label on it and even the price tag if we can. But this guy cuts the label right out in the store. He ships his suits to a clothing store, a high-class clothing store, and they sew their own labels right in.

The talented thief — the professional — had relatively little to worry about from the police. The risks of arrest were minimal. If a case came to court, the witness or the police officer could usually be bribed. Bail bondsmen were at times in collusion with thieves and their lawyers:

Teddy said that some of the guys had their own lawyers. They laid aside a certain amount from each job to cover the possibility of arrest. They even had their own bondsmen and never had trouble in getting bail set. There was one fellow who skipped bail, and nothing happened to him. These fellows didn't have much to worry about. If they got arrested, there were payoffs all along the line. At worst they served a short sentence.

The ranks of the first-class thief, in particular the "booster," were filled mainly by highly qualified persons. Certain groups and persons were unceremoniously denied membership in this select society by reason of race and presumed lack of skill. This was expressed by two members of the theft subculture in the following words:

KARL: Very seldom you find a good Negro booster.

LEFTY: Negroes, like, they walk the streets and see a person with a truck door open. They can grab a package out of that truck; or they walk by a store and they see the owner, like, walking in the back for a minute; and they can sneak in and grab a typewriter and run. That's what they call boosting.

Experience, knowledge, and skill were essential to the development of the good burglar and shoplifter. A certain pride of craftsmanship, developed early in the career of the delinquent, was useful later on:

Richie again spoke of breaking into cars. This could be done in various ways — through the side forward windows, with the aid of an ice pick and a screw driver. You had to know how to jump the transmission wires under the front hood. In other cars you started the motor in different ways.

Joey said when he was younger he made special "jump wires." He even had special tools to construct the wires.

Jackie recounted with much amusement how a bunch of keys had been stolen from the secretary at the settlement house. He had the locksmith make a duplicate of the main key and returned the bunch without the secretary ever knowing what had happened. They broke into the settlement house for three night running before the staff found out.

Karl insisted that some of the best "boosters" in the country were brought up and got their early training in his neighborhood. Sooner or later the skills of the older adolescent delinquent and young adult came to the attention of some of the older thieves. The reputation of the successful young thief spread, and he became eligible at a particular time and place for participation in a certain job.

Teddy said it wasn't a question of a young guy trying to join one of the older men's groups or of graduating formally. It was often that a young fellow's reputation came to the notice of some of the older burglars. "They want some one to come along, say, when someone else isn't available. If they think they can use him, the young fellow will be invited along . . ."

SUMMARY

The possibility existed in each of the three areas for the development of a variety of young-adult adaptations — conventional, quasi-conventional, and criminal. However, differential means structures appeared to set limits to the kinds of young-adult roles which could be played. The most extensive criminal opportunities were available in the neighborhood of the racket subculture. They stemmed from criminal organization, were safe, and offered even the young criminal operator large monetary returns. Extremely limited means of any variety were available in the conflict subculture. Here, ordinarily, young adults could enter upon careers of petty thievery and robbery and attain only low-echelon status in the rackets. In the theft subculture, it was possible for former delinquents to gain access to relatively lucrative careers as professional thieves — mainly as shoplifters and burglars.

In each area, delinquent subcultures appeared to equip young people in some measure with the knowledge, skills, and attitudes required to discharge functionally relevant and distinctive adult criminal roles. Criminal indoctrination, training, and selection processes were most systematic, rigorous, and efficient in the area of the racket subculture. Considerable care was apparently exercised in screening out those young people who were not eligible or were not likely to qualify as adult racketeers. Criminal induction and orientation processes were not nearly as well developed in the other two areas. In general, it was possible to say that although delinquent-group behavior appeared to be a necessary precondition, it was not always a sufficient one for the discharge of adult criminal roles later on. The availability of an adult-criminal means structure was crucial but not always sufficient for the development of criminal roles. It was apparent that even in the racket subculture, where the requisites of an active delinquent subculture and ample criminal means were met, there were young adults who did not pursue careers as racketeers. Personal motivation and the strength of adherence to conventional adult norms and values were variables that had to be considered as factors in young-adult adaptations.

CHAPTER VII

COMMUNITY ACTION AND DELINQUENT SUBCULTURES

The author is aware that this study has answered some questions while it has left others unanswered. Various significant aspects of delinquency from a particular sociocultural perspective of distinct subcultures were only partially examined. Ethnic, psychological, small-group, family, and situational variables were taken as implicit or considered only briefly. The examination of the multiplicity of factors contributing to delinquency in the case of any given individual or group was not considered as an objective of this work.

This exploratory study has, however, provided data indicating the association of certain highly important variables — anomie, opportunities, and delinquent patterns. The association of these variables has been clearly established. While the sequence of cause and effect has not been, at all times, drawn with unquestionable validity, nevertheless, on the basis of the present findings, it is possible to speculate profitably about community and social service programs which would modify delinquent subcultures such as Racketville, Slumtown, and Haulburg.

THE SOCIAL ORDER AND DELINQUENT SUBCULTURES

There is every reason to expect that the social, economic, and human costs of delinquency will skyrocket in the years ahead unless drastic remedies are undertaken. The growth of the youth population in low-income areas, the high rates of school failure and the large numbers of dropouts, and the increase of automation with its critical displacement of unskilled labor will accelerate the alienation of disadvantaged youths from the conventional norms of our society. The waste of youth power and the reduced potential of young people to pursue constructive adult careers will be enormous. The blight of delinquent subcultures will affect every highly industrialized and urban community in the country. Conflict subcultures, especially, may develop at a faster pace. Control measures will be only partially effective until the basic problem of inadequate opportunities for youth to achieve status, prestige, and self-respect is solved.

It is possible to argue that if the inequality of opportunities in our society leads to the development of delinquent subcultures, then equal or relatively equal opportunities should drastically inhibit the genesis and development of delinquent subcultures. The cultural injunction that success-goals be internalized by all would then be supported by a social system that provided equal access to the resources needed to make the race for success. Such a society would have to provide all age levels of its population with a very large number of prestigeful and respectable positions, limiting to a minimum the statuses that signify failure.

The allocation of resources or social opportunities would have to be planned in such a manner that the presently deprived segment of the population would be specially aided to attain the condition of life deemed significant and desirable according to dominant cultural standards. No doubt, unprecedented and comprehensive measures would have to be employed to develop such a social order. It is most unlikely that in our era of large-scale, complex, interlinked social problems, a local community could by itself bring about major changes in the condition of its lower-class population. State and national programs in support of local efforts would be indispensable. Such a social order guaranteeing equal access to success positions would tend especially to eliminate conflict subcultures.

A revision of the present system for making conventional opportunities available to young people would, however, be insufficient by itself to modify racket subcultures. A basic change in the value orientation of the dominant culture would also have to be made. An attack on the racket subculture and its entrenched parent racket culture would require, among other things, a change in certain generally accepted criteria for achieving success in our society. The racketeer's rules of "It isn't what you know but whom you know that counts," "Anything is all right if you get away with it," "A sucker is born every minute," and so forth are also the rules by which a great many successful conventional businessmen operate. The racket orientation, unfortunately, is only a variant of a major industrial and commercial tradition very much alive today in our society. Both are almost exclusively concerned with pursuit of the dollar. All things in life, and perhaps life itself, become ways or devices to achieve wealth and its derivative attributes — power, prestige, respect. Morality and legality are constantly subverted in varying degrees to the deliberate achievement of success at any cost.

That the value of success in market terms will lose its supremely dominant position in the scale of American values appears doubtful. Therefore, the reduction of the influence of the racket subculture is less likely to occur than the modification of the conflict subculture. The conflict orientation is not as strongly integrated into the prevailing system of dollar-cultural values as is the racket orientation. Furthermore, the accessibility of even some opportunities tends quickly to reduce the viability of the conflict subculture, already isolated from the adult culture — criminal or conventional. The destruction of the racket culture — since one cannot flourish without the other — presents a very difficult and perhaps even impossible undertaking in a highly business-oriented society.

Strictly local efforts to deal with the problems of subcultural delinquency are most likely to succeed in areas such as Haulburg, where delinquents tend to be oriented to a conventional middle-class style of life and have some access to legitimate opportunities. Major changes in the social or cultural structure of the community are not required. Manageable approaches to the problem of delinquency in Haulburg are available through improved planning and distribution of existing opportunities and services. A primary objective of social service programs in Haulburg should be to assist delinquent youths to make better use of available conventional opportunities. The theft subculture may therefore be regarded as the least undesirable form and, within limits, may be a more tolerable type of delinquent subculture than either the racket subculture or the conflict subculture.

Under even ideal conditions of society some disparity between youthful aspirations and expectations is to be anticipated. It appears doubtful that any society will ever be entirely able to prevent some individuals, families, and neighborhoods from gaining greater access to resources than other individuals, families, and neighborhoods. Elimination of the gross disparities in the number of opportunities available to youths would, however, restrict the development of the more aberrant youth systems to some bland variety of theft subculture.

COMMUNITY PLANNING AND DELINQUENCY [1]

A general design for improved living in particularly deprived lower-class areas should be based on three concepts: *opportunity, service,* and *organization.*

Lower-class groups, especially Negroes from the southern states, Puerto Ricans, Mexicans, and some southern whites, do not have equal opportunities or access to the means by which to attain culturally valued goals. In large urban centers, where newcomers — often they are not recent newcomers — are quick to accept dominant cultural aspirations, they are not equally quick to gain essential opportunities. Children of low-income groups are often ill prepared by education, training, family nurture, and guidance to find or make use of the limited means available. Lower-class parents may want their children to attend school, to graduate, and to become successful people; but the means available to their children, both within and outside the family system, to develop significant status may not be sufficient. Not only are schools in slum neighborhoods generally inferior in helping children to meet the intellectual and social demands of the society at large, but parents themselves are often handicapped in their efforts to help their children make use of

[1] The following section is adapted from Irving Spergel and Richard E. Mundy, *East Woodlawn: Problems, Programs, Proposals* (Chicago: University of Chicago School of Social Service Administration, March, 1963), pp. 89–100. (Mimeographed.)

available opportunities by defeatist attitudes and inadequate knowledge of the expected behavioral patterns. Appropriate social skills for effective communication and interaction with middle-class personnel at schools and agencies are not adequately understood or taught by parents.

In essence, positively enabling environments conducive to successful achievement, whether in the home, in school, or in the neighborhood, are not available to children of low-income groups, particularly those in deteriorated neighborhoods. For children, inadequate social environments constitute limited opportunity systems. Full and equal opportunities may be provided them only through the strengthening of family and community institutions. Family systems may be strengthened only as parents themselves receive special training and education and as the society provides more jobs, better housing, and improved opportunities for participation in constructive community life. Children themselves must be given a broader range of basic and special educational opportunities than they are presently receiving.

Since the provision of basic social and economic opportunities is not enough, however, a variety of significant social supports, through services, must be developed to insure that the expanded opportunities which became available to the child at school or to the parent through a better job are fully utilized. Social work, as well as psychological, psychiatric, health, and other community services, must be amply provided to many parents and children so that the basic opportunities are appropriately appreciated and used. Meaningful counseling services must be provided to certain children in order that they make productive use of the school experience. Children require adequate medical, dental, and other health services to function educationally at their best. Highly disorganized families need special help with domestic and family-management problems. The availability of basic educational, employment, and housing opportunities does not mean that they will, in all cases, be effectively used. Gaps in information on available opportunities, failures in motivation, and limited mental, physical, or emotional capacities may block the use of such basic resources. Services facilitate the use of opportunity systems and function to break through the barriers of apathy, dependency, and impulsiveness which have been defensively erected by members of lower-class groups to prevent even more serious personal and social disorganization. The primary goal of services should be to strengthen the positive motivations and abilities of people so that they may take full advantage of the greater social and economic opportunities which are afforded.

Unfortunately, socioeconomic and cultural poverty develops its own inertia; people — young and old — become accustomed to decay and deprivation. They learn to adjust and develop mechanisms of survival to meet the recurring crises of everyday living. Indeed, a measure of skill, excitement, and satisfaction may be derived from grappling with, and in part succeeding against, overwhelming social odds. But standards, values, and skills acquired in the battle for survival in the slums, against crime, corruption, and disease, are not only not useful in coping with adequate community opportunities when these are available, but are harmful. Services then function as important spurs to better use of conventional opportunities.

Even the provision of expanded opportunities *and* services may still not be enough to prevent social ills and to rehabilitate problem families and their children. Expanded opportunities and services must be efficiently *organized*. Administrative arrangements for the rendering of opportunities and services have been notoriously inefficient in our problem-ridden communities. Competing, overlapping, unrelated public and voluntary programs reduce the value of opportunities and services provided. Too often, problem youngsters and their families are shunted from agency to agency. They seem frequently to fall outside the reach and influence of middle-class-oriented teachers, welfare workers, counselors, psychiatrists, and good neighbors. Furthermore, many programs in deprived neighborhoods lack quality, imagination, and flexibility. Untrained and poorly supervised personnel are presented with intolerably heavy and difficult assignments which they cannot handle effectively. Stereotyped and inferior practices at schools and agencies are little better than no teaching or help at all.

There is need for effective rationalization and co-ordination of services within and between agencies — public and voluntary. Opportunities and service programs have to be organized and administered so that maximum use is made of the inevitably scarce skilled personnel through careful deployment. If the efforts of all agencies and organizations within a particular community were well integrated, professional, semiprofessional, and volunteer staff would be able to attain greater efficiency and effectiveness.

PROGRAM PROPOSALS

A community or neighborhood with serious social problems should be helped to change from a "have-not" or problem-ridden area to a "have" or socially effective area. It should, in the shortest time possible, be assisted to meet the standards of desirable urban living which characterize "solid" and "good" communities. A problem community should be helped to develop into an open, multiclass community. Middle-class whites and non-whites should be encouraged to reside in the area, since a fundamental condition for the development and the enhanced welfare of a lower-class community is the presence of a strong and stable middle-class population in the same area. Lower-income persons must be given adequate social, economic, and cultural opportunities to raise their standards of living; middle-class elements serve as an important leaven in this process. In the long run, an all-lower-class community constitutes a ghetto and, as such, a barrier to the creation of effective opportunities and positive patterns of living.

A pattern of community development, furthermore, should be a product of discussion and decision-making by public and voluntary organizations, both inside and outside the area, which are vitally concerned with the welfare of persons in that community. Local citizen groups, however, should bear a major responsibility for the policy and the development of a dynamic social and physical plan for the area. This does not deny the need for a variety of experts to formulate technical plans and implement policy decisions. Nevertheless, the development of a community plan should rest ultimately with an association of key public and voluntary agencies which represents clearly the will and power of the people in the local community and in the entire city. In setting up such an over-all community association or council, it is imperative that local organizations do not overassert themselves and that the city government, in particular, assumes bold and imaginative leadership in the solution of serious community problems.

The following is a very general outline of several basic kinds of programs and organizational structures suggested as integral to a needed community-development plan.

OPPORTUNITIES

HOUSING

New low-income and middle-income housing should be constructed in depressed sectors of the community and this should be accomplished in such a manner as to minimize dislocation and hardship for existing residents. Old commercial and industrial properties no longer in use should be targets for early clearance. They should be replaced as quickly as possible by low-income housing structures. The most blighted housing, unfit for rehabilitation, should be the next target for removal. Residents to be transferred to housing within or outside the area must *absolutely* be provided with housing accommodations equal to or better than those currently possessed by them. Strict enforcement of building codes must be undertaken with reasonable haste. The possibility of developing or using state legislation permitting public authorities to confiscate slum properties which are not rehabilitated within a state reasonable time should be energetically explored.

EDUCATION

1. Priority should be given to the improvement and expansion of school facilities to care for the flood of school-age children presently (and potentially) in the community. Educational opportunities for children and youths should be planned on a regional basis. Equal educational opportunities should be provided, in part, through full racial integration of junior-high-school grades and high-school programs. Whenever possible, children in overcrowded local elementary schools should be transported at city expense to schools in nearby neighborhoods which are operating under capacity.

2. High priority should also be granted to the development of special cultural and social enrichment programs for preschool children and those in the primary grades.

a) Programs of cultural and social enrichment should be established for preschool children (three to five years old) in need of such programs. Existing recreational, church, and volunteer agency facilities might be used in this project.

b) Special educational enrichment programs for primary-grade school children should be developed through the aid of auxiliary teachers, specialists, parent and community volunteers, including students from local colleges.

c) An interlinked school-and-social-center program should be established which would provide for the continued education and enrichment of the life experiences of children after regular school hours, particularly between 3:15 and 5:00 P.M.

3. Special work-study program geared to the needs of potential dropouts should be further developed at the local high school. Intensive small-group academic and vocational training programs, leading to specific employment possibilities, should be created or expanded, in both the day and evening schools.

4. A new educational institution, the Adult Education Development Center, principally for older teen-agers and adults who are presently unemployed, should be created in the area. The need for a system of education, training, and retraining is likely to be permanent in our very rapidly and continually changing society. Traditional bodies of knowledge and skill, as well as traditional attitudes, seem to become obsolete almost overnight. Basic and advanced programs in general education, commercial studies, and vocational training should be established in this center. Special attention should be directed to raising the literacy levels of persons who are functionally illiterate. A flexible, imaginative, and sensitively developed program should be able to attract older teen-agers and adults whose prior school experiences, on the whole, have been negative. A nominal subsistence scholarship plan should be worked out to further sustain the interest of students in this program.

The Adult Education Development Center should be organized and staffed by district personnel of the board of education in close consultation with representatives of business, industry, unions, the state employment service, and the local department of public aid. Existing school facilities may be utilized, although ultimately separate building facilities will probably be needed. Federal funds will very likely become more available for the implementation of such retraining programs.

5. Finally, teachers and teachers-in-training in the area should be systematically exposed to knowledge of non-white cultures and to specific ethnic-community social needs, interests, and problems; particularly, they should acquire techniques and attitudes for effective communication with, and instruction of culturally different and deprived people, young and old.

EMPLOYMENT

New employment opportunities must be developed for marginal workers, both by private industry and through a public works program. Federal planning and funds will be required for such job-creating projects. The local unemployment problem needs to be resolved as part of a regional or city-wide program. New ways of subsidizing industry and business, on the condition that marginal workers are employed and trained, will have to be found. Criteria for the selection of industries, businesses, and public and voluntary agencies for such programs will require the most careful exploration. National youth programs represent one attempt to provide employment for youths in a variety of public and voluntary service organizations. Federal work projects for the unemployed adult male and female, however, must also receive the highest priority.

A variety of urban-renewal and human-renewal projects can be devised that would be useful to the community and to the unemployed adult whose ultimate return to the competitive job market would thus be facilitated. New programs and increased services in hospitals, day-care centers, the park department, public schools, and housing would further this goal. Some programs would need to be permanent; others of only a temporary nature. For various reasons, some persons may not be able readily, or ever, to hold down a job in the competitive labor market. A new and permanent form of a Works Progress Administration would have to assure continued employment of such marginal workers.

SERVICES

A variety of service programs should be created to complement the opportunity programs which become available. Especially required is attention to the needs of predelinquent and delinquent children and their families. The purpose of all new demonstration programs should be clearly to facilitate the utilization of opportunity systems by socially and culturally handicapped persons.

1. Local Social and Health Services Centers should be established, each functioning under one roof, to provide referral, information, and guidance directly, as well as a variety of short-term services for a wide range of social, economic, legal, and medical problems. They would serve as readily accessible centers for people with emergency or immediate needs for help with the pressing problems of social reality. A major function of the staff would be to provide referral services and to assure that persons needing help were effectively connected with the right programs. Also, efforts to develop high-quality short-duration treatment programs would permit existing agencies in the area to deal more effectively with long-term problem situations.

Such service centers would ideally include representatives of the following types of agencies: board of health, Planned Parenthood Association, family service bureau, department of public aid, state employment service, housing department, board of education, and the police department. Whenever possible, these existing agencies, public and voluntary, should be encouraged to assign service personnel to the center, who will promote specific agency objectives as well as an experimental plan of co-ordinated services directed to the total welfare of the clients. New types of services and personnel which are needed and feasible, but not now available through existing agencies should be developed. Undoubtedly, new concepts of service patterns will have to be developed within the framework of such a service center. Services of the various agencies should be purchased on a contract basis by the Social and Health Services Centers, and the entire center operation should come under the general direction of a local Opportunity and Service Council, described later.

2. School social services (group work and casework) should be established in conjunction with the various school enrichment programs. Caseworkers and group workers should work with selected children and their parents, particularly in the preschool program, to promote maximum utilization of the educational and cultural opportunities afforded by the school. In addition, attention should be paid to children and their families in the primary, upper-elementary, and high-school grades.

For children of preschool age, services should be located either in the respective churches and agencies where preschool programs are conducted or in the Social and Health Services Center. In any case, direction of the social services project should come under centralized administration. For children of elementary-school age, services should be located in, and be under the jurisdiction of, the district public school system. Social and psychological services, especially academic and vocational counseling, should also be made available directly through the district school system to youths who are in danger of dropping out of school or who are not properly utilizing opportunities in high school.

3. Social service and vocational counseling units should be established in the Adult Education Development Center and in those industries, businesses, and public agencies which are developing employment projects for marginal workers. Experimentation with subsidized rehabilitation workshops in commercial and industrial establishments and possibly in unions should be attempted. These would use the services of professional and semiprofessional social workers and counselors to facilitate optimal use of the work setting by marginal employees.

4. Special "outreach" services for youths should also include the development of a street-club-worker unit to deal with gangs or delinquent groups on the streets, intensive casework-group-work projects for parolees and probationers, and a psychiatric unit for emotionally disturbed adolescents. These special programs should be highly integrated with each other as well as with existing social, health, recreational, and block-organization services. Existing agencies, such as the park department, the Boys' Club, the community center, the YMCA, and the

YWCA, should be called upon to sponsor or staff such projects wherever feasible.

5. Existing social, health, employment, recreational, and educational organizations should be helped through consultation and subsidization from the Opportunity and Service Council to strengthen, improve, and expand particular programs to better meet the needs of the population, particularly its youth segment. Special attention should be directed to creating new facilities and expanding the staff for the enrichment of the social and cultural experiences of youths.

6. The serious health problems of the population and the severe lack of adequate medical facilities and services will probably require a major investment of public resources in the deteriorated areas. Private clinics and hospitals should be urged and supported through subsidies to expand their facilities and services and to make them available to low-income residents of the area. Under city health department leadership, new mobile diagnostic and educational units should systematically operate programs particularly aimed at the prevention of serious childhood and maternal illnesses and to the detection of serious diseases, e.g., T.B., cancer, heart disease, and venereal disease, among the general population. Procedures for the effective referral of ill persons to clinics and hospital services should be worked out in conjunction with the Social and Health Services Center. It may also be possible, under certain conditions, to experiment with the use of mobile treatment teams to provide services to ill persons directly in their homes. New patterns of home care evolved in various cities provide models for this type of service.

7. The development of block organizations should also receive high priority. Present block organizations should be centralized, and their functions, particularly in the lower-income segments of the community, vastly expanded. The block organization should become a basic unit of self-government and self-help. It should become a means for the democratic participation of the people on each block in the policy decisions of agencies which affect their daily social living. The block organization, furthermore, should become a basis for the initial handling of

a whole range of social problems which confront local people.

Each block organization should have its own block agent or agents. Each such agent should be an influential person, preferably a resident of the block or neighborhood. He should have organizational ability, native intelligence, or adequate educational background, and a strong commitment to the welfare of the people and the community. The block agent's role will probably vary from street to street. It is expected, however, that he will mobilize and facilitate activities on local social issues and problems. He will also need to refer persons with complex social and personal problems to existing agencies. He should be able to counsel individuals burdened with certain simple social problems. He should be a "middleman" or "broker" between residents on the block and the agencies.

The block organization should give special attention to the problems and interests of youths through the development of special work and recreational projects. Youth should maximally be involved in the planning, execution, and staffing of such projects as building repair and maintenance, gardening, baby-sitting, supervision of younger children in playlots and playgrounds, and small business operations. Reimbursement should be provided to youths for their labors. Every effort should be made to find projects which afford meaningful opportunities to bridge the gap between adolescent diffusion and focused adult responsibility.

Individual block organizations should function as units of a larger association or associations of block organizations. Providing funds for block-organization agents and projects should be done through the community fund, private foundations, voluntary contributions, and nominal membership assessments. The possible use of special federal funds, independent of the federal funds provided to the local Opportunity and Service Council, should be explored. Every block organization should be granted maximum freedom to develop programs on its own terms. It is extremely important that block organizations be free to criticize and support public and voluntary agency programs, including those of the local Opportunity and Service Council. At the same time, each block organization or association of block organizations should appoint or elect representa-

tives and observers to the Opportunity and Service Council.
Block associations should be regarded as one of the basic units
of this council.

Block-organization projects and operations should be imagi-
natively developed. The creation of new programs and approaches which promise to meet the social needs of people
should be encouraged through the auspices of the block organization. Furthermore, consultation and training of block agents
for their important and complex functions should be given by
professional community workers employed by the association
of block organizations. Finally, the guiding principles of block
organizations should be creative, flexibile, and innovational
programs along with informal, simple, and rational procedures.

ORGANIZATION

Partly explicit and certainly implicit in the description of
agency programs just presented are patterns of known organizational failure which seriously limit the extent and quality of
available opportunities and services. The failures may be categorized as follows:

1. The general inability of agencies, public and voluntary,
to communicate with each other and to co-ordinate programs
effectively on a neighborhood or larger-community level. Local
organizational channels tend to be directed vertically to city
and state-wide centers of administration. Almost no major
program collaboration among local, branch, or independent
agencies has been effectively developed.

2. City-wide and local agencies fail often to be concerned
with, and to program adequately for, the distinctive local community needs of low-income groups. Socially and culturally
handicapped children and their parents are not, in general, pro-
ductively drawn into school, social service, public welfare, or
cultural and recreational programs.

3. There is almost a complete absence of democratic participation in the policy- and decision-making processes of local
organizational bodies. Very few agencies — health, social welfare, community organization, or law enforcement — make use
of local citizens in a significant advisory or policy-making

capacity. A functionally authoritarian and paternalistic spirit pervades nearly all agency arrangements in the lower-class community. The average citizen or agency client is relegated to the role of passive recipient of services.

The following is an outline of an organizational structure recommended for more effective determination and implementation of a program of community development in a socially deprived area. This is a tentative working proposal:

An Opportunity and Service Council should be the heart and muscle of local and city-wide concern for social and physical development. It should set major objectives, determine basic policies, and develop key programs for the improvement of living conditions of community residents. For the effective functioning of the Opportunity and Service Council, existing public and voluntary agencies may need to restructure patterns of service voluntarily and systematically and even to relinquish some degree of institutional autonomy.

The Opportunity and Service Council should facilitate the efficient development, distribution, and use of opportunities and services. It should be a co-ordinative, integrative, and funding mechanism for public and voluntary programs in the area. Existing agencies should comprise the base for the development of the council. It should include on its policy-making board and various committees representatives from all the major public agencies, including the department of planning, the department of housing, the board of education, the department of health, the commission on youth welfare, the police department, and the fire department, as well as representatives from the important local and city-wide voluntary agencies and local block organizations. A special status, for co-ordinating purposes, should be worked out for such county and state-wide agencies as the county department of public aid, the state employment service, and the state youth commission. The power to enforce co-operation among the various public agencies at the local level should be guaranteed at the top levels of city government. Wherever possible, however, emphasis should be on developing co-operative agency arrangements. The provision of service contract funds by the Opportunity and Service Council should further facilitate co-ordination of agency programs. A professional staff and appropriate committee structures containing representatives from public and voluntary agencies and local citizens groups should be established.

Specifically, the function and structure of the Opportunity and Service Council should be:

1. To develop community policy in regard to social and physical planning. A series of committees, e.g., housing, education, health, family service, delinquency and crime, employment, and recreation, should be developed to assist the council board and its executive to determine appropriate program goals and objectives.

2. To implement major policy decisions within a framework of co-ordinated community planning. The responsibility of the Opportunity and Service Council, through its committees and staff, should be to create systematic arrangements at different levels of agency administration for policy and program co-ordination and integration. For example, in relation to specific social problems, agency executives should collaborate in the development of interlinked programs of case-planning, collaborative practice, and "follow-up."

3. To operate particular service programs, such as those of the Social and Service Health Center.

4. To engage in the development of new and supplementary service projects which existing agencies are unable to undertake.

5. To develop devices for the representation of local opinion in the formation of significant policies and programs, including those of its own organization and those of the other public and voluntary agencies in the community.

It may be feasible for certain aspects of community planning that the Opportunity and Service Council extend its scope of operations to adjoining areas. The particularly deprived community would have much to gain from such an arrangement — greater housing, education, social services, and cultural facilities would be at the disposal of its residents. Planning for a larger geographical unit is essential, particularly if new housing and educational opportunities are to be developed for problem-ridden people.

The Opportunity and Service Council should be a special city governmental authority. The council program should be operated basically as a function of city government within a framework of controls and standards set by a federal agency or department such as the President's Committee on Juvenile Delinquency and Youth Crime or an Urban Affairs Department. The director of the council should receive his authority from the mayor's or deputy mayor's office. He should be appointed, however, on the recommendation of the board of the Opportunity Service Council.

The council should not become a vehicle for partisan or patronage politics. One means of insuring that the Opportunity and Service Council will properly pursue its goals and will effectively implement its programs would be the continued existence and independent development of major voluntary community-action groups, including revitalized block organizations. These groups should not only be represented on the board and various committees of the council but should continue to develop their own social-action programs in the manner which they deem most appropriate for furthering their community's welfare. It is important that the power to determine or affect the welfare of a community be shared responsibly by more than one organization, whether public or voluntary.

The Opportunity and Service Council should not be permitted to deteriorate into a "conscienceless bureaucracy." It should be a people's organization, representing the basic interests of the residents of the area. Every effort must be made to keep the programs and policies of the organization focused on the needs and interests of the people of the community, particularly those in the low-income, socially handicapped group.

The Opportunity and Service Council should be supported through federal funds from organizations such as the President's Committee on Juvenile Delinquency and Youth Crime, the National Institute of Health, federal urban renewal agencies, or an Urban Affairs Department and by local governmental and foundation grants on an indefinite basis.

Finally, a staging process should be developed to bring the Opportunity and Service Council and its programs into being. The most powerful and representative local community and governmental agencies concerned with the social and physical development of the area should take major responsibility for initiating and directing a community organization process, with participation by all other appropriate voluntary agencies, public departments, and community groups in the locality, through which a community social and physical plan and instrumental organization may be created.

THE SOCIAL WORKER AND THE DELINQUENT SUBCULTURES

A key assumption has been that social service programs are essentially committed to the enhancement of individual, group, and neighborhood interpersonal experience. Such programs tend to develop only residual and implicit commitment to major social structural change. Social workers normally operate within the framework of a given agency's purposes and objectives; such agencies, at best, attempt to extend services to a variety of groups and individuals, particularly those in need of help. Social work, as it is now practiced, is not primarily concerned with change in the community's basic social structure except in a limited amelioristic sense. Social workers tend to accept the basic organization of our society and community and seek mainly to enhance the positive potential of its constituent parts.

If the above assumptions are correct, then the most suitable context for a strictly social service approach would appear to be the neighborhood of the theft subculture, which has partial provision of conventional opportunities and a dominant commitment to legitimate values. Since the structural support of a viable community social and cultural system is already provided, the social worker need not exhaust his energies attempting to rectify a severe shortage of opportunities such as characterizes Slumtown or a severe distortion of values such as characterizes Racketville. Indeed, there is little he himself can do about these dysfunctions to begin with. At the same time, the social worker *is* expected to act in all three areas.

The social-work practitioner is capable of performing three major functions toward the modification of the delinquent adaptation: He can facilitate positive interpersonal relationships; he can also serve as a bridge or link to effective use of the opportunity system by the client or client group; finally, he can promulgate conventional values. Depending on the dominant delinquent orientation in the area, the social agency and its agent — the social worker — should emphasize that function most likely to produce the most positive change.

In a neighborhood such as Racketville, the social worker's efforts should be directed to stressing the values of the conventional society convincingly to the delinquent and his group. It must be assumed that at least a few delinquents, even in this kind of area, retain some identification with conventional values and role-models. Attempts must be made to strengthen such identifications. Where necessary, strategic efforts should be made to precipitate value conflicts in individuals and groups and to support those community elements seeking to strengthen legitimate institutions.

In a neighborhood such as Slumtown, the social worker's major function lies in the provision of access, albeit limited, to opportunities by which delinquents may achieve some measure of success as defined in conventional terms. Access should be extended as widely as possible to jobs; vocational training; and new educational, social, cultural, and recreational experiences. These youths should be helped to contact a variety of adults and organizations controlling conventional opportunities. Social service agencies should also directly provide opportunities to delinquents for prestigeful and respected roles as subprofessionals, assistants, or trainees within the agency program itself.

In a neighborhood such as Haulburg, as already intimated, the social worker's major effort lies in enabling or facilitating the delinquent, his group, and the neighborhood to make better use of available conventional resources. The individual delinquent may require special help in motivation or remotivation to make use of his own personal potential in relation to opportunities accessible to him. Individual and group-counseling programs would appear to be highly useful in this regard as well as the co-ordination of rehabilitative services on behalf of the delinquents.

None of the three ways in which social work functions, as just outlined, is exclusive of the others. Indeed, they are merely variations of the same basic social-work role. Specific agency arrangements and emphases in social-work services would seem to be indicated, however, in the light of the specific constellation of social problems confronted in a particular delinquent subcultural neighborhood.

Finally, regarding the narcotics-addict orientation, in the measure that the addict is a former delinquent, efforts directed at the alleviation of pressures which produce the delinquent subcultures should also reduce the frequency of the drug adaptation. It is unlikely, however, that the problem of addiction for the older adolescent or young adult may be more than only partially amenable to the influence of the social worker. It is possible that a recognition of the adjustive function of drugs will enable the worker to focus on and support the positive efforts made by the addict to get and hold a job, to stabilize a marriage or other family relationship, as well as to cut down on drug consumption. Perhaps further social breakdown and psychological deterioration might be mitigated through a rational and controlled system of medical distribution of drugs to addicts. It is assumed that drug-usage is reduced and even eliminated as the young adult learns to fulfil adult roles more responsibly and with greater personal satisfaction.

IMPLICATIONS FOR FURTHER STUDIES

Research on delinquent subcultures is still in a highly exploratory phase. Data on delinquents in their natural social contexts remain largely to be collected, and research theory and method are still in a rough and tentative stage of development. In the future, the researcher or research teams will have to use multiple theoretical and technical approaches if the full range of data and potential knowledge are to be acquired. Studies of broad theoretical and methodological scope, although expensive, may provide in the long run the knowledge and understanding for the development of the most economical programs for eliminating or constructively modifying delinquent subcultures. This volume provides only a small sample of the rich lode of material that awaits the investigator who would know the delinquent in his own community.

PROBLEMS
IN OBTAINING DATA
ON DELINQUENT SUBCULTURES

The problems which I met while conducting the study are considered sequentially, in the order in which they arose. At the outset I had to identify myself to the participants and define my role. During this period my role was often misconstrued and tested in a variety of ways characteristic of the dominant feelings, concerns, and interests of delinquents in each neighborhood. Once a relationship of trust was established, group information was shared more freely, and group behavior proceeded more naturally. Nevertheless, obstacles were still encountered. Efforts were periodically made to exploit my access to funds and services. Throughout the study I had to define and demonstrate the limits of my role repeatedly. Finally, toward the close of the participant-observation process, when fruitful role relations were firmly established, formal interviews were held with many of the group members. There were also difficulties in obtaining data at this later stage of the study.

PROBLEMS IN PARTICIPANT OBSERVATION

Role definition. — Relationships with groups were developed in several ways: Initial field contacts with the delinquent groups in Slumtown and with the narcotics-using group in Racketville were made with the help of introductions by street-club workers who had positive relationships with the groups. With delinquent groups in Racketville and Haulburg, I was compelled to establish my contacts through self-introduction, for agencies and their workers either had poor relationships with them or were unwilling to risk possible deterioration of the existing relationships through my involvement. In Haulburg I was able to re-establish contacts with various older delinquents and with members of a drug-using group known to me formerly when I was a street-club worker.

At first I introduced myself or had myself introduced as someone from Eastern University writing a book about neighborhood groups. In Racketville, because of the ever-present concern with detectives, undercover agents, and news reporters, special care was taken to stress the fact that the study was of a technical and absolutely confidential nature, useful only to social scientists and to social workers.

The role of a researcher had to be defined and redefined constantly to persons newly contacted and to those persons already known who were still uncertain and uneasy. In the neighborhood of the racket subculture I was at various times labeled as a policeman, a plain-clothes man, or a federal agent:

I saw Davey, Little Augie, and his girl friend, Phyllis, on the playground. Little Augie said that he, himself, had thought I was a federal agent. When I first came, he had run around the block.

The researcher was on one occasion identified as a reporter by a key member of the delinquent group in this area:

At one point I made a move, a rather unobtrusive one, I thought, to get closer to Blackie. Whereupon he said, in a derogatory tone, "You're just like a reporter. Why don't you get your pencil and paper out? And don't forget to take everything down." I had to assure him that I was not a reporter and that I did not have pencil and paper for taking down notes.

The novelty and lack of clarity about my role aroused not only suspicion but even hostility in some members of the group:

Little Augie raised a question about what I was doing in the neighborhood. He wondered whether I was a cop, a "stool pigeon," or a Youth Board worker. I tried to clarify again my role as a research worker. Little Augie said that what I was saying to him wasn't clear and that he suspected my real motives. He wondered how the work I was allegedly doing would benefit *him*. I said that if I could get the facts down as to what the fellows were like, it would help a lot of people, in the long run, perhaps including them. He then said that he did not want to become a guinea pig for me. I repeated that I was not there to do the fellows any harm.

On one occasion, I was falsely accused of informing to the police and causing the arrest of a key leader of a delinquent group. Actually, I merely happened to be in the vicinity when the youth was arrested (for assaulting two other boys). When the youth who had been arrested returned to the block (he was released at the precinct with surprising speed), he sought me out and said:

"You're a rat and a stool pigeon." I asked what he meant. He said that I had "ratted" on him and that the detectives had picked him up because of that. I denied this, saying that I was with the other fellows nearby and did not even know myself what was going on. He did not believe me and said that the police had surely been notified, since they usually were not in the block, and that I was to blame for this.

During the early stage of his work I was often misidentified in Slumtown as a street-club worker. More than once a member of the delinquent group pointed me out to an inquiring peer or adult as a "Youth Board worker":

A young adult asked Papo who I was. The question was put in Spanish, but the meaning of the words was clear. Papo said "Youth Board." Later, when I asked him about this, he said that I fit that category more than any other one and that, besides, it was the easiest thing to say.

Generally, in Slumtown, I was not identified as a representative of the law. On several occasions I was mistaken by prostitutes who lived in a row of apartments near the hangout of one of the delinquent groups for a "John" seeking a good time. On two occasions I was taken for a drug addict, and efforts were made to sell me heroin. On at least one occasion I was taken for a solicitor in behalf of a prostitution racket:

I was talking Barbara, who had been recently released from a training school for girls. She was formerly a member of a Debs group, a girls' affiliate to the Regals. He mother soon appeared at their ground-story apartment window and called her away. When

Barbara returned after a brief conversation with the older woman, she said that her mother was worried about to whom she was talking and had thought that I was trying to get her to join a prostitution organization, because there was a lot of that sort of thing happening in the neighborhood.

In Haulburg I was most frequently and correctly identified as "someone from Eastern doing research on neighborhood groups and juvenile delinquents." As in the other neighborhoods, however, misidentification did at times occur. Uncertainty and confusion over my role were related closely to focal neighborhood concerns and the presence of familiar adult types in the area. For example, the role of adult homosexual was attributed to the researcher more often here than in the other neighborhoods:

While we were in a luncheonette Jackie said that when I first came around he had thought I was a "gayer." I asked him what he meant by a "gayer." He said a homosexual, someone who was "gay." He added that he believed this to be the case until some of the boys explained that they had known me as a street-club worker and that I was now from Eastern University and was doing research.

Because of my previous relationship with members of groups I had known years before, I was asked from time to time to help with finding jobs, problems of drug addiction, court cases, interpersonal relations involving family, girl friends, probation officers, and so forth. Such requests for help were generally referred to Youth Board workers or social agencies in the neighborhood.

Meeting initial suspicion and hostility. — The groups tested me during the early stages of the relationship in various ways: by simple distrust, attempts to frighten me, "baiting" or "ranking" me, and by minor acts of physical violence. The testing behavior appeared to serve several functions: to demonstrate the group's uncertainty in the face of a new and strange relationship, to discover whether or not I was a "right guy," and to determine my areas of personal weakness and of personal strength. In Slumtown the period of testing was brief and its character mild:

Eddie, the street-club worker, introduced me as the fellow he had told them about the previous day. He said that I would be around the area for a while. The group was reticent and obviously suspicious. One of the members said, with a sneer, that some of the Noble Lords had been around earlier looking for trouble and to "watch out." One older-looking fellow who seemed to have leadership status looked darkly in my direction . . . I said I was glad to meet the fellows. After a moment or two of silence the group began to speak in Spanish. Later I asked Eddie if the group generally spoke in Spanish. He said "No" and added that maybe it was because of my presence there that they did so on that occasion.

The next day, however, when I was at the community center, Papo came up to me and said that he had been with the group the day before and just wanted to say "Hello" now.

The kind of testing I was subjected to in Haulburg was similar to that experienced in Slumtown. It was brief and mild. The initial reception was, at worst, cool and ambivalent:

I ran into three of the younger fellows. They were about to pass me by. I said "Hello." Herman said, derisively and uncertainly, "Here comes the social worker." I ignored the tone of the remark and asked if the boys had a good time over the Fourth of July. They said that they had and went into some detail about their activities. Herman then urged one of the other boys, half in jest and half-seriously, to take an interview which I had already administered to some members of the group. The boy to whom the remark was directed, however, made no response. In a moment the trio walked away.

The kind of testing practiced by delinquent youths in Racketville was entirely different. It lasted longer; it was open, intense, and quite sophisticated:

Angelo, Larry, and Frankie were in my car with me. They prodded me to drive faster. I stayed within the speed limit. Soon Angelo began to play a "game" which involved slapping the back of my neck and head with the palm of his hand. (This game was at times played by members of the group with each other.) Frankie joined in on a limited basis; however, he confined his aggression mainly to teasing. The boys were told to quit. They laughed and made a big joke of it. The tapping continued with increasing force. I pulled the car over to the side, warned the group there would be an accident if they continued, then started on the road again. Angelo said that I didn't understand them, "You don't know anything about guys like us. You were just raised in a nice neighborhood. You don't know how it feels to be on the street and kicked around by people . . ." Frankie continued his teasing only a short time longer. Larry was completely silent. When we got back to the block, I told the group to get out. I expressed anger — especially with Angelo. I said I thought Angelo was drunk and didn't know what he was doing. Just at this time Monk and Big Tony approached and told Angelo and the others to get out and to act right.

Contrary to my expectations, the narcotics-using group in Racketville was initially more aggressive and hostile than the delinquent group in the same area.

Countering group exploitation. — From time to time there was pressure by group members on me to obtain money for food, refreshments, and special favors. In general, all requests were refused except for refreshments and for driving group members around, which were granted on a limited basis. The nature of requests for favors was diversified — from driving group members around the block to taking them to my home for dinner, buying stolen goods, or getting a drug addict a job in a hospital.

In each area, characteristic kinds of exploitation were attempted. In Racketville one such effort to exploit occurred during the initial contact with several young adults who were regarded as leaders in a network of delinquent groups:

George (twenty-five years old) was deadly serious as he spoke: He said he would be glad to sit down and work out a business proposition with me. I asked what he meant. He said that for a certain sum of money he would tell me the whole story, the truth about the club — from the very start — how they had recently killed two people. (Actually such killings had occurred but they were not related to gang-fighting activity.) Arnie interrupted and said that for $500 — that is, for $250 apiece — a deal could be worked out. Georgie silenced Arnie, saying that he would quote no price but maybe a percentage could be agreed upon. I said that I was mainly interested in the younger fellows and particularly in what they were doing now. George said the information they would give me would be the whole story and would include what the kids could tell me.

He said that only the older guys had the real story and told me to think it over and that he would be around. I thanked them and said that I doubted if anything could be worked out but that I hoped to see them in the neighborhood.

The following was an example of intended exploitation by members of the delinquent group in Slumtown:

I volunteered to drive several members of the group to a dance on the West Side. Several of the boys remained in the car and said they had come along for the ride. As we drove back I was asked to go along ————— Street so they could "burn" on the Noble Lords. I also noticed a narrow object about a foot long, wrapped in rags, that was secretly passed from one boy to the other. I guessed it was a gun or a rifle of some type. I told the boys I was going straight back to the neighborhood, which I did.

Finally, a type of exploitation most common in Haulburg was the following:

Frankie, who was about nineteen or twenty years old, said he had a traveler's check from his father which he wanted me to cash. I said that I was not able to do this and suggested that he try a bank. Frankie insisted that the check was good and that his father had meant it for him. After about twenty minutes of haggling he admitted that the signature wasn't his father's. Finally, when I had been silent for a long while, he said he had really taken the traveler's check from his father and that it had to have his father's endorsement, which it didn't.

Setting limits on behavior toward researcher. — Implicit in the above discussion was the function of the researcher in setting at least minimal controls or limits on the behavior of the group members with whom he was interacting. It was extremely difficult for me to maintain the role of passive observer with the group at all times. It is nearly impossible in an open community setting for a single researcher not to interact directly with delinquents, letting them know what he stands for and how far they may go in various situations. Not only had the role of codelinquent to be avoided, but the role of an adult authority figure had to be played with restraint. At times I felt compelled to interfere and to help stabilize a particular pattern of interaction in order to acquire certain data. The following situation occurred in Slumtown:

A few minutes earlier, the boys had seen a pushcart filled with bananas coming down the street. Wally, Phil, and Mexico suddenly took off after the pushcart. I knew that they were after the bananas and that a chance to have a good informal interview might be thus lost. I told the boys to wait a minute and gave them a quarter. They bought the bananas, and the talk continued.

The next day I stood at the corner with Wally when the same pushcart, again filled with bananas, came by. I asked what would have happened if I hadn't given the fellows a quarter the previous day. Wally said, boastfully, that if the guys were right here now they would probably steal the bananas. I asked what would happen then. He said they would run in different directions. I asked whether the pushcart owner would chase them. Wally said that if he did it would be even worse for him. The fellows would then run in different directions, and some would double back and take more of the bananas. I asked what would be the consequences if the cops were around and picked them up. Wally said, "All they could do would be to rap us around a little."

PROBLEMS IN OBTAINING FORMAL INTERVIEWS

The members of the narcotic group in Racketville were split over whether to grant me permission to obtain formal interviews and, indeed, whether I had a right to ask for such information to begin with:

Angelo said he thought the guys who gave me interviews were crazy and that the information would surely be used against them. Teddy said that if any of the group were "busted" I could never show my face in the neighborhood and they would get even with me. Marty then joined in. He was furious at my asking Harry and Paul "these kinds of questions." He said that he might have been sitting in the car and a couple of numbers men or "button men" (racketeers) might have come over and said, "Hi, Marty, what are you doing there," picked up one of my sheets, and asked what it was. In a situation such as this, if he said, "Just answering questions," probably he, the researcher, and all the guys in the group would get killed.

Teddy took a copy of the questionaire, saying he wanted to look at it. Later when I asked for it, he said that he had burned it. He took me to the playground and showed me the small pile of ashes.

Just the same, there was a vigorous effort by several members of this particular group to co-operate fully with me in the completion of the interviews:

Paul came over and said he trusted me and thought I was a "right guy." He knew I wouldn't do anything to hurt him. Actually, Paul had given me a great deal of information about his father, who was an important racketeer in the neighborhood and involved in loan-shark and numbers operations.

Sal came up to me later and "bawled" me out for asking Marty whether I could interview Sal and the others. Sal said it was up to him and nobody else whether he would be interviewed and about what. He then not only volunteered that his father was a racketeer but that he had two uncles who were also in the rackets.

Some of the problems connected with the process of formal interviewing in Racketville extended to non-delinquents as well:

Father G. of the ——— Church said that he thought the youngsters in the Youth Council would co-operate. He had one concern, however, and that was with the section on racketeers. He said that everyone knew there was a great deal of involvement with rackets in the neighborhood, but the youngsters might not want to answer these particular questions. He thought that the information would quickly get around that there was a detective at the church who was asking questions. He would probably get a great many phone calls from worried parents and neighbors. Father G. thought, therefore, that the best procedure would be to give the youngsters the option of answering or not answering various questions.

In general, there was relatively little difficulty in obtaining data through the participant-observation or the formal interviewing process with groups in Slumtown or Haulburg. There was considerable difficulty in acquiring data in Racketville.

INDEX

Access to means. *See* Opportunities
Addiction. *See* Drug-addict adaptation
Adult Education Development Center, 177–78, 180
Adult thieves. *See* Thieves, adult
Adults:
  conflict among, 14, 19–21
  as guardians of status, 124
  influence on delinquents of, 146–47
  measures of relationship with, 125–26
  neighborhood, 144–45; *see also* Integration, neighborhood
  as opportunity sources, 117–22
  relationships with significant, 124–47
  See also Controls; Young adults
Age:
  and community-center attendance, 132
  of delinquents, 8, 10, 11
Age-level integration, 22–27
Agencies:
  citizen participation in, 175–76, 183–84, 185
  failures of, 174, 183–84
  organization of, 184–87
  See also Community center; Community planning, organization of; Services
Aggressive behavior. *See* Brawling; Fighting; Gang-fighting

Anomic gap, xvi
  of delinquents, 106–12
  and disparity between income aspirations and expectations, 109
  and disparity between occupational aspirations and expectations, 107–8
  as illustrated by graphs, 109–12
  of narcotics addicts, 106, 108, 111–12
  of non-delinquents, 106, 108, 111
  See also Aspirations; Delinquent subcultures; Expectations
Anomie theory, xii, xx, 93–94, 107.
  See also Anomic gap
Aspirations, 93, 95–101
  of delinquents, 29, 33, 95, 96, 97–100, 101
  of narcotics addicts, 95, 96, 97, 101
  of non-delinquents, 29, 95, 96, 97, 101
  and the social order, 170–72
  See also Anomic gap; Income; Occupation
Automation, 169–70
Automobile theft. *See* Car theft

Benzedrine, 57
Betting, off-track, 30, 154. *See also* "Horse parlors"
Big City Youth Board, xix, 5 (Table 3 n.), 40 n., 41 (Table 10 n.)
Black Claws, 67

199

Block organizations, 181–83
Bookie. *See* Bookmaker
Bookmaker, 6, 21, 100, 145, 161
Booster. *See* Shoplifter
Bopper. *See* Slumtown gangs; Gang-
    fighting
Bopping. *See* Slumtown gangs;
    Gang-fighting
Bopping club, 64 n.
Brains, 159–60
Brawling, 42, 45–46, 82–83
    as distinguished from gang-fight-
        ing, 38, 40
    and drinking, 46
    over girls, 89
    tradition of, 46
    See also Fighting
Bribes, 15, 20, 21, 142–43, 144, 165,
    166
Broken homes, 7, 8, 27, 129, 130–31
Building codes, 176
Burglary, xiii, xvii, 17, 21–22, 49–50,
    66, 100, 116, 149, 152, 164, 167,
    168
Business and the rackets, 18, 32, 33,
    96, 97, 100, 103, 104, 170–71
"Button men," 197

Car theft, xvii, 16, 66
    and criminal intent, 49
    frequency of, 48
    function of, xvii, 48–49
    learning value of, 49, 167
Church attendance, 9, 10, 11
Cloward, Richard A., xi, 114
Cloward, Richard A., and Ohlin,
    Lloyd E., x, xii and n., xiv n.,
    94, 108 n., 155 n.
Cocaine, 57. *See also* Drug-addict
    adaptation
Community center:
    age of attendance at, 132
    kinds of, 132
    relationship with, 132–36
Community-center workers, 132–36,
    137
    ambivalent relationship with, 135
    compared to street-club workers,
        139–40
    distant relationship with, 134–35
    and racket values, 133–34
    unfriendly relationship with, 133

Community development, 175–76
Community planning:
    and community organization proc-
        ess, 186–87
    and delinquency, 172–75
    and local governmental leadership,
        175–76
    objectives of, 17
    and opportunities, 172, 176–79;
        see also Education; Employ-
        ment; Housing; Opportunities
    organization of, 172, 183–87; *see
        also* Agencies
    program proposals for, 175–76
    and responsibility of local groups,
        175–76
    and services, 172, 179–83; *see al-
        so* Services
Con man, xi
Conflict subculture, xii, xv, xvi, 27,
    28, 61
    access to means in, 114, 123, 151,
        152
    age-level integration of, 24–25
    anomic gap in, 106–12, 122
    community planning and, 170,
        172–87
    delinquent-group formation in,
        65–66
    family income in, 4
    family relationships in, 130–32
    girls and gang-fighting in, 88–89
    and illegitimate means, 114, 151,
        152
    indexes of social breakdown in,
        4, 6
    life experiences in, 77, 78
    narcotics addiction in, 56–57
    neighborhood integration of, 19–
        21, 144, 145
    neighborhood life of, 13–15
    neighborhood racketeers in, 114–
        17, 145
    neighborhood thieves in, 115, 116,
        146
    occupation of male breadwinners
        in, 3
    patterns of ganging in, 73
    population characteristics of, 2
    qualifying for rackets in, 159, 160,
        161, 162–63

researcher's problems in, 190, 192–93, 196, 197

social clubs in, 82, 83

social order and, 170

social worker and, 187, 188

young-adult conventional adaptations in, 150–51, 163–64

young-adult criminal adaptations in, 154, 163–64

young racketeers in, 156–57, 158, 159

Conflict subculture relationships:

with community centers, 132

with community-center workers, 132, 134–35, 136, 137

among delinquent groups, 81–82, 83

with fathers, 128, 130–31

with girl friends, 87, 88–89, 90–91

with mothers, 127–28, 130–31

with neighborhood adults, 144–45

with non-delinquent groups, 84–85, 86

with police, 142–43, 144

with significant adults, 125, 146

with street-club workers, 137, 138–39

Conformity and realistic aspirations, 94–95. *See also* Non-delinquents

Connections, xiii

family, 31, 100, 150, 151, 155, 160–61

in Haulburg, 53, 151

and narcotics-addict adaptation, 56, 57

in Racketville, 31, 37–38, 150, 155, 156

in Slumtown, 156–57

See also Integration; Values

Controls, 92, 149–50, 155

adult, 18–20, 92, 133–34, 146, 163, 197–98

criminal, 18–20, 75–76, 134, 163, 197–98

See also Integration

Conventional adaptation. *See* Young adults, conventional adaptation of

Conventional opportunities. *See* Opportunities, legitimate

Conventional values. *See* Index, value-norm; Values

Conversation analysis, 118–22

method of, 118–20

references to adults evaluated by, 120–22

"Cowboy," 10

Crew, 64 n.

Criminal adaptation. *See* Young Adults, criminal adaptation of

Criminal indoctrination, 168

Criminal opportunities. *See* Opportunities, illegitimate

Criminal values, 22, 30, 33, 35–36, 47, 52–53, 57, 61, 80–81, 171. *See also* Integration, of criminal and conventional groups; Index, value-norm; Values

Crowd, 64 n.

Cultural deprivation, 178

and defeatist attitudes, 172–73

in Racketville, 13

Culture structure, xiii-xv, 93–95, 148, 170–71 *passim*

Czechs, 2, 79

Debs, 88, 89, 192–93

Defeatist attitudes, 60, 104–5

Delinquency:

causes for, xx, 92, 94, 127–28, 129, 131, 169; *see also* Anomic gap; Anomie theory

costs of, 169–70

functional and dysfunctional, 30–38, 47–53, 61, 98, 149, 155, 156–57

See also Poverty; Cultural deprivation

Delinquent behavior. *See* Delinquent norms; Drug addicts; Haulburg delinquents; Racketville delinquents; Slumtown delinquents

Delinquent norms:

and delinquent behavior, 30, 34, 168

index of, 34–35, 47, 52–53, 57, 61

See also Criminal values, Values

Delinquent subcultures:

and cultural pressures, 93–94

defined, xiii

and differential relationships with
adults, 124–25
and neighborhood conditions, 1,
27–28
and social conditions, 93–94
social order and, 169–72
theory of differences in, ix–xvi
See also Conflict subculture;
Racket subculture; Theft subculture
Demerol, 57
Deprivation. *See* Cultural deprivation; Poverty
Devils, 46
Diddy bopping. *See* Gang-fighting
Dolophine, 57
Double standard, 87–88, 90
Drinking patterns, 78–79
Drug-addict adaptation:
as alternative adaptation, 60
and anomic gap, 106, 108, 109,
111–12
commitment to, 55–56
consequences of, 56, 60
as conventional adjustment, 153–
54
and delinquent subcultures, 53–55,
80–81
among delinquents, 53–55, 153–54
gang status as related to, 60–61
initial use of marijuana in, 53–55,
57, 153
meaning and sequence of, 54
motivation for, 55
neighborhood pressures against,
53–54, 55
as transitional adjustment, xii,
xviii, 60, 95, 106
Drug addicts:
ambivalence of, 57
aspirations of, 57, 95, 96, 97
criminal patterns of, 56, 60
escapism and retreatism of, xii,
62, 112
expectation levels of, 101, 102,
103
gang-fighting of, 58, 80
group cohesion of, 58, 82
pattern of narcotics-use by, 55–
56, 58–59
and racket orientation, 57
among Racketville group, 57–60

and relationships with mothers,
127 and n.
use of alcohol by, 59–60
use of heroin by, 56–57
Drug-selling, 19, 30, 33–34, 59, 84,
105, 145, 154, 155, 157, 163,
192

Eastern University, 191, 193
Education:
and Adult Education Development Center, 177–78, 180
community planning and, 172–87
passim
of delinquents, 9, 10, 11
of parents of interview subjects,
6–7, 8
as qualification for rackets, 160
and school program of delinquents, 9, 10, 11
value of, 37–38, 47, 53, 57, 97
Educators, xi, 97, 178
Empirical expectations:
for accessibility to means, 113–14;
see also Opportunities
for actual achievement, 101–2;
see also Expectations
for aspired achievement, 95; *see
also* Aspirations
for relationships with adults, 125;
see also Adults, relationships
with significant
for size of anomic gap, 106; *see
also* Anomic gap
Employment:
and community planning, 173,
178, 180, 181
of delinquents, 9–10, 11
of neighborhood residents, 3–4
of parents of interview subjects,
6, 7, 8
See also Aspirations; Expectations;
Occupation; Unemployment
Ethnic origin:
of delinquents, 8, 10, 11
of neighborhood population, 2
of parents of interview subjects,
6, 7–8
Expectations, 93, 101–5
assumptions in regard to, 101
of delinquents, 101, 102, 103, 104,
105

of narcotics addicts, 101–2, 103, 105
of non-delinquents, 101, 102–3
See also Anomic gap; Empirical expectations; Income; Occupation; Opportunities
Exploitive sex arrangements, 17. *See also* Homosexuals; Prostitution

Family:
extended, 129–30
income of, 4, 6, 7, 8
name of, 49–50
and racket control, 18–19
strengthening of, 173
See also Connections, family; Broken homes; Fathers; Mothers; Parents
Fathers:
education of, 7
occupation of, 6, 7, 8
relationship with, 125, 128–29, 130, 131
See also Connections, family; Family; Parents
Federal controls, 186
Federal funds, 178
Federal planning, 178, 186
Federal urban-renewal agencies, 186
Fences, 21–22, 49, 116, 145–46, 164, 166
Fighting, 29–30. *See also* Brawling; Gang-fighting
Forgery, xvii, 164, 196
Francione, Russell, xix n.
"Fruit," 10
Funeral parlors, 12

Gambling, xv, 154
Gang-fighting:
and achieving "rep," xvi, 38, 42, 43, 61, 71–72
frequency of, 40
in Haulburg, xviii, 45–46, 47, 82–83
interethnic, 42, 64–65
patterns of, 38
and preparation for conventional career, 149
and preparation for criminal career, 98
in Racketville, xviii, 40–42

in Slumtown, xvi, 42–45, 61, 88–89, 134, 160, 196
Youth Board records on, 40 n.
See also Brawling
Gang genesis and development, 63–66
in Haulburg, 65–66
in Racketville, 64–65
in Slumtown, 65
Gang girls. *See* Girls
Gang members:
confusion over, 67
identification of, 66–68
Gang membership, 70–75
for achieving "rep," 71, 72, 73
character of, 73–74
for criminal gain, 72, 73
for friendship reasons, 71, 72, 73
integrated pattern of, 71
means of severing, 91–92
multiple, 71–72, 81–82
recruitment for, 74
scope and intensity of, 73
shifting character of, 68
voluntary character of, 73–74
Gang names:
and quest for prestige, 81–82
and subcultural values, 68, 70, 72
See also Nicknames
"Gayer." *See* Homosexuals
Genovese, 98
Gerard, Donald L., 127 n.
Germans, 2, 11, 79
Girls:
"good" and "bad," 87–88, 90
leaving gang for, 91–92
relations with, of gang boys, 86–91
role of, in conflict subculture, 88–89
role of, in gang, 88–89
See also Prostitution
Graft money, 15, 20, 21, 142–43, 144, 165, 166
Graphs, discussion of, 109–12

Haulburg, xv, xvi–xvii *passim*
description of, 15–17
population characteristics of, 2
See also Theft subculture
Haulburg delinquents, 11
brawling by, 46
burglary by, 49–50

car theft by, 48–49
drinking by, 78–79
gang-fighting of, 40, 45–46, 47
loan-shark activities of, 31
narcotics-selling by, 33
narcotics-use by, 54–55, 153
policy-racket activities of, 31
stickups by, 50
tattooing of, 76
theft by, 52
value-norm index of, 35, 53
See also Haulburg gangs; Haulburg youths
Haulburg gangs:
coercion into, 73, 74–75
identification of members of, 67–68
initiation rituals of, 76
names of, 70
personal names in, 69
purpose of membership in, 72–73
severing relations with, 92
See also Haulburg delinquents; Haulburg youths
Haulburg youths:
aspirations of, 37, 53, 96, 97, 99–100, 101
distinctive antisocial behavior of, 47–51, 52
expectations of, 101, 102, 103, 105
near-hipsterism of, 153
and orientation to adults, 120, 121, 122
parents of, 7–8
role-models of, 36–37, 53
See also Haulburg delinquents; Haulburg gangs; Theft subculture relationships
"Heart," 43–44, 159, 160
Heroin, 56–57
"Hick," 10
Hijacking, 164
Hipsterism, 152–54
Hock shop, 22
Holdup. *See* Robbery
Homosexuals, 17, 79, 193
"Horse parlors," 21. *See also* Off-track betting
Housing:
condition of, 11–12, 13–14, 15, 16
improvement of, 173, 176
public, 11, 13, 176

Human-renewal, 178
Hungarians, 2
Huxley, 153

Illegitimacy, 87, 88, 90
Illegitimate opportunities. *See* Opportunities, illegitimate
Income:
aspirations for, xv, 95–101, 122
expectations for, 101, 102, 104
of delinquents, 10, 11
family, 4, 6, 7, 8
graphs based on, 109–12
as indicator of anomic gap, 106, 109
of racketeers, 97, 98, 100, 150, 157, 158, 165
of shoplifters, 165–66
Index:
of disparity in income, 109; *see also* Anomic gap
of disparity in occupational status, 107–8; *see also* Anomic gap
of social breakdown, 4–6
value-norm, 34–35, 47, 52–53, 57, 61; *see also* Values
Initiation rituals, 75–77
purpose of, in Racketville, 75–76
purpose of, in Slumtown, 76
Institutional means. *See* Opportunities
Integration:
of criminal and conventional groups, xvi, xvii, 17, 18–22, 27–28
of delinquent and non-delinquent groups, 24, 83–86
of delinquent groups, 24, 25, 26–27, 71–72, 79–83
of neighborhood, 17–27, 27–28
of offenders of different age levels, xvi, 17, 22–27, 27–28, 92
racial, and the schools, 176
See also Connections; Controls
Irish, 2, 11, 64, 79
Italians, xviii n., 2, 6, 8, 11, 12–13, 14, 27, 34, 64, 65, 80, 127, 157

Jitter-bugging. *See* Gang-fighting
Jobs. *See* Employment
"Joy-riding." *See* Car theft
Jukebox racket, 159

Kerouac, J., 153
"Kicks," 49, 51, 69, 77
Kobrin, S., xiii n., 114

Lashers, 84
Legitimate opportunities. *See* Opportunities, legitimate
Legitimate values. *See* Index, value-norm; Values
Leopards, 84, 155
Loan-shark racket, xv, 6, 30, 32–33, 34, 154, 198
Lobos, 161
Lower-class neighborhoods, xi–xviii, xx n.
Luck, 37, 47, 99

Mailer, N., 153
Marginal workers, 178
Marijuana, 53–55, 57, 153
Means, 112–22 *passim. See also* Opportunities
Merton, Robert K., xii, xiii n., 47 n., 93 and n., 94, 108, 112, 112 n.
Mexicans, xii
Miller, Walter B., 47 n., 172
Mixed conflict-theft subculture, xix, 109 n., 111
Morphine, 57
Mothers:
    education of, 8
    relationship with, 125, 126–29, 130, 131
    See also Connections; Family; Parents
Mugging, 66, 86, 152
Multiclass community, 175
Mundy, Richard E., 172 n.

Names. *See* Gang names; Nicknames
Narcotics-addict adaptation. *See* Drug-addict adaptation
Narcotics-selling. *See* Drug-selling
National Institute of Health, 186
National youth programs, 178
Near-hipsterism, 152–54
Negroes, xiv, xx n., 2, 14, 64–65, 80, 130, 166–67, 172
    as "boosters," 166–67
    sample of delinquent, xix, 109 n., 111

Neighborhood appearance, 11–12, 13–14, 15–16
Neighborhood integration. *See* Integration, of neighborhood
Neighborhood life, 12–13, 14–15, 15–17
Nicknames, 68–70. *See also* Gang names
Noble Lord Debs, 89
Noble Lords, 20, 40, 43, 44, 65, 69 n., 74, 82, 85, 159, 194, 196
Non-delinquents:
    anomic gap of, 106, 108, 109
    aspiration-expectation curves of, 111
    aspirations of, 94, 95, 96
    attendance at community centers of, 132, 134
    cultural pressures on, 95, 108
    as deviants in Racketville, 36–37, 115
    expectations of, 101, 102, 103
    group structures of, 83
    and relationship with delinquents, 24, 79, 83–86
    and relationship with fathers, 128
    and relationship with mothers, 127
    See also Young adults, conventional adaptation of
Norms. *See* Delinquent norms; Index, value-norm; Values
Numbers, xv, 6, 19, 21, 30, 31–32, 98, 104, 144, 150, 161

Occupation:
    aspirations for, 95–101
    of delinquents, 9–10, 11
    expectations for, 101–5
    of fathers, 6, 7, 8
    of female breadwinners in neighborhoods, 4
    an indicator of anomic gap, 107–8, 109, 109–10
    of male breadwinners in neighborhoods, 3–4, 6, 7, 8
    pattern in past decade, 4
    See also Employment; Unemployment
Off-track betting, 154
Ohlin, Lloyd E., and Cloward Richard A., xii and n., xiv n., 94, 108 n., 155 n.

Open community, 175
Opportunities:
  access to, through social workers,
    125, 132–40, 187–89
  community planning for, 172–87
  in delinquent subcultures, xii, xv–
    xvii, 124. *See also* Drug-addict
    adaptation
  and education, 172–87 *passim; see
    also* Education
  and employment, 173, 178, 180,
    181
  and housing, 173, 176
  organization of, 172, 174–76, 183–
    87
  through relationships with adults,
    124–47
  services, as links to, 172, 173–74,
    179–89
  the social order and, 169–72
  as socially structured capacities,
    xiii, xx, 113–14
  success-goals and, 93–123
  theory of, xii–xv, xx, 93–95
  See also Opportunities, illegiti-
    mate; Opportunities, legitimate
Opportunities, illegitimate:
  and delinquents, 30–62, 96, 97–98,
    100, 113–23, 125, 129–31, 145–
    46
  as intervening variable, 107–8, 114
  and narcotics addicts, xvii–xviii,
    57, 60, 62, 101–2
  and neighborhood integration, 17–
    22, 27–28
  and non-delinquents, 37
  theory of, xiii–xviii, 114
  and young adults, 154–68
  See also Connections
Opportunities, legitimate:
  and delinquents, 9–10, 11, 29, 93–
    94, 104–5, 122–23, 124–25,
    146–47
  development of, 169–89
  theory of, xiii–xvii *passim*
  and young adults, 148–52, 163–
    64, 167
Opportunity and Service Council,
    179, 181, 182, 184–87
  funds for, 186
  and partisan politics, 186

purpose of, 184–85
and regional planning, 185
as special city governmental authority, 185–86
structure of, 185–86
Organization. *See* Agencies; Community planning, organization
  of; Opportunity and Service
  Council

Parents:
  of interview subjects, 6–8
  relationship with, 129–32
  See also Broken homes, Connec-
    tions, family; Family; Fathers;
    Mothers
Parole, 9, 10, 11
Payoffs, 15, 20, 21, 142–43, 144,
  165, 166
Petty theft, 16, 19, 26, 50, 56, 66,
  167, 168, 197
  for "kicks," 51, 52, 197
  as preparation for criminal ca-
    reers, 47–48, 50–51, 52, 168
Pimp, 164
Pocket-picking, 164
Polack, 161
Police, 14, 16, 23, 25, 50, 125, 141–
  44
  accommodative relationships with,
    141–42, 143, 144
  harassment by, 142–43
  payoffs of; *see* Payoffs
Policy racket, xv, 30, 31–32, 154
Polish, 2
Population:
  changes in, 2, 12–13
  characteristics of, 2–11
  density of, 13, 15
  growth of youth, 169
  influx of non-white, xx, 2, 172
  size of, 2, 13
  size of youth, 2, 3
Poverty, 7, 14, 27
President's Committee on Juvenile
  Delinquency and Youth Crime,
  186
Probation, 9, 10, 11
Professional thievery, xvii, 148, 168
  craft ability and, 47–48, 152
  organization of, 21–22, 49, 164–67

and racketeering, 164–65
systematic element in, 49, 50, 66, 164–67
Program proposals, 175–89
Prostitution, 14, 30, 79, 90, 98, 154, 164, 192–93
Protection:
  from other gangs, 73–75
  racket of, 98, 154, 158
Puerto Ricans, xiv, xx n., 2, 7, 10, 13, 14, 15, 42, 64, 65, 71, 79, 80, 130, 157, 158, 172
"Pushing." *See* Drug-selling

Qualifying for the rackets, 35–36, 159–63
  by brains, 159–60
  by connections, 159, 160–61; *see also* Connections
  by education, 160
  by toughness, 159, 160
  by trust, 159, 161–63

Racket subculture, xii, xiv, xv–xvi, 27, 28, 61
  access to means in, 114, 122–23, 150, 152
  age-level integration of, 23–24
  anomic gap in, 106, 107–8, 109, 110, 111, 112, 122
  community planning and, 170–71
  delinquent-group formation in, 64–65, 66
  family income in, 4
  family relationships in, 129–30, 132, 150
  girls and brawling in, 89, 90
  and illegitimate means, 114, 150, 152
  indexes of social breakdown in, 6
  life experiences in, 77, 78
  narcotics addiction in, 56–57
  neighborhood integration of, 18–19, 144, 150
  neighborhood life of, 11–13
  neighborhood racketeers in, 115, 116, 117, 145
  neighborhood thieves in, 115, 116, 146
  occupation of male breadwinners in, 3

patterns of ganging in, 73
population characteristics of, 2
qualifying for rackets in, 159, 160, 161–62, 163
researcher's problems in, 190–92, 194–96, 197–98
social clubs in, 83–84
social order and, 170–71
social worker and, 187, 188
young-adult conventional adaptations in, 150
young-adult criminal adaptations in, 154
young racketeers in, 154–56, 158, 159, 163
Racket subculture relationships:
  with community centers, 132
  with community-center workers, 133–34, 135–36
  among delinquent groups, 79–81, 83
  with fathers, 128, 129–30
  with girl friends, 87–88
  with mothers, 126, 127, 128, 129–30
  with neighborhood adults, 144, 150
  with non-delinquent groups, 83–84, 86
  with police, 141–42, 144
  with significant adults, 125
  with street-club workers, 137, 146
Racketeers, 47, 97–98
  and conventional institutions, 12, 15, 18–19
  and family structure, 18–19
  and non-delinquents, 115
  number of, 114–16
  and relationship with delinquents, 20, 30–34 *passim*, 145
  and settlement workers, 19, 134
  as source of norms and values, 19
  successful status of, 12, 15, 114–17
  young adults as, 154–59
  See also Connections; Racket subculture; Rackets
Rackets, xii–xviii
  bookmaking 6, 21, 100, 145, 161
  and bureaucratic structure, 30–31, 31–34 *passim*

as a business, 18, 32, 33, 96, 97, 100, 103, 104, 170–71
drug-selling, 19, 30, 33–34, 59, 84, 105, 145, 155, 192
gambling, xv, 154
ineligibility for, 163
jukebox, 159
leadership, 13
loan-shark, xv, 6, 30, 32–33, 34, 154, 198
long-term involvement in, 163
numbers, xv, 19, 21, 30, 31–32, 98, 104, 144, 150, 161
off-track betting, 154
policy, xv, 30, 31–32, 154
preparation for, 30–34, 35–36, 47
as preparation for a legitimate career, 163–64
prostitution, 14, 30, 79, 90, 98, 154, 164, 192–93
protection, 98, 154, 158
qualifying for, 159–63
union, 154, 158
See also Racketeers
Racketville, xv–xvi *passim*
description of, 11–13
population characteristics of, 2
See also Racket subculture
Racketville, alternate area, xix, 2 n.
Racketville delinquents, 8–10, 11
brawling by, 42
burglary by, 49
car theft by, 48
drinking by, 78, 79
gang-fighting of, 38, 40–42, 45–46
loan-shark activities of, 32–33
narcotics-selling by, 33–34
narcotics-use by, 53–54, 55
narcotics-using group of, 57–60
policy-racket activities of, 31–32
stickups by, 50
tattooing of, 76
theft by, 30, 51
value-norm index of, 35–36
See also Racketville gangs; Racketville youths
Racketville gangs:
coercion into, 73, 74
identification of members of, 67
initiation rituals of, 75–76
names of, 70

personal names in, 68, 69
purpose of membership in, 71
severing relations with, 91
See also Racketville delinquents; Racketville youths
Racketville youths:
aspirations of, 37–38, 96, 97–98, 101
distinctive antisocial behavior of, 30–34
expectations of, 101–5, 122
and orientation to adults, 120, 121, 122
parents of, 6–7, 8
role-models of, 36–37
See also Racket subculture relationships; Racketville delinquents; Racketville gangs
Ranking, 80, 131, 193
Regal Debs, 88, 89, 192–93
Regals, 20, 24, 40, 42, 43, 44, 54, 65, 69 n., 74, 76, 81, 82, 85, 89, 91–92, 104, 134, 142, 143, 158, 159, 192
Regional planning, 185
Religion of delinquents, 9, 10, 11
"Rep," xvi, 38, 42, 43, 61, 69, 71–72, 73, 81–82
Research:
assumptions of, 94, 101, 113, 118
basic premise of, xiii
exploratory nature of, xi, xx, 169
implications of, 189
limitations of, xx, 92, 169
method of, xviii–xx
problems in, 31 n., 136 n., 190–98
reliability of, xix–xx, 31 n.
validity of, xix–xx, 31 n.
Researcher:
attempts at exploitation of, 195–96
meet with suspicion and hostility, 193–95, 197, 198
role definition of, 190–93
and setting limits, 196–97
Residential stability of delinquents, 8–9, 10, 11
Retreatist subculture, xii
Robbery, 17, 50, 56, 66, 84, 163, 164, 166, 168
Role-models, 36–37, 47, 53, 57
Rothenberg, Robert, xix n.
Running away from home, 66

Safecracking, 17, 164
Schools. *See* Adult Education Development Center; Education
Second sample of delinquents (Haulburg), xix, 109 n., 116, 125 n., 145–46
Services:
    and Adult Education and Development Center, 180
    and block organizations, 181–83
    and community planning, 172, 173
    financing of, 179, 180, 181
    for health, 173, 181
    and Opportunity and Service Council, 179, 181, 182, 184–87
    organization of, 174–75, 183–87
    psychiatric, 173, 180
    purpose of, 173–74, 179
    referral, 179
    school, 180
    social, 169, 171, 173–75, 179–83 *passim*
    and Social and Health Services Center, 179, 181, 185
    See also Community-center workers; Social workers; Street-club workers
Settlement workers, 19, 134. *See also* Community-center workers; Street-club workers
Shoplifters, xvii, 22, 51, 60, 100, 146, 164, 165, 166, 166–67, 168
Shylock. *See* Loan-shark racket
Slumtown, xv, xvi–xvii *passim*
    description of, 13–15
    population characteristics of, 2
    See also Conflict subculture
Slumtown delinquents, 9, 10–11
    burglary by, 49
    car theft by, 48
    drinking by, 78, 79
    gang-fighting of, 38, 40, 42–45, 46
    loan-shark activities of, 32
    narcotics-selling by, 33
    narcotics-use by, 54, 153
    policy-racket activities of, 31
    stickups by, 50
    tattooing of, 76–77
    theft by, 51–52
    value-norm index of, 35, 53
    See also Slumtown gangs; Slumtown youths

Slumtown gangs:
    coercion into, 73, 74
    identification of members of, 67
    initiation rituals of, 75, 76
    names of, 70
    personal names in, 68–70
    purpose of membership in, 71–72
    severing relations with, 91–92
    See also Slumtown delinquents; Slumtown youths
Slumtown youths:
    aspirations of, 37, 53, 96, 97, 99, 101
    distinctive antisocial behavior of, 38–45, 46
    expectations of, 101–5, 122
    near-hipsterism of, 153
    and orientation to adults, 121, 122
    parents of, 7, 8
    role-models of, 36–37
    See also Conflict subculture relationships; Slumtown delinquents; Slumtown gangs
Social activities, 77
Social breakdown, indexes of, 4–6
Social Gents, 84
Social and Health Services Center:
    functional structure of, 179, 181
    in relation to Opportunity and Service Council, 185
Social planners, xi
Social scientists, xi
Social workers, xi–xii
    aspiration to be, 53, 96, 97, 98
    and delinquent subcultures, 187–89
    and social change, 187
    See also Community-center workers; Settlement workers; Street-club workers
Southern whites, 172
Spanish Counts, 85
Spergel, Irving, xiv–xv, 172 n.
"Square," 10
"Stand-up guy," 157, 162–63
Stealing. *See* Thievery
Stickup. *See* Robbery
Street-club workers, 136–40
    authoritative function of, 137–38, 139, 140
    compared to community-center workers, 137, 139–40

positive relationship with, 136, 137, 138, 140, 146
as providers of access to opportunities, 11, 136, 139, 140
special approach of, 136
subjected to abuse and violence, 137–38, 140
See also Community-center workers; Settlement workers; Social workers
Stompers, 40
Success-goals, xiii, xv–xvii, 92, 93–101, 122
and the anomic gap, 106–12
and the social order, 170–72
See also Aspirations
"Taps." *See* Payoffs
Tattooing, 76–77
Teachers, xi, 97, 178
Theft subculture, xii, xiv, xvi–xvii, 27, 28, 62
access to means in, 114, 123, 152
age-level integration of, 25–27
anomic gap in, 106–12, 122
community planning and, 171–72
delinquent-group formation in, 65–66
family income in, 4
family relationships in, 131, 132, 147, 151
girls and brawling in, 89
and illegitimate means, 114, 152
indexes of social breakdown in, 4, 6
life experiences in, 77, 78
narcotics addiction in, 56–57, 60
neighborhood integration of, 21–22, 144, 145, 151
neighborhood life of, 15–17
neighborhood racketeers in, 115, 116, 117, 145–46
neighborhood thieves in, 115, 116, 145
occupation of male breadwinners in, 3–4
patterns of ganging in, 73
population characteristics of, 2–3
researcher's problems in, 190–91, 193, 194, 196
social clubs in, 83
social order and, 171–72
social worker and, 187, 188

young-adult conventional adaptations in, 151–52
young-adult criminal adaptations in, 154
young-adult thieves in, 164–67
Theft subculture relationships:
with community centers, 132
with community-center workers, 132, 135, 136
among delinquent groups, 82–83
with fathers, 128–129
with girl friends, 87, 89–90, 91
with mothers, 126–27
with neighborhood adults, 144–45, 151
with non-delinquent groups, 85–86
with police, 143–44
with significant adults, 125, 146–47
with street-club workers, 139–40
Thievery, xvii, 21–22, 47–53, 62, 72
petty, 16, 19, 26, 50, 51, 52, 56, 66, 167, 168, 197
professional, xvii, 21–22, 47–48, 49–50, 66, 148, 152, 164–67, 168
See also Burglary; Car theft; Shoplifters
Thieves, adult:
relationship with, 21–22, 49, 116, 145–46, 167
and bail bondsmen, 166
and lawyers, 166
and police, 21, 142, 166
See also Fences
Toughness, 35–36, 61, 70, 155, 160, 161. *See also* "Heart"
Town Marauders, 66
Truancy, 66
Trust, 159, 161, 162–63

Ukrainians, 2
Unemployment, 3–4, 169–70, 178
Union racketeering, 154, 188
Urban Affairs Department, 186
Urban-renewal, 178

Values:
criminal, 170–71, 187–89
illegitimate, 13, 14–15, 16–17, 36–37, 47, 52–53, 57, 61–62, 75–76, 154–63

index of, 34
integration of conventional and criminal, 17–22, 27–28, 163–67
legitimate, 37–38, 47, 52–53, 57, 61–62, 149–52
market, 170–71
See also Aspirations; Connections; Rackets; Role-models
Vandalism, 66
Vultures, 23, 40–42, 64, 71, 73, 80, 81, 84, 91, 97, 133, 138, 155, 159
Juniors, 23, 67, 75
Seniors, 23, 67, 75
Tots, 23, 75

Warriors, 71, 73, 80–81, 84, 155
Seniors, 57–60, 71
Tots, 71
Works Progress Administration, 178

Young adults, 148–68
conventional adaptation of, 149–54
criminal adaptation of, 154–68
racket adaptation of, 154–59; *see also* Qualifying for the rackets; Racketeers
theft adaptation of, 164–67; *see also* Thieves, adult

Zen, interest in, 153